PASSION FOR THE POSSIBLE

If I could wish for something,
I would wish for neither wealth nor power,
but for the passion of possibility;
I would wish only for an eye which, eternally young,
eternally burns with the longing to see possibility.
(Søren Kierkegaard, The Moment)

I dwell in possibility.
(Emily Dickinson)

Daniel J. O'Leary

Passion for the Possible

A SPIRITUALITY OF HOPE FOR A NEW MILLENNIUM

the columba press

First published in 1998 by
the columba press
55A Spruce Avenue, Stillorgan Industrial Park, Blackrock, Co Dublin

Reprinted 2000, 2002 & 2006

Cover by Bill Bolger
Origination by The Columba Press
Printed in Ireland by Colour Books Ltd, Dublin

ISBN 1 85607 235 5

Acknowledgements
The author and publishers gratefully acknowledge the permission of
the following to use material which is in their copyright: Veritas
Publications for quotations from *Christ at the Centre* by Dermot Lane;
Darton, Longman and Todd for quotations from *God of Surprises* by
Gerard Hughes (1985), *The Heart of Creation* by John Main (1988), and
from *Jesus Before Christianity* by Albert Nolan (1977); The Liturgical
Press for quotations from *Mystery and Promise* by John F. Haught; Fr
Tony Kelly for quotations from his *An Expanding Theology;* Reed
Consumer Books Ltd for a quotation from *True Resurrection* by Harry
Williams; Image Books for a quotation from *In a Time for Love* by Eugene
Kennedy; SCM Press for a quotation from *Models of God* by Sally
McFague; HarperCollins Publishers for a quotation from *Hymn of the
Universe* by Teilhard de Chardin and from *A Spirituality Named
Compassion* by Matthew Fox. We have also applied to the following for
permissions: Phoenix Publishing for a quotation from R. S. Thomas;
Eleanor Friede for a quotation from *The Education of Little Tree* by
Forrest Carter; Bear & Company for a quotation from *Original Blessing*
by Matthew Fox; Triumph Books for a quotation from *Search for the
Meaning of Life* by Willigis Jager; Barrie & Jenkins for a quotation from
Pope John Paul II; Phoenix Paperbacks for a quotation from *Birds of
Heaven* by Ben Okri; Burns & Oates for a quotation from *The Eternal Year*
by Karl Rahner; Transworld Publishers for a quotation from *Siddartha*
by Herman Hesse.

We have made every effort to contact copyright holders and seek their
permission to use their material. If any involuntary infringement of
copyright has occurred, we offer our apologies and will correct any
error in future editions.

Contents

PART 3
The Moment of Creativity and Healing
A Theological Glimpse about Experiencing Resurrection

*Awakening our Energy. Releasing our Imagination. Co-creating with God.
Being Empowered by the Present Moment. Emerging as Soul-friend
(Anamchara) and Wounded Healer. Experiencing Resurrection.*

PART 4
The Moment of Compassion and Transformation
A Theological Glimpse about Living Pentecost

*Releasing Compassion. Seeing my Neighbour as Myself. Revealing the
Interdependence of all Creation. Conspiring for Transformation. Touching the
Soul of the Universe. Announcing a Vision of Justice and Freedom.
Celebrating the Mystery. Telling the New Story of Cosmic Connections.
Eating Bread and drinking Wine.*

Acknowledgements

I feel indebted to so many people for the final version of this book. *Passion for the Possible* was a decade in the making. It gathers together so many strands of my own journey among the communities of islands, parishes and monasteries around the world. Through all of this it moves towards some kind of synthesis – theological, spiritual and psychological. Everyone who helped to make sense out of my life, has served to create and craft the four *Moments* of this book.

I have also tried to distil, in these pages, the essence of earlier writings, in the light of my experiences up to now. I have been encouraged to continue with this quest by members of my family, by many of my friends, by members of our parish here in Yorkshire, and by our Bishop David Konstant (even though he may not agree at all with the drift of my reflections!). A number of the book's personal reflections have been published in various magazines and newspapers in these countries.

Together with many others, my *anamchara* Margaret Siberry has co-created the content, sequence and structure of the main argument of the book and has written *Awakening to the Possible,* a personal reflection in the fourth *Moment.* Doreen Mills has meticulously checked the text for errors and Philip Davis has shown remarkable self-control and understanding where my approach to computers is concerned. From these dear friends, and from many other parishioners here at St Benedict's, even while completing our new gem of a church, I have learned so much about loving and forgiving, about trusting and believing – the very graces and blessings that are the incarnate presence of God in our community. These are the people to whom I dedicate *Passion for the Possible.*

Introduction

Because you have picked up this book about spirituality you are probably searching for something to nourish your inner needs, to feed your spiritual hunger, to bring more meaning into your life, to affirm the reality of your daily experiences of hope and joy, despair and pain, fear and forgiveness. Whether you are a church-going person or not, disenchanted with religion or not, 'lapsed' or not, my only desire is to bring a new springtime, a new energy to your life. Because the mental, spiritual, emotional and physical aspects of our days and nights are so intertwined and so mutually dependent, I truly believe that the holistic inter-weaving of what you are about to read will transform your faith, your joy in life, and your understanding of what it means to be a Christian.

At the right time, they say, the right idea is invincible. This book is written to offer a way forward for the Christian churches that are rapidly becoming irrelevant to the spiritual needs of the multitudes of God's people. The churches we have known, particularly the Roman Catholic Church, are undergoing a profound crisis. This desperate situation is largely due to the institutionalism and clericalism, the triumphalist attitudes and sin-centred emphases, the terrible focus on fear and judgement, all of which are currently being replaced by a more positive and creation-centred theology and spirituality, a more life-affirming belief in the unconditional loving of a compassionate God. Such a rediscovery of that lost revelation of Jesus will fan into flame the good spark that still smoulders in our churches today. And it is the source of whatever enlivens and quickens the pages of this book.

As clerics, we are desperately (and, I suppose, understandably) reluctant to acknowledge the huge damage done to countless souls at the receiving end of a Catholic upbringing that was often a caricature of the message of Jesus. In the face of relentless evidence about the almost unbelievable distortion of God's original blessing called creation and incarnation, and of the untold harm done to so many innocent souls by a travesty of mis-interpretation of that first revelation, why do the powers that be continue to defend their position, and seem to deny the urgency for a spirit of repentance with the possibility of a new beginning?

Passion for the Possible is about finding another way of understanding our faith, of reflecting on the mysteries of creation, incarnation, the church and its sacraments. It is about restoring a lost trust in humanity and in all of creation on the part of the official churches; it is about fanning into flame the forgotten spark of divine dignity in everything that God has created, at a time of ecclesiastical distrust of human nature and of 'mere' created and material things.

This book is written for Christians who are losing hope in their churches, who are hanging in there but at the end of their rope, who are disillusioned at the lack of vision in their ecclesiastical leaders, who have lost their confidence and are wondering where next to turn to. The theological glimpses in the following pages are set out as a very small, humble, but hopeful contribution to the possibility of a brave new beginning for our Catholic Church, for an exciting discovery for individual souls, for a forgotten revelation of spiritual empowerment that will shape, sustain and inspire the dramatic challenges and changes that await us all in the new millennium.

The theological emphasis throughout the book is on stimulating our divine, creative energy, on setting free the passion and the compassion that still stirs in our souls, on celebrating the beauty, the darkness and the newness of everything that grows. It is a theology that sees suffering as birth-pangs rather than as 'the wages of sin', that sees procreation as the source of blessing rather than of original curse, that sees salvation and healing in terms of the liberation and transformation of people and of the whole world. It is a theology that values the gifts of prophecy, ecstasy and hospitality rather than the conditions of guilt, duty-filled compliance and fear of pleasure. It is holistic and life-centred rather than based on a dualism that separates God from creation, body from soul and human loving from divine loving. Without such a radical shift in our understanding of the Christian revelation, our wise thinkers tell us that there will be no institutional church to belong to.

One of the main aims of this book is to bring to God's people the outline of a simple but profound theology, together with what is now called a spirituality of the heart. Because such an aim is thoroughly incarnational, its heart is the limitless experiences of the human condition. The book is written, therefore, out of a theology of creation and is structured along the four *Moments* of creation spirituality. The first of these, the Way of Wonder, is about the original blessing and original joy at the core of created things. All creatures reflect the beauty and wonder of God. Creation, according to Thomas Aquinas, is like a book of scriptures, revealing God as one who fashions the universe after God's own heart. Having become human in Jesus, God is forever becoming human in all life.

Then there is the familiar *Moment* of emptiness and pain – the Way of Darkness. Along this path, we are asked to believe, lies the surest and swiftest way to participate in God's sheer joy and freedom. There is a dignity to darkness; there is a freedom hidden in pain. So much suffering comes from trying to avoid the necessary losses and fears of each day and each decade. In the silence and the waiting we experience something of the mystery of God.

The third *Moment* reveals how human beings, through Jesus Christ, become 'wounded healers' and thus co-creators with God. Even though this holy process is called a *Moment*, it can take ages of time. The place of suffering in the finest creations wrought by human hands, is evident in the masterpieces of our world's artists, known and unknown. When we're aware of God in our dark times as well as in our noon-times, pain and healing and creativity come together. Writing about this 'Creative Way', Father Bede Griffiths believes that 'the sense of the presence of God in the world around us and in our own hearts awakens the creative powers in our nature and calls us to express our joy in art and poetry, in music and dance, and to order our lives in justice and truth.'

The fourth *Moment* is about social, universal and cosmic transformation. It follows on from the more personal growth and self-awareness of the preceding paths in this spirituality of the heart. Again, Bede Griffiths describes the Way of Transformation: 'The mind and the will are transformed by the indwelling presence of God, particularly by the Holy Spirit. This leads to social transformation as justice and compassion are seen to be the expression of the inner response to God's grace and love in human affairs.' This *Moment* has immense implications for those with deep concerns for the environment and for the future of mother earth. The possibilities are exciting, challenging and full of real hope.

Each of the four *Moments* begins with a theological 'glimpse' to underpin the claims I make throughout the book. There is an important reason for this. Over the past three decades of working with people in search of love and meaning in their lives, I have come to the conclusion that most people's theological difficulties, defensive arguments and initial resistance regarding renewal and change in themselves and in the the world, arise from the dangerously flawed, dualistic set of doctrines fearfully carved into young minds and hearts. So, for our first steps into an exciting, orthodox and incarnational theology of revelation, I point to a number of Christian theologians, particularly to two of our finest – Thomas Aquinas and Karl Rahner. We could have no safer 'guardian angels' for our journey, even though I know only too well that I have not done them justice.

After the initial 'glimpses' of each *Moment*, I then offer a number of personal reflections. In these I try to 'process' the thoughts of my head into the feelings of my heart; to transform the knowledge of my mind into the wisdom of my soul; to express something of the actual experience of the lived grace of the Holy Spirit; to push out the boundaries of human experience for it is precisely there that we will discover God and encounter grace. These reflections form the core of my prayer these days, as I try to become, in my most human living, what I know and believe to be true about God-made-flesh, and also as I try to be attentive to the divine revelation of an amazing love, emerging from within my most ordinary and most intense experiences. Prayer then becomes an unending discovery of the intimate presence of the God of surprises at every single moment of our lives.

PART I

The Moment of Beauty and Wonder

Rediscovering Incarnation

'God became human so that humans could become God.' Even though this beautiful truth was first expressed and believed during the early years of Christianity, most of us today have a different understanding of the incarnation. At a huge cost to our quality of life, we have lost sight of this initial and exciting revelation. For some strange and shadowy reason the amazing mystery of the fleshing of the Word gradually became centred on a tougher, legalistic kind of transaction between God and a fallen race. Even today, redemption is generally regarded as a kind of rescue operation by God – a desperate last-ditch effort from outside to salvage a world gone adrift. The death of God's Son was part of the terrible bargain. When the core of Christianity is based on such narrow, sin-centred motivations, then the consequences are immense and, to my mind, often quite damaging.

For instance there is a common belief that the incarnation happened only because of human sinfulness – that is to say that original sin is the sole reason for God's decision to become human. I feel sure that this is profoundly misleading. God's people have suffered deeply because of this unbalanced but perennially popular theory. Another deadly legacy of a sin-based theology of redemption is the pervading dualism in Christian preaching, teaching and general understanding of creation and incarnation. By this I mean that over the centuries the whole point of the divine-human union has so often been misrepresented or even seriously missed. Instead of 'locating' God at the heart of God's creation, there is a persistence about maintaining the separation between the divine and the human, between grace and nature. Also, there are far-reaching implications for our understanding of church and sacraments and of our interpretation of many doctrines and teachings, when we rediscover some lost insights into the love and meaning at the heart of incarnation. In these theological glimpses at the beginning of each section, I hope to open a few windows on to some delightful scenes to warm our faltering hearts.

We are God's delight

After a lean and fairly barren period in the history of Christian thinking, a new dynamism is once again beginning to colour our understanding of revelation. The initial insight of the early Church Fathers is gradually being recaptured. Revelation is again seen as the amazing love-story of God's desire to be intimately among us in human form. Full of intense compassion, God wished to create out of pure love, and then, in time, to become that creation. That becoming happened in Jesus Christ. In him it was revealed that God's heart beats in all our hearts, that all our bodies are temples of the Holy Spirit, that every creature is a divine work of art. How different that is to the awful picture painted for us of the angry God in search of vengeance!

Revelation is now seen to be about the beauty of being human since humanity is the 'raw material', so to speak, of God's presence in the world. Revelation is about the unbelievable possibilities of humanity, graced at its centre from the very beginning. It is about God's desire to be known and loved in the humanity of Jesus Christ. It is about God's delight in being visible and tangible in human form. This is how it became possible for God to be close to us, to share completely in the experiences of creatures, the fruit of God's own womb. We can say with saints and theologians from the time of Christ, that the incarnation happened not just because creation went wrong at some early stage, but because in God's plan to share God's own divine joy with others, creation was first necessary so that incarnation could take place. I hope that this does not sound complicated.

Think of a married couple. Out of their mutual love they conceive a child into whom they will pour their deepest care and affection. The child is 'full' of its parents, grown from the seed of their love, nourished in the womb of the mother, bearing its parents' image, reflecting so much of their personalities. The child is 'a copy of its parents' to quote St Paul. So too, in this 'new' way of looking at the meaning of creation and incarnation, we are, so to speak, 'copies of the glorious body of Christ', a kind of rough-draft of the shape of God. In the *Office of Readings* this very morning, (Vol 3, p 510) I came across the following gentle exhortation in a sermon of St Leo the Great; 'O Christian heart, recognise the great worth of the wisdom that is yours, so that the creator may be shown forth in the creature and that, in the mirror of your heart as in the lines of a portrait, the image of God may be reflected.'

When God was creating Adam, Tertullian reminds us, as do

both Vatican Councils, it was the human form of the Son, the ever-present Word, that was motivating God. Adam was the long-term preparation for Jesus – a sort of proto-type of the lovely Saviour who was to come later. All of this we have tumbled to in the revelation that is Jesus. Now we know that all humanity is heading towards divinity. You and I are growing into God, as the mystics put it. In fact all of creation is already sacred, and reveals something of the glory and splendour of God. That is why we say that the event of incarnation has ended all dualism. Heaven and earth are forever mysteriously intertwined since the Word became flesh. And deep in our own inner being the kingdom of God forms an intrinsic part of our true nature.

The dearest freshness

The poets and artists are never tired of playing with this fascinating theme. Unlike many of the official teachers of religion, they have never lost the sense of wonder at the mystery of the indwelling of God in creation. For them, the smallest particle of creation becomes a window on God's beauty. Their intense energy is spent on revealing 'the dearest freshness that lives deep down things'. They see 'his blood upon the rose and in the stars the glory of his eyes'. Like 'flaming from shook foil', God's splendour radiates from all creatures for those who stay blessed with the original vision of childhood. The artist and the mystic use images and symbols to catch the fire-fly glimpses of the extraordinary presence of a Spirit of Wonder beneath the seemingly superficial and ordinary. Once we become sensitive to the meaning of the birth, life, death and resurrection of Jesus, then everything is changed. We see the world differently. We finally get the message. The human holds the key to God. 'Salvation,' as the Church Father said, 'hinges on the flesh.' All things are made new. From now on, our vision and our focus will be trained on discovering the God of surprises hiding and playing at the heart of life.

'Through every cleft, the world we perceive floods us with riches – food for the body, nourishment for the eyes, the harmony of sounds and fullness of the heart, unknown phenomena and new truths – all these treasures, all these stimuli, all these calls coming to us from the four corners of the world, cross our consciousness at every moment. What is their role within us? They will merge into the most intimate life of our soul, and either develop it or poison it.'[1] There is no dualism here. God is so intimately one with the world. We are not healed from outside in. Grace is not something on top of, or part of, or added to nature. Unbelievably, what we keep forgetting, or denying, or failing to understand is that *nature itself is intrinsically graced from the beginning*. Because of the revelation that happened at the incarnation, we can now be certain that the kingdom of God is within, that the Holy Spirit is at work and play in our inmost being, that we look for God not 'out there' anymore, but waiting to be discovered in our deepest self.

Even a partial awareness of this unbelievable mystery of divine surrender to our hearts brings a challenging responsibility to the way we live. Our style of life is profoundly affected by our belief that God somehow needs us to continually keep co-creating the world with him. We begin to realise that the kingdom of God is first built by us in each others' hearts. Our worldview is immediately and radically altered. Our relationship to ourselves, to each other, to the world and to God is fundamentally impacted. In God we live and move and have our being. Empowered by the Spirit, nothing is impossible anymore.

You are God's seed
A rediscovery of incarnation theology reminds us of the inseparable unity between God and us. It reminds us too that without *our* commitment there will always be something forever incomplete about the redemption of the world. Jesus is unambiguous about this when he refers to those who failed to recognise the divinity of the poor and needy, the loveless and the marginalised. St Simeon wrote, 'These hands of mine are the hands of God; this body of mine is the body of God because of the incarnation.' The mystic Meister Eckhart preached, 'You are God's seed. As the pear seed grows into the pear tree and the hazel seed becomes the hazel tree, so does God's seed become God.' And St Teresa made the well-known affirmation, 'Christ has no body now on earth but yours; no hands now but yours; no feet but yours; yours are the eyes through which Christ shines his compassion to the world; yours are the feet through which he is to go about doing good; yours are the hands through which he is to bless people now.'

Gone forever is the dualism that would see our time on earth as a brief testing-time of punishment in an alien place until our escape home to heaven. The incarnation has revealed what true humanity is, to be realised not by running away from the world or turning our backs on it in indifference and fear. Christ does not reveal what it is to be divine but what it is to be human. That our God-likeness might become complete is the purpose of creation. And the way to human fulfilment is to penetrate right to the heart of the world, in all its sufferings, ugliness and desolation as well as its joys, beauty and integrity. In Christ our humanity has undergone transformation. This transformation is not something added on to our nature – a divine layer on top of our humanity. It is rather the revelation of the intrinsic meaning of our lives. We are God's dream coming true. We are God's delight. God rejoices in our humanity and God is the energy behind every heartbeat of our lives.

Another way of putting this is to discern the activity of grace within our souls. At our very centre is the address of the Holy Spirit. God has taken up residence in our innermost place. Again, the incarnation liberated God from the prison of the heavens, chained by God's transcendence. The Vatican Council's document, *The Church in the Modern World,* makes it clear that in the past we over-emphasised the notion of two distinct worlds, one sacred and one profane. We forget that the old distinction between the holy and the human has been overcome in the person of Christ. In Christ it is revealed that God's home is now in people. In him it is made clear that God speaks in and through the words and actions of all God's creatures. Our prayer and sacramental worship are the necessary means of remembering and celebrating this profound truth. We will explore later how Christian liturgy is the continuing revelation and confirmation of this deepest dimension of human life – namely that God's gift of self-communication and healing compassion is happening to us in every event and at every moment of our 'ordinary' lives.

One could say that nothing is outside the reach of God. Even before we begin to be present to others and to the world, we are already held in God's embrace. We do not, for instance, have a relationship with God *in addition* to other relationships. We experience God and relate to God, in and through all our relationships. Our relationship with God is inseparable from *every* relationship we experience. 'We experience God most completely by experiencing ourselves and other people, and whenever we experience ourselves or other people, we also experience God. In fact, we give glory and praise to God most fundamentally by routinely living in a way that quietly affirms the original goodness to be found in every moment of life, no matter how ordinary. The renewal that is needed takes place when our daily lives become an implicit and unselfconscious affirmation of God.'[2]

At this point many readers may be wondering about whatever happened to the doctrine of original sin. It is unfortunately alive and well! But there is a balance to be regained. In *Redemptor Hominis*, one of our present Pope's first letters to the church, he does not dwell on this doctrine. He includes it, of course, but does not make it the sole cause of the incarnation. Karl Rahner, too, maintains that the fall of humanity was not the first and only reason for revelation and salvation. He reminds us of the Scotist school of thought which holds that the most basic motive for revelation was not 'the blotting out of sin', but that the incarnation was already the goal of the divine plan even apart from any divine foreknowledge of freely incurred guilt and sin. The incarnation may be seen as the most original act of God's will to create and then to redeem (if necessary), so that redemption from sin would be 'included' in the first desire of God for the *hypostatic union*, for another way of being God's self, which necessarily called for creation and its completion. What is important here, from the point of view of church doctrine, is that the victory of the *Logos* (the Word) over sin should never be denied. But it is freely permitted to regard the incarnation, in God's primary intention 'as the summit and height of the divine plan of creation, and not primarily and in the first place, as the act of a mere restoration of a divine world-order destroyed by the sins of mankind...'[3]

Grace in Winter

We are here in the land of grace. Grace is always and everywhere available to us. It is only we ourselves who prevent it from transforming us more truly into that image of God in which we were first created. God's gracious gifts surround us on every side. It is important to remember that grace does not only travel on fine days. On wintry evenings, especially, grace is never far away. By this I mean that very often the greatest strides in holiness are made in the darker happenings of our lives. We will explore this aspect of the mystery more fully in the next section.

Rahner puts the closeness of grace in this way: 'Grace is simply the last depth and radical meaning of all that the created person experiences, enacts and suffers in the process of developing and realising himself as a person. When someone experiences laughter or tears, bears responsibility, stands by the truth, breaks through the egoism in his life with other people; where someone hopes against hope, faces the shallowness and stupidity of the daily rush and bustle with humour and patience, refusing to become embittered; where someone learns to be silent and in this inner silence lets the evil in his heart die rather than spread outwards; in a word, where someone lives as he would like to live, combating his own egoism and the continual temptation to inner despair – there is the event of grace.'[4]

Some people sense this exciting shift in the dynamic of grace with open wonder, joy and thanksgiving; others struggle with it. Hermann Hesse's novel *Siddhartha* contains some of the most evocative passages on this theme in recent literature. In one of these passages which describes the remarkable experience of a disciple at the deathbed of the Master, our understanding of the inevitability and universality of the grace of Christ is deepened and clarified.

> He no longer saw the face of his friend Siddhartha. Instead he saw other faces, many faces, a long series, a continuous stream of faces – hundreds, thousands which all came and disappeared and yet all seemed to be there at the same time, which all continually changed and renewed themselves and which were yet all Siddhartha. He saw the face of a fish, of a carp, with tremendous painfully opened mouth, a dying fish with dimmed eyes. He saw the face of a newly-born child, red and full of wrinkles, ready to cry. He saw the face of a murderer, saw him plunge a knife into the body of a man; at the same moment he saw this criminal kneeling down, bound, and his head cut off by an executioner. He saw the naked bodies of men and women in the postures and transports of passionate love. He saw corpses stretched out, still, cold, empty. He saw the heads of animals – boars, crocodiles, elephants, oxen, birds. He saw all these forms and faces in a thousand relationships to each other, all helping each other, loving, hating and destroying each other and becoming newly born ... Govinda bowed low, right down to the ground, in front of the man sitting there motionless, whose smile reminded him of everything that he had ever loved in his life, of everything that had ever been of value and holy in his life.'[5] Grace is indeed this 'smile of unity over the flowing forms' of our experiences of life.

For many of us, nature and grace are seen as two distinct entities. The image of the world that this suggests is that of a two-storey house, where grace and nature are on separate levels, grace building on nature, but never really belonging to it or penetrating it. Today we are asked to make a 'paradigm shift' whereby the secular world is from the outset always encompassed and permeated with the grace of God's self-communication. God invites us, and every part of the cosmos, to enter into communion with the divine Self, according to its own capacity. 'The world is permeated by the grace of God ... The world is constantly and ceaselessly possessed by grace from its innermost roots...Whether the world knows it or not, this is so.'[6]

Grace has been offered to the world from the very beginning of its existence, by virtue of the fact that it is created as a potential recipient of divinity. Grace is, therefore, available always and everywhere, at least as an offer. The love of God does not become less a miracle by the fact that it is given to everyone. This extravagant offer is without conditions. St Benedict, the patron saint of the parish I now serve, in his advice to the cellarer of the monastery (chapter 32 of his Rule for monks) states that the person chosen by the abbot should 'regard all the utensils and goods of the monastery as sacred vessels of the altar'. Monastic tradition tried to bridge the gap of dualism between the sacred and the human that plagued, and still plagues, the Christianity of our times.

Celebrating our humanity

From its very beginning twenty billion years ago, the world was already permeated and filled with God's compassionate presence. There never was a time or space in the history of evolution when God was absent from the world. In the person of Christ this tremendous love-story has been finally revealed. The human is now the home of the divine. The redemption has happened. Salvation has taken place. What was begun in creation is completed in the incarnation. The long-awaited healing has brought a stunning vision to human awareness. The search for God is no longer a dualistic journey outwards; it is the recognition of what is already throbbing within us. That is what we celebrate in the sacraments. The immediacy of the eternal God keeps slipping our mind. It is divine power that energises our daily lives. Grace is life fully lived. God's basic gift to us is the lives we live and the good earth from which we make our living.

In *The Furrow* James Mackey writes, 'The life which is now being called God's grace to man *(sic)* is precisely the life of everyman's everyday experience. It is man's working and eating, walking in the fields or on the seashore, playing for his team or dancing in his club, sleeping with his wife or talking with his friends, suffering the slings and arrows of outrageous fortune or holding out a helping hand to his fellow man, deciding what is best with the best guidance he can get, and getting up for Mass on Sundays. All that is grace.'[7]

In *Doctrine and Life* Sean Fagan explains that Francis of Assisi, with his eyes of faith, had no difficulty with this kind of vision. For him the sun and the moon, fire and water, animals and humans, all spoke of God. As Christians, this insight is offered to all of us. The smallest particle of creation is a theophany, a revelation of God – the acorn, the grain of sand, the shrill siren of a passing train. All too often our act of seeing stops at appearances, failing to explore the love and meaning, 'the dearest freshness' at the core. We need eyes to read the wind, the stars, people's faces as they pass, new roads as they are made, in such a way as to go below the surface. But there are moments which stand out from all others, moments which come like a gift, moments when 'the focus shifts and a single leaf becomes a universe, a rock speaks prophecies and a smile transforms a relationship.'

We call such moments sacred, because in them we glimpse something of the sacredness of life, the wonder of God. Following on from this 'what needs to be emphasised is that our sacramental celebration becomes more meaningful when it is seen as a high-point, a peak moment, a special occasion in a life that is already sacramental in its own right. The sacraments are of a piece with the rest of life and reality, not eruptions from a different world. In this sense it is more helpful to approach them from the context of life as a whole. They are moments of insight, bringing home to us, each in its own way, the deeper meaning of our life and destiny. The sacraments declare forth what is otherwise hidden in the darkness of the world, in the routine of everyday. They bring into focus and draw our attention to what we tend to ignore and lose sight of when we are busy about many things.'[8]

In time and space, in ordinary signs and symbols, the scattered fragments of our lives are gathered up and for a moment given meaning in the light of Christ. John Macquarrie writes, 'In the word and sacraments, the divine presence is focused so as to communicate itself to us with a directness and intensity like that of the incarnation itself...'

Encompassed by love

People are sometimes a little anxious by this kind of presentation. Forgetting what happened in the incarnation, they fear that such theology is 'too human'. They have the uneasy feeling that God is somehow diminished when creation is raised to such a holy state. Are parents jealous when their children are honoured? We are so unfamiliar with unconditional love. Most of us have experienced only conditional acceptance. We are gently challenged by the incarnation to trust in the extravagance of the divine heart. At all times this beautiful world is encompassed by God's love.

Even if we wished we would be hard put to avoid the experience of God. The experience of God is practically inescapable. We cannot help coming into the embrace of divine compassion whenever we experience anything. 'We do not sometimes have experiences of love, fear, ourselves, or anything else and then also have experiences of God. The basic, original experience of God, on the contrary, is the ultimate depth and radical essence of every *personal experience*...'[9] Until this is clearly understood it is very difficult to truly grasp the essential meaning of worship or liturgy or the celebration of the sacraments. If we cannot see God in the ordinary events of life, we cannot expect to see God when we gather to worship. To the extent that we have a sensitivity to the presence of God in every daily experience, we will experience the richness of the Spirit in the liturgical assembly. Before the Sunday eucharist can be a celebration of spiritual and joyful healing and empowerment, every human encounter must be an encounter with God.

The Irish poet Patrick Kavanagh finds God 'in the bits and pieces' of daily life. Writing about the loving mystery that is easily ignored or overlooked because of its hidden nature, Karl Rahner feels the need to 'dig it out, so to speak, from under the refuse of the ordinary business of life'. This detection of the quiet gift of the abundant life, waiting to be discovered in the shadow and light of each night and day, is the work of the mystic. There is no doubt that we are called to awaken and nourish the mystic already alive and well within each one of us. To deny this child of wonder within us, to refuse to acknowledge our lonely mystic is to reduce our life to a grey dullness, to starve our imagination, to stifle the Holy Spirit and to make God sad.

Mysticism has to do with the search for the hidden love and meaning, for the experience of the abiding, absolute mystery of God, in the ordinary things that happen during our days and nights. This is particularly true of the positive and wonder-filled moments that come our way.

The beauty, joyfulness, or goodness of a particular experience might well be a compelling revelation of the presence of God. For example, experiences in which we witness a majestic sunset, celebrate with a faithful friend, are overcome by the immensity of the ocean, are unconditionally loved by a parent, wonder at the splendour of the stars, play with a child, marvel at the grandeur of a mountain range, or delight in the passion of a lover, can all be powerful experiences of the absolute mystery. Our desire to be increasingly attentive to the presence of God would lead us to contemplate moments such as these and all the everyday instances of joy, peace, beauty, and goodness that we so often take for granted.[10]

If we cannot see God in the ordinary events of life, Rahner holds, then we cannot expect that we will suddenly be able to see God when we gather to worship. To the extent that we have a heightened awareness of the absolute mystery in all the joys and sufferings of life, we will have little trouble in finding God in the liturgical assembly. Before worship can be an explicit experience of God, daily life must be an explicit experience of God. This theologian is convinced that we all carry a child-mystic within us; that mysticism, in its real meaning, is not as remote as we often assume; that Christians must become mystics who are attuned to the mysterious light that shines behind all that happens.

Original beauty

The point of the 'theological glimpse' at the beginning of each of the four 'moments' of the book is to render translucent to our eyes of faith, the original beauty beneath the surface of this world and all our experiences of it. There can only be a realistic passion for the possible when we are convinced of the divine power that drives our energies beyond limited horizons. Until we re-vision our theology, substituting a more enlightened model of revelation for the dualistic thinking that has dominated our teaching and preaching for centuries, we will never succeed in making that liberating 'paradigm shift' that transforms us to the core of our lives. And until our theology is renewed to bring it into line with the truest traditions of the church we will never understand the divinity of humanity. We will forever hesitate about transcendence and immanence, following endlessly uncertain cul-de-sacs about false distinctions between 'God and man', and falling into ambiguous traps about nature and grace.

In these 'theological glimpses', I try to reflect the thinking of two of the finest Christian theologians of all time. My general interpretation of incarnational theology is drawn, as you may have gathered, from the work of Karl Rahner, widely regarded within the church as the most influential thinker of this century. I end this section with a number of supportive quotations from Thomas Aquinas, Doctor of the Church and still *the* Roman Catholic theologian of divine revelation: 'Every creature participates in some way in the likeness of the divine essence ... In all creatures there is a footprint of the Trinity.' 'God is not threatened when creation is honoured.' 'To hold creatures cheap is to slight divine power ... In a certain sense, one can say that God is more closely united to each thing than the thing is to itself.'

Matthew Fox has uncovered many lovely insights of the 'Angelic Doctor'.[11] Referring to the energy and image of God in everything, Thomas writes, 'All natural things were produced by the divine art, and so may be called God's works of art... Just as flaming up comes with fire, so the existence of any creature comes with the divine presence.' God's delight in the interconnectedness of creation is also made clear. 'God contains all things and hugs them in an embrace insofar as all things are under the divine providence ... The Godhead is both a place and foundation and chain connecting all things.'

St Thomas had such a profound sense of the holiness of life, a sense that has largely been destroyed because of a dualistic mentality that dominated later theology. '...it is not possible to find something that does not have (some) being and perfection and health ... There is nothing that does not share in goodness and beauty.' Regarding beauty and light he had much to say. 'God is beauty itself, beautifying all things ... with a holy beauty ... God puts into creatures, along with a kind of sheen, a reflection of God's own luminous ray, which is the fountain of all light ... From this Beautiful One, beauty comes to be in all beings, for brightness comes from a consideration of beauty...'

There is something earthy and deeply satisfying in the

incarnational approach of Aquinas. He reminds us of the intoxication of the Celtic people in their awareness of God's delight.
There is a sense of divine ecstasy in his description of creation.
'The Godhead, who is the cause of all things, through its beautiful and good love by which it loves all things, according to the
abundance of divine goodness by which it loves all things, becomes outside of itself.' Divine love produces ecstasy. Aquinas,
so often misrepresented as 'dry', loses this image in the poetry of
his expression. Referring to those who are restored in God's
spiritual 'sweetness', he writes, 'But what is more, they will be
drunk, meaning their desires will be filled beyond all measurement of merit. For intoxication is a kind of excess, as the Song of
Songs says, "my beloved, you are drunk with love".' Maybe the
composer Schuman, for instance, carried mountains of this
music within him. During the last year of his life he wrote over
140 songs, more than his total tally until then. 'I will die,' he said,
'like the nightingale, from singing.'

Seeds of Glory
Once we move into this way of thinking, we find reminders of
our origin, destiny and true nature at every hand's turn.
Yesterday's Divine Office carried this verse:
O Godhead, here untouched, unseen,
All things created bear your trace;
The seed of glory sown in you
Will flower when we see your face.

And on the previous day, September 8th, the birthday of Mary,
St Andrew wrote, in the Office of Readings, about the meaning
of the incarnation as 'the unveiling of the mystery, this nature
made new ... and the *deification* of human nature assumed by
God.' There is great joy in this Christian vision of creation. It
works wonders for our self-esteem! 'To be crowned is to reign,'
wrote Aquinas, 'God made human beings like royal persons of
lesser creatures, and human beings are "with glory", namely
with the clarity of the divine image. And this is a kind of crown
for humanity.' Moreover, God is at play when creating all things
and 'God delights. God is always rejoicing and doing so with a
single and simple delight. In fact, it is true to say that love and
joy are the only human emotions that we can attribute literally
to God.' Aquinas also writes about our natural aptitude for understanding and, in a way, for becoming, the beauty and good-

ness and wonder of God. This is the 'glory' of the human body-and-soul unity.

Many of you will be wondering, 'But what about sin and evil? Where do such realities fit into the picture?' In the next *Moment* we will consider this immensely important question. For now, a few remarks from St Thomas will set us thinking! He is convinced of the sacredness of all creation from the beginning. His language is almost disturbingly forthright. Creation was completed in Christ. 'The incarnation accomplished this, that God became human and that human beings became God...' This conviction is repeated again and again. Even evil he sees as a 'good' with a defect. And 'if all evil were prevented, much good would be absent from the universe. It is the concern of divine providence not to safeguard all beings from evil, but to see to it that the evil that arises is ordained to some good.' Once we repent of our sins he counsels against being swallowed up 'with overmuch sorrow'. He warns that sins against hope are more dangerous than sins against faith or love – for when hope dies we lose heart. There is nothing more dangerous than teachings that would 'cast people into the pit of despair'. He quotes Isaiah: 'Lift up your eyes on high, and see the joy which is coming to you.' Finally, 'Remember this,' he assures us, 'God's love for us is no greater in heaven than it is right here and now.'

Sin is blind

In *The Colour Purple*, Shug reminds us how fed-up God must be when we walk through a field of poppies and fail to notice the colour purple. Rabbi Lionel Blue refers to an admonition in the Talmud. On the final Judgement Day we shall be called to account for all the beautiful things we should have enjoyed – and didn't. Patrick Kavanagh, one of Ireland's finest poets, explains why a parish priest worried about the spirituality of his new curate. The younger man was never afraid when the sun opened a flower. Sin is blind to beauty. It is grey and has no imagination. Sin shrinks before surprise and excitement. It sees no magic in creation. The vibrant presence of the Holy Spirit in all things is denied. Cynicism replaces trust. Sin lives in a flat world and fears the edges. Like a depressed soul, it does not notice colour.

Sin is more than lots of sins. It is not a 'one-off' mistake in an otherwise perfect life, a clearly defined stain on a white surface. It is more like a way of being that we follow, an attitude of refusal to the invitation to wholeness and holiness. Sin is a draining thing. It has no growing in it. It is ugly because it is graceless. It cannot bless or rejoice or be passionate. Nor does it want to see very far. Shades of this negative state are alive and well in all of us. To believe anything else would be mad beyond measure.

Sin is the choice to live in illusion, to avoid the truth of existence, of light , of one's dark side. Many people experience sin as being trapped, tempted to despair, being held captive. Others speak of sin in terms of fear, fear of self, of others, of taking risks, of speaking out. Such sin is the refusal to trust that God is good and that therefore we are good too. This results in a life of excessive control, of hanging on, of clinging to self, to others, of grasping for more. Sin is giving in to self-hate and to the insecurity that results in a life whose main focus is self-protection at the expense of others.

When I think of sin, at least in so far as the *via positiva* is concerned, I think of fear – the fear of beauty, of pleasure, of change and of being open. Closedness must be the sin against the Holy Ghost. Deliberate insecurity keeps the shutters tight. There is no light where there is no trust. Many of us were brought up in a climate of fear where to be different was to be avoided. We lived in a two-tiered world where only the top tier mattered. Lie low here and fly high in heaven. Steer clear of all risk in this life so as to enjoy the no-risk existence to follow. There is something sinful about this blind attitude towards the divine invitation to live life to the full, in the here and now. In scriptural terms sin is seen as 'missing the mark'. It misses the miracle. There is no mystery in the life of sin. 'By sinning in this way we refuse to fall in love with life, to love what is loveable, to savour life's simple and non-elitist pleasures, to befriend pleasure, to celebrate the blessings of life, to return thanks for such blessings by still more blessing.'[12]

The fleshing of God

What we are trying to do here is to offer new categories of thinking, of language and of imagery to make the mystery of the humanising of the Word more accessible to Christians today. We are still working out of the classical presentation of the incarnation as defined by the early councils of the church, particularly the Council of Chalcedon (451). Without getting bogged down in the perennial theological debates of the centuries, it is clear that there is an urgent need for a new framework to hold an unchanging truth. In *Gaudium et Spes*, the Vatican II *periti*

pointed out that 'the human race has passed from a static concept of reality to a more dynamic, evolutionary one. In consequence there has arisen a new series of problems, a series as important as can be, calling for new efforts of analysis...'

Among the difficulties to be faced in a re-presentation of this
mystery is the fact that in our everyday understanding of the
meaning of Christmas, the incarnation is often seen to be con-
fined to the actual moment of the Messiah's birth, and is also
seen to have taken place in separation from God's all-pervasive
presence in the world. Another misapprehension is the limiting
of the implications of the incarnation to humanity alone. The
wider universal and cosmic impact of the mystery has profound
consequences for the ecological crisis in which we find ourselves
today. This aspect of incarnation will be looked at more closely
in the final part of the book, the *Moment of Transformation*.

In this first section of the book, much of our re-focusing of the
significance of incarnation for our world today, arises from passages such as the following from the Documents of the Second
Vatican Council:

> The faith is that only in the mystery of the Incarnate Word
> does the mystery of man take on light ... Christ, the final
> Adam, by the revelation of the mystery of the Father and his
> love, fully reveals man to man himself and makes his
> supreme calling clear ... For by his incarnation the Son of
> God has united himself in some fashion with every man. He
> worked with human hands, he thought with a human mind,
> he acted by human choice, and loved with a human heart.
> (*Gaudium et Spes*, art 22)

The Irish theologian Dermot Lane notices how John Paul II takes
up this emphasis of the council and adds significantly to it when
he wrote in 1986 about *The Holy Spirit in the Life of the Church and
of the World*:

> The incarnation of God the Son signifies the taking up into
> unity with God not only human nature, but in this human
> nature, in a sense, everything that is flesh ... the incarnation
> then, also has a cosmic significance, a cosmic dimension: the
> 'first born of creation' unites himself in some way with the
> entire reality of man, within the whole of creation. (art 50)

The incarnation, then, is not a one-off intrusion into the course of
history, an interruption from outside like a 'bolt from the blue'.

It is of a piece with the first creation. Neither is it about human beings alone. It embraces the whole of the universe in all its evolutionary dimensions. In some respects, Lane insists, the question about the meaning of the incarnation is as much about the general and intimate presence of God in the world, as it is a question about the particular presence of God in Jesus of Nazareth.

Further, not only the human person but also the world around the person is understood to be radically relational, processive, and interdependent. The world in which we live is a vast network of web-like relationships, dynamic processes and organic inter-connections. A fundamental unity is perceived to exist between spirit and matter, self and world, subject and object – a unity that has been significantly enlarged and enriched by the findings of post-modern cosmologies...[13]

Karl Rahner's theology is forever weaving around the twin threads of the incarnation tapestry – the story of God's gracious self-communication to the individual, the community, the universe, on the one hand, and, on the other, the world's efforts to respond to this invitation. What is of supreme importance for the Christian to remember and believe, is the fact that this eternal offer, this spoken word of love, from the Godhead to God's creation, has been perfectly heard and responded to, once for all and irrevocably, in the life of Jesus, in what the Council of Ephesus called 'the hypostatic union'.

The following three *Moments of Passion for the Possible* will explore how this once-for-all event in history is lived out, (or not) in the continuing human and cosmic story of today.

Angelus over Carron

This is my first day in Carron, Co Clare. Many years ago I explored some of the renowned wonders of the nearby Burren and was captivated by its quiet and strange atmosphere of power and beauty. But I had never even heard of Carron. Just now I have walked the lonely, brooding road from Mooney's Perfumery back here to Fr John O'Donoghue's hospitable home where I'm spending a weekend after a few hard weeks on Inis Mór.

If it is true, and of course it is, that the *slua sidhe*, the faery-folk of Celtic mythology, eventually went underground and now have their habitation in mushroom-shaped mounds and around large flat rocks, then Carron must have an immense invisible population. Not even one human dwelling place could I see, only layer upon layer of endless, low, silent slabs of ancient limestone. It was one of those still, eerie evenings when vague fears set in, like the half-remembered nightfalls from childhood when we would suddenly run home as fast as our bare feet could carry us, not quite sure of why we were so frightened. And so it was with me now, in that threshold-moment, when thin shadows were hovering expectantly at the approach of the autumn dusk.

And then, as though it had no source, and stronger than a tinkle and gentler than a peal, the Angelus rang, like a muted melody across the fields of Carron. The clear, quiet, full tones echoed off the hills and slid down the rocks; they pierced the twilight mist and flowed in waves all around me. It felt like a friend had come to greet me in my confusion, like a compass in the desert to direct and guide me. And my eyes were drawn to the first strong evening-star above me, pulsing its light with calm authority and a fierce confidence. Voices were conspiring to comfort me and then, carried by the sound of the bell, just before it became silent, these words were whispered into my anxious heart:

You are not alone – because I love you. Do not be afraid – because this land is safe. I have walked this road before you. I have looked under every stone and behind every tree. You are surrounded by a circle of protection, the Celtic *caim* of my compassion. That is why I became human like you – that you might not know fear. You cannot see them now, but the sky around you is full of angels. They protect your every move and they clear the air before every breath you draw. They light your way; they guide your steps. Like Gabriel did, they announce my desire to make my home with you, to cherish and nourish everything that I, your divine Lover, ever made.

When you hear the Angelus bell, remember these things. I became like you so that all of you could become like me. The road you are walking is a sacred way. The darkening sky over your head is a sacrament of my protection. That stream between the flat rocks you spoke about, is playing a tune of praise to me. And the small birds flying home give me perfect delight.

Because I dwelt among you and made my home with you, you are, therefore, sons and daughters of Infinite Power. Because I am your Father, your Mother, you are flesh of my flesh and heart of my heart. And yes, even the *slua sidhe*, your invisible companions, they also have their place in my grand scheme of things.

And when you till the land and build your bridges, and when your skills create the cities of tomorrow, so wondrous beyond all telling, and your super-highways of communication will reach beyond the stars, somewhere, suddenly, a little bell will ring. It will ring to remind you to enjoy what you are doing, because all your work is holy. And it will ring to remind you that unless you do with a loving heart whatever you are doing, it will not be beautiful. Nor will it last for long.

And don't forget to play. Remember me, once the child of Nazareth. How I loved to play like all children do. I became a human child just to feel the joy of a child. And there is something in every child that will tell you more about me than all the books and learned sermons. You may be older now, and serious too, no doubt. The lines of fear and doubt criss-cross your lovely face. And so the bell will ring to remind you of your neglected child – the little wondering one who is waiting for you to return to find her. You do not know it, but her eyes light up at every new surprise that comes your way, at every time you see a rainbow in the night. She holds the key to all your joys. She never misses that singing bell, the small sacrament of how much I love you.

And so it will ring to shock you with the extent of my obsession with you. You are the rhythm of my breathing; the apple of my eye. You are the lines on the palms of my hands. My love for you knows no bounds. There is nothing I will not do for you. My wildest pleasure happens when you allow me to love you. The Angelus bell reminds you that this intimacy happened once-for-all, at a certain place and time, and to a certain Person, not so very long ago. Because it happened to him, it is happening in you, if you let it.

And between you and me, I would also like to think that when the Angelus bell peals out across the hills and valleys, the seas and lands of wider worlds, across the planets and galaxies of outer space, that people will remember another little bell that rings around the bread and wine of every Mass. Tuned by the same Artist, they both are urgent with the lyrics of a certain day and the music of a certain night when I became one with you forever.

Giolla mo chroí, you are nearly home now. Walking with me, you will always be nearly home. I beg you to leave your fears aside. I have dismantled every possible trap they could set for you. I fill you with my own divine energy. How much I want you to dance your way into every new day, every new place, every new encounter.

Before I leave you, I want to tell you this. Wherever you go, and as long as life will last, there will always be a sudden moment in the middle of your busy life, when from the heart of everything in creation, from the tiniest insect to the epicentre of unexplored space, for a precious moment of wonder-filled pause, a little bell will ring. And only your eternal child of faith and wonder will hear it – and remember.

Celebrating my delight

I was climbing over rocks near Eochaill village on Inis Mór, a small island off the south coast of Co Galway, with a fierce drive in me. I pounded onwards, head down, across the square fields of Aran, laid out like a chessboard of grass and stone on the western brink of Europe. Intent on completing my two-hour work-out within a competitive fitness-plan, I only gradually became aware of a vague but persistent query playing around the verges of my mind. 'What are you doing to yourself?' it asked, 'Is this really necessary?' Why, I began to wonder, was I straining, forcing, comparing? And against whom was I competing? Where was the invisible enemy to be defeated? Or was I partaking in some kind of race to prove something I wasn't aware of?

This was a Sunday evening at about five o'clock. My senses were full of November. Having slowed down because of my self-questioning, I noticed the lights go on in a nearby pub – Deochlann Joe Watty. My decision came quickly. Soon I'm sitting inside. The fire is crackling; small children are playing on the warm stone floor to the background music of a Kerry polka on the radio; the locals are eyeing the visitors with kind interest. What a grace this moment is! Thoughts and feelings press swiftly in on me. How easily we miss what is important. I had forgotten to be comfortable with myself, to accept myself, and most certainly, to celebrate myself. The children around the fire were simply delighted with themselves. Was I? Why was I continuing to punish myself so much? What was wrong with me? Yet here I was, in my fifties, still alive, still sound in wind and limb, and still excited about the mystery of love. I reflected for a while on those observations.

In the first place I was alive. For this I offered a swift and deep prayer of gratitude. The odds, I'm told, are billions to one against any of us being here at all. Then I realised that in a world of sudden and tragic illness, disease and death, all my senses were in reasonably good working order, my heart and lungs were faithful to me, my body was a true and often forgiving friend. Had I ever thanked them, appreciated them or had I perennially taken them for granted in my blinkered and ignorant drive for some unrealistic or unworthy goal of unattainable perfection? But this particular evening I was truly grateful for my life. Death had not claimed me.

Then I remembered that death has many faces. There are other kinds of dying. Across my mind flitted glimpses of near-escapes in my various encounters with creeping bad habits and incipient addictions. These had to be spotted, encountered and at least provisionally dealt with. By 'provisionally' I mean that it isn't so much a question of vanquishing such diminishments forever, like a climber who leaves the low-lying valley-mists behind in reaching the higher mountain plateaus. Rather is it a matter of keeping oneself calmly in a state of expectancy for both the sudden mists and occasional plateaus that have to be encountered every living day. For this hard-won wisdom I also celebrate my divine energy this evening.

While on this theme of journey, I briefly remembered, too, some aspects of my spiritual stumblings through the decades, even though I now regard all my life as a quest for the spiritual. There were times when my journey took me down some cul-de-sacs of the soul that served only to force me back on to places and spaces that opened on to ever-new and beckoning horizons. That kind of death or failure often seems necessary to bring us safely home. There are other angels too that point the way – friends, poetry, moments of beauty. Even the darkness itself can lead us to the many-splendoured thing. And so, for this too, for still being intent on learning more about the mysterious journey of love, I saluted my battered heart.

Yes, above all for this. Because I marvel at the innate capacity for being enthusiastic about loving that I carry. Sometimes the fire burns low; often it crackles brightly. At a time of understandable pessimism in many church circles, I find it easy enough to get excited about new and urgent possibilities. I have often feared that I might lose the energy that powers my being. Once or twice I have. Those were slow, dark days of danger. Often they were full of fear. They were a wasteland without mystery, a cold place without love. I hope they never return. Each night now I pray to wake up in the morning like the child with a new look of hope in her eyes. 'If God be for us who can be against?' as our Sunday hymn asks.

Our fire flickers out only when we try to self-generate the fuel. Once we surrender to the infinite sources of dynamic life, drawing forever on God's extravagance, we will shine with a holy brightness and vigour and vision. The horizons of enclosure move away. The only limits now are those we set ourselves. God-bound, we can blaze a trail of attraction and liberation for those around us. And the key is to do it together. 'In a straight line ' (and alone), as the Little Prince reminds us, 'nobody goes very far.'

I look at Joe Watty's clock. There's time for another pint.

The chapel and the mountain

I was heading for Galway; on my right lay a treeless yet beautiful tract of land in North Clare, and on my left, as untamed as on the day of creation, beyond the elegant Cliffs of Moher brooded the blue-black Atlantic Ocean. Some lines from the previous evening's brochure for a most enjoyable Ballyvaughan *Storytelling and Folklore Festival* were stealing into my mind bringing much delight. They referred to the *slua sidhe*, the 'little people' of Celtic folklore.

> Down from the deepest glens of the Burren they padded. Up from the crevices in the grey limestone they slithered, uncounted hordes of them. And then, in the darkness, they faced for Ballyvaughan, determination and anxiety written in every face.

I began to reflect on those Celtic stories about the intermingling of the living and the dead, those who belonged to the present human race and those who were members of the *slua sidhe*, the people of the underworld. Their comings and goings were frequent, especially at certain times of the year and in certain places. For them, heaven and earth, life and death, were not mutually exclusive, chronologically different or categorically distinct modes of being. There was a blurring of the edges of both stages of existence, an ambiguity about details of such things as calendars, maps and addresses. In the mythology of the *Tuatha de Dannan* for instance, concerning the after-life, we find that they did not so much disappear *away* from this world as *into* it.

Maybe we have much to learn from our wise ancestors here. Could it be that the whole mystery of death is far more subtle than we think? Maybe, instead of clearly leaving us, moving definitively out of range into another realm until Judgement Day, those who die disappear *out* of our surface sight but *into* our deepest selves and our environment in an intimacy not recognised by either faith or senses alone. If love, the most spiritual of energies, reaches such profound levels of bonding and unity in our normal human condition through the medium of our embodied creaturehood before we die to this earthly life, there seems to be good reason for keeping a very open mind about how such intimacy continues to deepen after bodily death.

Fr Noel Dermot O'Donoghue, that fine writer, theologian and scholar of Celtic spirituality and traditional Christianity, first opened up these questions for me at a talk he gave some years ago in Dingle, Co Kerry. His words, whether written or spoken, never fail to draw so many of us a little deeper into mystery. Because of his unique attunement to the ultimate intimacy of all creation, since all creation is the fruit of the same divine womb, he forever seeks to gather rather than to scatter, to include rather than to cut off. I sense his humility, as with shoes off, cap in hand, and full of respect, he gazes around him at the inviting mountains of tradition, anxious lest he dislodge the slightest bit of shale. Deep within him he carries, reverently, the life-giving secrets of the ancient spirit-world and re-members them into our current experiences.

It was in the context of his reflections on theology and environment – *the Chapel and the Mountain* – that he reached back into history and enlivened for us the kind of Celtic milieu into which early Christianity was received. He described how Celtic Christianity was, and still is, at home in the world of nature, one of the homes of the immanent God. When our ancestors showed respect for the faery-folk and listened intently to stories about them, or when they took part either in a spirit of play or of reverence in the various rituals at the four high-points of the Celtic calendar, they were doing something very important and sacred; they were building an essential bridge of vision between one great tradition and the beginning of another.

They had, said Dr O'Donoghue, '....a kind of vision that saw *into* nature, that discerned in and through and around it a real sphere of living presences, at once physical and spiritual, having physical shapes and colours but not held or contained by the conditions of the stable yet corruptible everyday world.' Referring to the spirit-world of the Bible, full as it is of beings called angels, naturally taken in their stride by the people of that time, he goes on to say, 'It is because we have lost the faculty of attunement to the region these beings inhabit that we are all too easily persuaded by certain scholars, so-called, that these beings are no more than imaginary or mythical.'

Now to get back to our question about what happens when people die. O'Donoghue continues, 'There is an ambiguity here that Christian theology, from the time of Augustine until today, has never quite resolved. Are the dead alive in another region, or do they somehow, somewhere, await an awakening? Are they still somehow part of nature, or do they dwell in a spirit-world which may be near to us but is yet of a totally different substance? Are the men and women who walked the hills of Dana, and laboured in its fields and uplands, now without any presence in this place, now unremembering and unconcerned?'

At the foot of those very hills of Dana – the Two Paps, as O'Donoghue and we, locals, call them – because I, too, was blessed to be born in their mysterious shadow – I visited a very elderly couple, a brother and sister, one wintry evening. They confided in me. Regularly, they whispered, a 'ghost' came and sat by their fire without uttering a word. Could it be one of their ancestors in search of something? Was he always around but only sometimes seen? How many more were living at the same address? Is a more intimate kind of union possible between those who die and those who love them? Is there a liberating and strengthening way in which we possess the departed in our very hearts, closer than during separate, earthly life? Is it perhaps *necessary* for death to happen before such a break-through of essential being can push forward the civilisation of love? Could this have something to do with what Christ meant when he said, 'It is for your own good that I am going because unless I go, the Advocate will not come to you. He will lead you to the complete truth and your sorrow will turn to joy ... in a short time you will see me again.' (Jn 16)

Buddhists celebrate *satsanga* – a universal kind of gathering where past and present souls form a pool of Godliness and one-ness. Buddha was once giving a talk in the forest and he asked his disciples to make room for the many heavenly spirits that had come to listen. 'You cannot see them,' he said, 'but the forest is filled with divine beings at this moment.' Like St Columcille's conversations with the crowds of angels that encircled him in the valleys of Iona, so also these other spirits descended into the aura of Buddha, to listen to him speaking and to enter the vibrations of Godliness.

Since I began thinking along these lines, everday brings new evidence of the immediacy of resurrection. Only this morning I was reading these exciting revelations in the Daily Office. 'The Lord God says this: I am *now* going to open your graves. I mean to raise you from your graves, my people, and lead you back to the soil of Israel. And you will know that I am the Lord, when I open your graves and raise you from your graves, my people. And I shall put my spirit in you, and you shall live and I will re-settle you on your own soil...'

Finally, I remember a poem I came across some years ago. I
was drawn to it then. I think I understand it better now.

> All Hallows
> It was just another day on which
> the pew-length spaces filled the church,
> one person here, another there, equal
> but opposite in their accustomed place.
> Nothing much distracted from routine
> turnings of the page. We were content
> to limit things to what we had the breath for,
> until, counting out the bread, I looked
> and saw the church was full of people,
> all alert and tall and ready.
>
> Some long dead have now returned to sing,
> some recent friends, all light and shining
> in the latticed sun. I could not move
> for those that loved the place.
> They needed welcoming, and so I stepped
> beyond the rubrics, and said my stumbling piece:
> 'what threadbare hosts caught unexpectedly,
> how they had as much a right as we,
> how valued for their clothes of white and gold
> and pale green'. Only half was I remembering
> the wedding and the followers that
> just the day before had been arranged
> with never this in mind.

(David Scott in *LOGOS*, Welsh Theological Journal, p 54, Vol 1,
No 2, 1991. Also, for an introduction to the thought of Noel
Dermot O'Donoghue on relevant aspects of the Celtic tradition,
see *The Mountain behind the Mountain*, T and T Clark 1993.)

Hooked on beauty

Bachelor pads are often drab. A friend had given me a small collection of flowers in a pot for my kitchen window. Yesterday I was reading the accompanying instructions. 'Keep turning the pot', it said. I wondered why. Today I know. Already, like crowds at a street incident, or fans at a Papal walk-about, the small emerging plants were leaning towards the light, crowding over each other as they strained to face the window. They were not drawn by the light-bulb, by the mirror, or by any other shiny substance. Only the true light of the sun commanded their full attention. How could I resist the temptation to start thinking about our growing hearts and the light of God!

A lifetime of false beauty confuses our instinct for the real thing. Like the fragile plants, we are born with a sense of what is good for us, an innate feel for truth and beauty, for justice and wisdom. We lean towards health and wholeness when we're small, even as we lean towards our mother's breast. There is no school for telling tiny plants where the sun is, for showing the way down to the river, for pointing the way up to the fledgling, or for teaching the wind how to blow. Our hearts, too, need no teachers. They are coded for what is essential to growth and freedom – namely, beauty. For beauty are we born. By beauty are we nourished. Without it we decay.

As God's own offspring, we inherit the readiness to appreciate, integrate and become, ever more fully, the beauty in whose image we are fashioned. But like the silent mystery behind all our wisdom, like the divine face behind every face, true beauty is not easy to discern. Not because it is in itself a complicated or puzzlesome thing. On the contrary, there is nothing more simple or transparent. The reason for its seeming ambiguity lies in the blurring of our spirit's focus. We go out of tune, out of true. The airwaves are scrambled, making identification almost impossible. Counterfeit attractions are set up to captivate our hearts, to mislead our spirits. When out of tune, even our souls can pick up false melodies. The one song of songs is rarely sung. Most people live their lives without ever tumbling to the amazing mystery of their beings, without ever knowing the healing powers of their hearts, without ever suspecting that their familiar (and often unaccepted) bodies are God's body too.

So astray can we go, so deeply damaged can our innermost antennae for true beauty become, so ingrained can our acquired tastes for instant gratification and therefore false fulfilment be, that often only a major shock will draw attention to a life-time's mistakes. Only then will some kind of dawning realisation of misunderstood values and misread directions for healthy living begin to grow upon us with increasing conviction. The task that follows is not so much towards acquiring new information but towards shedding the information already etched into the naïve mind, by bad education and worse advertising. From the moment of birth our greed has been pandered to. Our flaws are brutally exploited. Our inherent weakness is relentlessly bombarded. 'These cigarettes will give you pleasure,' the adverts run, and then in parenthesis they add (because they must) 'they will also kill you.'

The good news is that once the layers of indoctrination, of ignorance, of blindness – of all the hallmarks of original sin – are gradually peeled off and revealed for what they are, the homing device of our hearts begins again to hum into life. The flame had never really gone out. It was buried, but it stayed alive. And its heat and light are good as new. The natural instinct is naturally unerring. And so the weaning away continues. Like it must. We are weaned from the womb, and then from our mother's milk, and the weaning is never easy. There are always new things to be weaned away from. The trick is to spot them before they become part of our heart's furniture.

There are always incipient bad habits, the birth of a new addiction, the invitation to another bright temptation, the last beguiling whisper to justify the first false step. Most of us get hooked by mistake. We are enticed by what *seems* to be the good and the beautiful. Nobody I know *chooses* evil. So many sad endings begin through ignorance, attachment or blindness. That is why early awareness repays so handsomely. Because the more firmly we are hooked by betraying beauty, the more bitter the war of weaning. There will be outraged protest from deep within us, there will be resistance and ridicule, cajoling and threatening. The mysterious counter-forces to growth and life will fight to the death before releasing an inch of the precious ground they have captured.

Once in Rome, Horace said 'Non omnis moriar.' It means 'I shall not wholly die.' Whatever Horace may have meant by it, I read into it the inspiring truth about the infinity of the human spirit. The darkness is never total. The fire is never completely out. Death is never the last definitive word. That is why I am always lifted by St Paul's hymn of hope. In a letter to his people he assures them that we may be hassled and hounded but never cornered; battered and bruised but never destroyed; accused and attacked but never defeated; threatened and tormented but never killed.

When I came to this Priory in 1991, there was a dead-looking plant tucked away in the corner of the spare room. I often wondered why Mary, my friend, had never chucked it out. Five years later it blossomed in radiance to reveal its purple uniqueness as an African violet.

Our seeds of beauty may sleep through many a winter, but they never die.

Kicking for home

Runners know the feeling well. It happens when you 'hit the Wall'. This moment holds true for the fittest. Your legs, your chest, your spirit give up. You face a blank wall. It happened to me. It was an Irish August afternoon in Barraduff – the dark Kerry hill. The annual 'Human Race' was underway. Everyone was welcome. There was room for all – the fit, the hopefuls and the fun-people. And there was a medal for every finisher. It was here, on this very stretch of road, that a little-known Sonia O'Sullivan set her first major record. And here was I, a few years later, following in her footsteps – and there the similarities end! So here was I, a 'wannabe' champion, hitting the Wall. 800 metres to go. Old men were passing me in cold triumph. Small children were compassionately and sensitively stealing ahead of their priest. Middle-aged women, also aware of my embarrassment and agony, were unobtrusively sidling past. Even the 'professional walkers', with their strange, ground-devouring arm-and-leg action, were showing me their clean, relentless heels.

It was then that the voice within me said 'Kick for home'. And suddenly a new energy filled my body and mind. And my heart too heard the message. Everything changed. Within minutes I found myself striding down the suddenly-friendly village street towards Tadhg O'Donoghue's eternal petrol pump which marked the end of the 'Human Race'. I came 101st – out of the running, out of the prizes and very much out of breath. But unknown to the crowd, to the judges, to the condemning electronic time-keeper and to the ubiquitous and ominous ambulance that somehow always seemed to be watching me, I had won. I had won a huge victory over my resistance, over my shadow, over my private 'wall' and over myself.

At home, that night, in my nearby village, I reflected on the strange power of that 'voice within' – the one that whispered 'kick for home'. I then thought about the French cycling champion, Eddy Mercxs, who held the 1988 world championship for distance covered in one hour's cycling. He was asked about what went on in his head during that sixty minutes of sheer, unforgiving effort. 'My only thought,' he said, 'was that I was cycling home. The village of my childhood was dancing before me. My family and friends were willing me urgently to come to them. As I pumped the resisting pedals, the image of welcome overcame the pain. *I was always racing home.*'

More recently, Mike Powell, the world long-jump record-holder, was interviewed about the source of the energy that carried him airborne for a longer time and distance than any other mortal. This is what he said just before his most celebrated leap: 'In all my jumps, I am jumping home. When I was a kid, I would run down the hallway of our humble house, plant my leading foot just outside the kitchen door and jump into the dining room over the green, shag carpeting. I would land somewhere in front of my Mom's red, leather easy-chair. It was on these occasions, as I danced around the room, imagining that I had broken the world record, that my Mom, who was a real comedian, would point out that I had missed the take-off mark or that my jump was wind-assisted. Now I'm 27, and today I'm competing at the real Olympics. The scoreboard tells me that I'm in second place. So I take off down the runway, hit the board clean and leave the ground. And then everything goes really quiet. And, at the peak of my jump, as I stare at the horizon, I see, for a second, my Mom's red easy-chair at the end of the pit.'

These vignettes from the stars about one of the sources of their motivation, indicate that a dimension of excellence in the world of athletics (and in many other disciplines,) lies, not just in doing well what one does, but in doing it also in the context of a wider background. There is a choice between carrying out our work or play within fairly limited parameters, or doing what we do against an infinite horizon. A few examples might help to explain what I mean. A social-worker can perceive her work within the community as a series of individual tasks, of disconnected (and worthy) events, or she can see them, as well, as part of establishing God's reign in this world. An artist might regard her job as that of providing a number of beautiful objects to sell or to give away, or she might see her vocation, also, as one of revealing the beauty hidden within all creation. A teacher might regard himself as teaching a child to read or write, or he might see himself, too, as a kind of mid-wife, releasing the image of God from within the womb of humanity.

There is a story told about the journalist who interviewed two stone-masons at work on the same building-site. She asked them what they were doing. The first said he was making a wall. The other said that he was building a cathedral. And the grander vision would have added a richness, an accuracy and a quality to every stone he cut and to every brick he placed. In early Celtic Christianity we find endless examples of how the most routine and menial tasks of each day were carried out against an infinite background. Every journey, every preparation of food, every cleaning task, were all prayed into an eternal significance. It is possible to be too close to what we are doing. In achieving a necessary detachment from the immediate task, in placing a liberating space and perspective around what we are doing, in pursuing a richer vision of the routine chores, a new vibrancy and a more effective focusing of our energy begins to happen. In theological terms, every ordinary event becomes the sacrament of an extraordinary reality.

To return to the world of athletics. Sergei Bubka is the current world record-holder, and the greatest of all time, in the pole-vault event. He has no happy childhood memories as the son of a hard and unforgiving father, an old-style Red Army sergeant in a tyrannical Russian regime. So out of the captivity, poverty and unhappiness of his environment, Bubka took to the sky, again and again. Up there it was all silent freedom until he landed on his back to an explosion of applause from the grandstands of the world. But as well as that powerful motivation for his relentless training and committed devotion to his goals, Bubka had another agenda. He transcended both his immediate aims to jump higher than ever, and his wider aims of achieving a better quality of life for himself and his family, by his determination to turn his life-long pursuit into a thing of beauty, a work of art. After his recent success at the world championships at Athens (1997), he wrote, 'It would be a lie to say that the money is unimportant. Money has changed the lives of my family. But I have always wanted to be more than an athlete. I want to be an artist of the pole-vault. I want to create something new, something which will endure. I pole-vault from the heart.'

Whether expressed in terms to reaching for a deeper reality called 'home', or in terms of an awareness of the artistic and the beautiful, many athletes, at certain moments of their commitment and total effort, admit to an experience of body and soul as working in perfect harmony, in complete unity. It is not difficult to imagine the immense difference that this experience and understanding makes to the whole approach of athletes to their art and to their chances of excellence in competition. Before the world swimming championships in Seville (1997) Alexandre

Popov, double Olympic sprint champion, was asked if he had recovered from the stab-wounds he had received one evening in Moscow when he intervened at a fight in the interests of keeping the peace. He could see no reason for not continuing with his unbroken run of successes. His spirit was intact. There was a kind of spirituality about his description of the grace and healing he experienced while training with his dolphin friends. He assured his interviewers that the source of his energy would keep him swimming faster than ever, because 'no knife can touch my soul'.

There will always be, I reflected, something in our hearts that draws us home. While often forgotten, the pull of our childhood reality will surface with amazing vividness, at the most unexpected moments. There is a homing instinct, a divine imperative coded into the matrix of our psyches. We come into this world fresh and new, and the shapes and silhouettes of the human homes and hearths we are sent to will be indelibly imprinted, for good or ill, in our open, impressionable minds forever. But beyond our perennial call back to our happenchance geographical, cultural or religious homes on earth, there is, I truly believe, an even deeper and more mysterious nostalgia for our very first home in another place called heaven. It is here that the radical orientation of our deepest soul is lovingly and eternally fashioned for all time.

This awareness came home to me in a new light when I first saw the much-loved film 'ET'. One scene especially tapped into our collective unconscious. When the abandoned ET whispers to himself 'Home, Elliott, home,' his words touch the image that evokes our deep longing for that homeland playground of heaven. When ET whispered 'Home, Elliott, home,' millions of watchers in every nation wept, and will probably continue to do so for a long time.

The popular writer John Bradshaw holds that we weep because we are still divine infants in exile. This unarticulated awareness distresses us. No matter how secure and how connected we become in the communities of our lives here and now, there is still a more mysterious journey home we all have to make – a journey whose end we can only glimpse, as St Paul reminds us, through a glass, darkly. This divine coding will not be denied. For no matter how completely we fulfil our earthly goals and dreams, even when we arrive just where we have always longed to be, there will still be an inexplicable tinge of disappointment. Even after being deeply moved by the creativity and artistry of a Dante, a Michelangelo, a Shakespeare, a Mozart, (and maybe even *because* of such experiences) there will always be an echo in our souls asking, 'Is that all there is?'

Like the homing pigeon that transcends the distracting barriers of distance and direction in its returning home, so do we. Try as we will to fill our very being with the loveliness of the world, to convince ourselves that we have arrived, perhaps unconsciously to settle for less, inevitably and relentlessly, if we leave any little soul-space open, a small angel will enter. Out of the mysterious centre of our deepest being, this small angel will remind us that we came forth from a most beautiful Love – a beckoning God who calls us back – and forwards. We have come from God, I believe, and we belong, at the end, to that God.

No matter how good it gets, we are still not home. Maybe Joel, in the First Reading for Ash Wednesday, was listening to his lost and confused child, before he heard the Lord say 'Come back home to me with all your heart...' And that other 'wounded child', St Augustine, no stranger either to the delights and allurements of a temporary satisfaction, said it well in his final, graced clarity: 'Thou hast made us for Thyself, O Lord, and our hearts are restless till they rest, at home, in Thee.' It is in this richer context that I now understand that little voice which whispered at a crisis-moment in my 'Human Race' at Barraduff, 'Donal, kick for Home'.

So there it is. The human race and the human heart are full of mystery. We live our lives out of profound meaning. It is never just a race and we are never all alone. We are all part of a wider marathon, a more universal journey, a pilgrimage of all humanity. Hermann Hesse, one of our more unacknowledged, yet prophetic writers of this century, wrote in his *The Journey to the East*:

> I realised that I had joined a pilgrimage to the East, seemingly a definite and single pilgrimage – but in reality, in its broadest sense, this expedition to the East was not only mine and now; this procession of believers and disciples had always and incessantly been moving towards the East, towards the Home of Light. Throughout the centuries, this movement had been on the way, towards light and wonder, and each member, each group, indeed our whole host and its great pilgrimage, was only a wave in the eternal stream of human beings, of the eternal strivings of the human spirit towards the East, towards Home. The knowledge passed through my

mind like a ray of light, and immediately reminded me of a phrase which I had learned during my novitiate year. It was a phrase by the poet Novalis, 'Where are we really going? Always home!' (Quoted in *The Tablet*, June 14th 1997)

True to nature

I was 50 before I could swim. Even though I lived near enough to the Atlantic, I was so slow to commit myself to the water. There were two reasons for this. I did not trust it, and I was trying too hard. For decades I struggled around in the shallow end of the pool, in the baby part of the beach, fearful of letting go. When I did work up enough courage to take a tiny risk, I would swiftly sink in a hopeless and counterproductive flurry of flailing arms and legs, my mouth filled with water and my heart with panic. Clinging to the safe railing of the pool, gripping the bar for learners at the three-feet-deep limit, how I envied the swimmers.

One May day I slid into the pool and swam. It was effortless – so natural. I was overjoyed. It was so easy. Maybe it was because of the lovely friend who swam beside me. Maybe on that day I was ready to listen to the wisdom of play. Whatever the reason, the graced moment happened and it was a special blessing to me.

This morning, my mind goes back to that San Francisco day, because just now I feel that I am at the shallow end of the pool of prayer. There is some kind of similarity here, some kind of connection. As with my initial, futile and desperate efforts to swim, so too with my attempts at prayer. I'm trying too hard. I think I can make it happen through my frenzied attacks on the frontiers of meditation. Nor do I trust in the support of the Spirit of silence any more than I trusted in the support of the healing water. Today, after Mass, I find it so difficult to let go of the bar-grip that keeps me upright and in control, my feet secure on the safe and reassuring tiles of my own limits and boundaries.

On another May day I will trust my spirit to the water and the water will protect it. One San Francisco morning I will risk playing with the silence, and the silence will embrace me. Because they are made for each other – my body/spirit and the God/spirit. This is what we learn when we take the risk, when we leave the shore – that we are but arriving to make a whole. And it happens naturally, it comes without trying. It has its own coherence; it makes total sense; it needs no defence. Justification is superfluous. You simply know you're home. When asked

51

what it was like to be finally enlightened, the holy man said, 'It is like having spent your life trying to find a way into your house by climbing the walls, breaking open the roof, squeezing down inside, to eventually find that the front door was wide open all the time.'

With love and respect, but without fear, we move into the deeper water. The more of it there is, the more filled and supported we feel. The shallow-end, the hand-rails, the life-bouys – all that once were the centre of our attention – rapidly recede and are soon forgotten. This happens, not because we tried hard to forget them, but because something infinitely more sublime has filled the soul. For this new life, for this bright ocean of pure bliss, the spirit was created. It all feels so right, so light, so easy, so natural. The transformation is true to nature. The caged bird is set free; the dying fish is released back into the sea. For the liberated soul, the pain of frustrated hopelessness is over. There are many more challenges to be met, dangers to be overcome. But from now on, at least, they will all take place at home, that is, right at the boundary where the burning is brightest.

Begin with the heart

Where, then, shall we begin? Begin with the heart. Any effort to grow that by-passes the heart is in danger of losing its way. To try to circumnavigate the heart is not the way of incarnation. To search for God apart from the centre of human emotion is to seriously misunderstand what little we know of the Christian mystery. To place God's heart over against the human heart is to get it wrong from the beginning. There is a story about God's desire to play hide-and-seek with human beings. Having discussed all the possible hiding places with his angels – in the caverns of the depths of the ocean, behind the glaciers in the mists of the distant mountains, in a deep crater, he cried, 'I will hide in the human heart. No one will think of looking for me there.' Few have.

In our efforts to grow holy and wholesome, it is not difficult to get confused. Our impetuous hearts so quickly find trouble. Discerning the truth of what allures us is no easy option. Counterfeit beauty beckons on all sides. But of this I'm sure – any simplistic decision based on a preference for the 'spiritual' over the 'material' is fatally flawed. The mystery of incarnation signalled the end to such dualism. The human is now the gateway to the divine. The life of the heart is the life of the soul. 'It is on the flesh,' wrote Tertullian, 'that salvation hinges'.

And so, this morning, I ponder. Is there a way in which what appears to be a distraction from God becomes a way to God's very heart? What I mean is this. We often see the love of others as a counter-attraction to God. We struggle with this dilemma – is this or that person coming in the way of my relationship with God? As usual, I have a choice here. A dualistic understanding of incarnation would lead me to see each love, human and divine, as separate and 'over against' each other. This is a deep-seated attitude that many church people never lose. But when I see the love of those who hold me close, as God's incarnate love blessing me with enriching, tangible life, how simple it all becomes. The mystery of salvation becomes more wonderful, not because of its complications but because of its profound simplicity. We let God be God in us, not by cutting off our connections with creation and creatures, but by recognising the divine source and substance of created love.

Somewhere here lies the uniqueness of Christian revelation. It is a dramatic paradigm shift. What we once perceived as one thing, shifts into another form. Have you ever walked along a country road on a misty night-fall, your footsteps cushioned by the fog? Ahead of you is the silent dim figure of a stooped old man standing by the fog. As you slowly approach, your anxiety evaporates at the revelation that the shape is really that of a leaning bush, hunched in stillness. Can you recall the precise moment of changed perception, the timeless instant of recognition, the disclosure of reality? So it was for me this morning. The hearts I anxiously perceived in the fog of ambiguous and contrasting allurements as threats to my growing, I now rejoice over as lovely, touching incarnations of divine infatuation.

I began to see more clearly now that my prayer would not be about moving away from human relationships to find the divine. I would try, instead, to be fully involved in all dimensions of this exciting human condition with its network of relationships, but to do so in such a way as to recognise the potential for fallenness in our flawed humanity and not to deny its need for purification. There is a sinister dualism lurking in all our hearts which refuses to accept the obvious implication of the incarnation for finding the way to God. Because the vibrant humanness of Jesus led him to drink deeply of his incarnate condition, burning with a passion for the possible until this passion inexorably drew him through the darkness of a certain Friday into freedom, so too with us. It is in the whole-hearted grasping of our humanity, not in its denial, that the way through God is revealed. 'O God of human hearts, forgive me for not learning your first lesson taught to us in the mystery of the sacred, human heart of Jesus.'

Virindia: Land of the dream

Daniel Dancing Fish, my soul-friend, was sitting next to me as we powered our way over the Atlantic Ocean. To the background of the safe thrum of the jet engines, we were talking about the birth of dreams, about the breaking of hearts, about love and war, about healing and change. After a long silence I asked my friend to tell me a story. When Dancing Fish spoke, his voice came from somewhere deep inside.

Virindia is the Land of Love. It is full of beautiful, bright spirits. They are light and flowing and always moving. But they have no real shapes; they make no sound; they are without any colours. They are present everywhere but you cannot see them or touch them because they have no bodies. Because they have no bodies they do not eat anything and so they never really change. But they fill Virindia with light and sheer joy. That is why Virindia is called the Land of Love.

Once upon a time, the Virindians dreamt about a faraway planet they called Mother Earth. There were spirits living in that land too, but there they had shapes. The shapes had different colours. You could feel them too, because these spirits were bodies that came in all sizes and forms. These bodies were called humans. They had eyes to enjoy each other's colours, and hands to touch each other with, and ears to hear the sounds they made. To keep these spirit-bodies alive they had to eat food with different but delightful tastes and smells. In fact everything on Mother Earth had amazing outlines and patterns of colour. The Virindians dreamt, too, that Mother Earth herself was a beautiful ball of blue spirit rolling around in space with her playful, loving circle of cosmic friends.

These were the most exciting dreams that the spirits of Virindia had ever enjoyed. They longed with all their love to create such a Mother Earth. How they yearned for difference, for separateness, for choices in taste and texture, in work and play! They longed to be able to change – from red to orange to green and blue like the shimmering rainbows of winter; from golden light to rich darkness like a summer nightfall; from yellow to brown like autumn leaves.

The Virindians also longed to grow – from small to bigger to big. They dreamt of caterpillars that become chrysalises that become butterflies; of tadpoles that become frogs and go 'redit, redit' in the dusky silence before sleep-time; of lambs that grow strong; of baby snakes that grow long; of the small giraffes that grow tall; of stringy little streams that spread very wide and become great rivers; of blue whales that dive so deep; of acorns that grow so high and of elegant eagles that fly even higher. But most of all the spirits of Virindia wanted to become tiny babies with small bodies that grow into bigger people with bigger bodies. So you can see, Virindia was the place where Love wanted to take many new shapes.

Dancing Fish fell silent. I closed my eyes and waited for him to continue.

It came to pass that their wish was granted. Because Virindia was the homeland of pure love and sheer joy, the spirits now had the power to be born into Mother Earth. At the good news of their new birth, the happiness of the spirits was unbounded. Soon Mother Earth and all her dancing family of planets were dreamt into being by the love and joy of the Virindians. Mother Earth was pregnant with her children of wonder. They filled every space and place with their own delight and their new freedom. It was their spirits of Love that created and sustained every happening in the world. It was their spirits that rustled mysteriously in the midnight grass, that celebrated wildly in Handel's *Messiah,* that exploded triumphantly in the music of the spheres. It was the same Love-spirits that every year woke up the crocuses and told them that the winter was over, and that reminded the squirrels to go to sleep before their beds got too cold. The spirits from the Land of Love became billions of different things and lived and loved in the playground of their new mother. The days were always young and long; the nights were full of welcome.

Even while breathless with amazement at all the possible experiences, and all the different ways to play with change, a dark cloud was gathering over the lovely countryside of the Virindians. There was a sadness coming over the spirits as messages came back about what was happening to their sisters and brothers on Mother Earth. Many of them were mislaying or losing the one special gift entrusted to them for their time spent with Mother Earth. Someone or Something was stealing the Dream from the human-spirit people.

Dancing Fish paused again. He shifted in his seat. He looked at me from a great distance. He was wondering if I could understand this troubled secret of his soul.

There is a beautiful mountain in Virindia where all those spirits, waiting before dawn for their turn to sail across the sea of destiny to the shores of Mother Earth, gather to be blessed with a special gift. Each morning, just before the mists cleared, the beautiful spirits would receive a special memory, their ever-living souvenir of Virindia. This happened so that the deep happiness they knew all their timeless lives would always sing within them, until their journey in space and time with Mother Earth was over. This memory was 'the Dream'.

The Dream had great power over the hearts it lived in. Whenever the spirit-humans listened to it, a great joy came over them and waves of harmony flowed around them like its aroma surrounds the rose. That is why the young spirit-people trusted their hearts. Even their elders would get up and dance whenever they heard the distant mystic-music of Virindia. They were all so delighted with themselves and with everyone and everything where the Dream was becoming a reality. In fact they felt that one day the whole world would become the Dream – the New Virindia.

But remember, the Virindian spirit of Love that had become human was now sorrowing because something was going wrong. The community of the Dream was not growing as it should. The spirit-people were getting anxious. They were forgetting about riding on carousels, about playing and laughing like dancing fishes, about imitating angels and about colouring pictures of circus clowns. They were no longer telling stories about princesses and dragons, about heroes and heroines, about the amazing, invisible Spirit who was there from the beginning but keeps appearing in disguise all over the place; neither were they learning any more magic tricks about playing down the rainbows when the sun and rain embrace, nor about dancing up the moon when the day grows tired.

After much discussion, the spirit-humans whose Dream was still alive and well, decided that there were Dream-stealers on Mother Earth. Night after night, they figured out, while the spirit-children were sleeping, these thieves of the Dream creep silently into the small hearts, and carry away the dancing memory from the mountain of happiness, the precious souvenir-memory of Virindia. What happens then is a tale of tears. When those spirit-children grow into spirit-adults, they forget who they really are. They lose the memory of their true selves – that part of them that once fell in love with their dream of life on Mother Earth. The destructive power of fear takes hold in them, and because they are frightened – without their Dream – they make others afraid as well. Without the Dream they are lost. Without the Dream to warm them, they grow cold. There is no more hugging, nor do people do things together anymore.

And the news was getting worse. These spirit-people, without their Dream, were beginning to fight – about things like power and money and winning. No longer could they tell the difference between their enemy and their friend. Not alone were they attacking each other's Dream, they were destroying the beauty of their Earth Mother, who lived only to protect and nurture the wonder-filled promise they once carried. When the Dream is lost, a kind of wild madness takes over. Without the Dream, nothing is holy anymore. Nobody feels special, or worthwhile, or beautiful; there is no reason to be caring and compassionate, to be filled with a passion about the mystery and miracle of being alive. In their greed, not only do they destroy each other, but they plot and plan to mutilate the graceland of their own Mother Earth, the beloved planet that brought them to a new birth and whose only wish is that they find their true home in the heart of the Great Spirit, who longs for their return. Back in Virindia they are calling an urgent council. All the wisdom-spirits and the Dream-makers are there. They are deeply disturbed. 'In the beginning was the Dream ...' What had gone wrong? What would heal and moisten the wounded, dry hearts now gone astray without the Dream? Could the broken body of Mother Earth ever be nursed back to health again?

Hanging on his every word, I felt that the sad mood of Dancing Fish was beginning to change. Some angel was touching his soul. His voice now had new hope.

After much soul-searching, the Great Spirit of Virindia began to speak:

'Dreams are stolen from my spirit-people not just when they are children but whenever people are hurting. When people are hurting their hearts are breaking. That is when the thieves creep in through the open wound and carry away the troubled Dream.

'Not everyone knows, however, that the pain-time, the time when hearts come apart, is also a special time of blessing. Hearts must be broken if they are to grow stronger. Even as the Dream can be lost through the open wounds of the heart, it is through these same open wounds that it comes home again. When this happens the Dream grows stronger. I hope you can understand this. It is very important. But those who are careless about their Dream will lose it completely at the time of hurting. This is the greatest tragedy that can befall a human spirit-person. The heart without its Dream is like a morning with no sun, like a baby with no smile.

'Humans fight each other, not because they have a bad dream, but because they have no Dream. Without the Dream, love goes astray. Without its Dream, the heart is lonely.'

The Great Spirit of Mystery is weeping now. Silent tears of compassion are flowing from the winter skies above Virindia. Mother Earth is dying at the hands of her angry sons and daughters. They cannot hear the pleading voices of those whose Dream is still fresh and green – the very young and the very old. The Great Spirit is speaking again ...

'There must be an outbreak of loving immediately. Let there be a gathering of lovers, networked around Mother Earth. I have a secret. It is this. Pain and love come and go together. Light and darkness are close friends. That is my secret. The people-without-a-Dream will not learn this wisdom. They do not want to befriend their darkness. They will not listen to this secret of their hearts. Yet it is the only way to be healthy and joyful and to make others happy too. This is what we must teach them. The wounds they have shared on Mother Earth are now the only way for their inner brightness to be set free. This is not easy to understand. Did you notice, when you were there, how brilliantly the stars shone even though the sky was very dark? Or how beautifully Mother Earth smiled when Spring said 'hello' before Winter said 'good-bye'? For our spirit-people to become really human in time and space, they must learn a new dance. It is called the dance of darkness and light.'

And then, high on a mountain of praise, before the throngs of her wonder-filled family, the Great Spirit of Mystery carefully removed her garments. Like fires in a forest at night, seven blazing wounds blinded their eyes. Once more she spoke.

'As spirits we cast no shadow. But now we have bodies that do, temples of my Great Spirit that catch the light of the sun and the moon. Our shadow is as real as ourselves. It is our best but most difficult friend. Even in the hearts of those who are lost, it will find a fragment of the Dream – a fragment left behind by those thieves who steal our lovely memory – a fragment that can grow into an even more splendid temple.

'But what can we do? How can we, like holy spiders, build a web of compassion around Mother Earth, a web that will protect and nourish her, that will encompass her once again in divine beauty, that will restore our original vision and our special Dream?

Dancing Fish reached into the top pocket of his orange waist-coat. From a tattered piece of paper he read the last words of the Great Spirit of Mystery.

I myself will Dream again my Dream within you.
My Dream seems impossible.
It is not for the fearful spirit-human.
Your strength will come from my Dream within you.

Then you will risk
and wonder at your daring.
Run, and marvel at your speed.
Build, and stand in wonder
at the beauty of your temple.

You will meet me at every moment:
– in your soul-friends who share your Dream
– in your wounds that make it stronger
– in your sisters and brothers who
– find their lost Dream
  – in your brave heart.

Because you are now children of the universe
you will have sun even as it rains;
You will have your winter even while spring
is planning to surprise you;
You will be always dying a little
only to make room for another beginning.

And so, my lovely spirit-children,
Never lose your heart and its Dream.
It is my Dream you dream.
It is my light you shine.
It is with my love you love.
And when you are hurting
I am there too.

You will never walk alone.
And that is the heart of the Dream.

When we arrived at Philadelphia – the City of Love – I cannot remember saying goodbye to Daniel Dancing Fish, but I will never forget the story he told me.

New vision – Same place

It was still dark. Later, morning would uncover a grey frost over south Limerick. Wearily I respond to the early Abbey bell – the *vox Dei* – and struggle across the courtyard for Matins in the chapel. Hooded and brown, the monks enter. They move to their stalls. The chanting begins. And so do my distractions. After several weeks here at Glenstal Abbey, enjoying the hospitality of the Benedictines, I face a few questions. For how long could I live as they do? What is their secret? Is there a way of being in the world other than the fragmented and uncertain one I know – a different way of predictability, an even progression of time, an unfailing routine that tempers the volatile temperament? Here, today is like yesterday, tomorrow like today, each morning a continuation of the evening before. Or so it seems.

For how long, if I were to throw in my lot with them, as I have often wanted to do, would I miss the familiar sign-posts of my life – the opportunities to be different, the new encounters, the exciting possibilities, the little risks and modest ego-plans for the future? Why do I feel a chill in the warm sanctuary when I think of letting go of these dependencies? How deep the attachments that send a pang of horror across my stomach at the thought of losing them? What, I wondered, is the secret of the monks? What is that other way of being in the world? To live without the props, to trust the routine, to stop clinging, to transcend the fragmentedness of my possessiveness – is that what the *abundant* life is about? Is there a new way of *living out* there or *in here* somewhere, to which we move when we are sufficiently purified – a state of being, above and beyond the passing nature of flawed experience, an acquired distance from the unpredictable vicissitudes of a fallen world? Could I ever be fit to train for the final contest in such a sanctuary for saints, slimmed down of all my ordinariness, fine-tuned for God through breathing the rarified air of high-altitude discipline?

I shifted uneasily in my stall. The low and holy murmur of the chanting monks checked my panic. There was a radical change of direction in my next reflection. Maybe the Spirit-life, this separate and privileged state of grace that I felt drawn to, wasn't at all like I had imagined. Maybe this other way of living was not really at a new address in some extra-ordinary place, but simply a matter of our *perception* of the ordinary, our *manner of presence* to the excitements and boredoms of each week, our *apprehension and perception* of what's going on?

An image-example may help. I make a habit of getting lost – all over the place. Because of a faulty sense of direction I often go astray. But sometimes, when I think I'm lost, quite surprisingly, I recognise where I am. It is always an amazing moment when I suddenly realise that I am, in fact, safe in familiar surroundings. The strange is now friendly. The threatening is no longer so. Everything is perceived differently. Nothing has changed around me; only my way of looking at it has changed completely. New vision: same place.

We often use a phrase about 'knowing something by heart'. An idea becomes comprehensible, Tolstoy says, only when we are aware of it in our souls; when it gives us a feeling that we know it already and were simply recalling it. This was how he felt when he read the gospels. 'It all seemed so familiar,' he wrote, 'it seemed that I had known it all long ago, that I had only forgotten it.'

Maybe living in God's presence, this other way of being in the world, is not to take up residence *above* the world, or *beyond* it, or *apart from* it, but to enter ever more deeply *into* it, to acquire a totally new vision of what the same place is all about. Maybe that is what incarnation and redemption means – that Jesus did not make any essentially new alternative or radical second beginning as totally distinct from God's original creation and evolution, but disclosed to us a previously unknown *consciousness* of creation – an exciting and unique way of approaching and understanding it, of being part of it.

Maybe we don't have to travel to any holy mountain because where we stand is already holy. The sacred shrine where pilgrims gather has no meaning if the sacred shrine in our hearts is not honoured first. Maybe we do not have to court the attention of certain holy people in certain sacred roles. Sitting at the feet of the current guru will gain us little if we ignore the Holy Spirit already guiding our own hearts. The revelation of the Incarnate Word is forever incomplete without the revelation in every word of truth. Communicating with the Sacred Body of Christ during the eucharist in church on Sunday is of little value if divorced from the daily communicating with that other body of Christ in the vibrant eucharist of the world.

I lift my head. The monks have gone. And with them my contemplative vocation! The morning light is slanting across the space between the stalls. It splashes a feast of colour everywhere. The stained-glass window, dull and dark when we began, has now revealed itself as a thing of intense beauty. In the new light of Sister Sun, what looked so ordinary as to be unnoticed, now erupts into something wonderful and lovely. This visitation before my eyes is like a small sacrament of the wider mystery – an epiphany to confirm me in my hunch about incarnation. Christ does indeed play in ten thousand places, lovely in light and colour and shape and sound; green and round in every common bush and tree.

But not all take off their shoes or their blinkers.

Addicts like me

'I don't smoke.' I never said that before. I say it today, Oct 25th 1997. I have often said 'I've given up smoking for Lent, for Advent, for a month, for a year.' But I then continue again. This time it is different. Because I haven't 'given up' anything. To say 'I've given up smoking' (or any other addiction or diminishing condition) is, according to my bishop David, to convey the wrong message to our subconscious mind. It implies that we are missing something, struggling with a loss, engaging in a desperate strategy to live without something on which we are dependent, as though we were outwitting a deadly enemy. We are immediately placing ourselves at a disadvantage. Much better, our bishop suggests, to see the decisive moment in terms of a release, a freedom, a new beginning full only of promise. The decision to quit any addiction or 'bad habit' is, in the end, a spiritual thing, a moment of grace.

The bishop is right. Over the decades I have relied on white-knuckle will-power and on moment-to-moment techniques of avoidance. This is like walking on a tight-rope where any sudden change in the surroundings can send one crashing down to old habits. Far better to shift one's pattern of thinking radically – to think of gift rather than threat, of release rather than captivity, of break-through rather than the status-quo.

There is, of course, a place for discipline and effort. Nobody denies that. But there is a kind of trying that is counter-productive. The more we fight with 'the enemy' the more power we give to it. The more plans we make – the avoidance, for instance, of our smoking companions, the rerouting of our way home so as to avoid the pubs, the changing of our daily newspaper for one less committed to racing and gambling, the control of the kitchen environment so as to lessen the eating-binge temptation, the sharing of financial accountability to make compulsive shopping-sprees more difficult to get away with, the refusal to bring home work for every week-end so that a reasonable, life-balance can be achieved – the more uptight and unsuccessful we may find ourselves to be.

Effort, whatever form it takes, does not always lead to growth or positive change. It may even lead to severe disillusionment if it is no more than a covering over of the root disease. Effort may change the behaviour for a time; it does not change the person's soul. Yet there is undoubtedly a readiness for change, a timing for new growing. But we cannot arrange this solely by our own manipulation of the environment. We cannot lift ourselves by our own boot-laces. Jesus's decisive 'hour' of transformation was the culmination of his life; it was created out of his hard-won vision and awareness; the timing of his 'hour of destiny' was precise and crucial. Such readiness has nothing to do with whims or hunches, but begins with the long journey of inner awareness.

It may sound odd, but there is something to be said for embracing the source of our distress; for availing ourselves of the negative energy of our addiction rather than hopelessly trying to block it off; for a harnessing of the power of the addiction rather than the fruitless attempt to deny it. The wisdom of ages recommends the befriending of what frightens us, the acceptance of our weakness in the knowledge of a greater strength. Our shadow, they say, holds the key to our freedom, as it did for Jesus Christ, in the desert, in the garden and on the cross. The new freedom stems from our awareness of what is going on in us, our honesty in examining our consciousness regarding the positive and negative sources of our energy. And energy and grace are never far apart.

Whatever the addiction, whatever holds us trapped, (and there are none so trapped as those who deny any such condition) at the end, most of us still have some kind of vision of what God wants us to be. This beckoning God is calling us towards wholeness and holiness, and gifting us with all the wisdom and courage to achieve that abundant way of living. It is helpful to keep reminding ourselves of the fruits of the Holy Spirit, of the graces of redemption, of the freedom of God's children. Despite the cynicism of many, I find that affirmations are a very powerful form of prayer and self-transformation. Here are some of those I use at the moment:

I don't smoke (insert addiction or habit.)
I do not damage my life. I choose life, by the power of the Spirit.
I have broken my shackles; I am free again.
I am aware of divine energy flooding my being. I can do all things in him who makes me strong. I am now beginning a whole new approach to my life at many levels.

I am more efficient, more attentive, more accurate, more vibrant without …
My whole existence is lifted, lightened and energised by not …
Because I am open before God and others, there is no alienation, closedness, furtiveness or fear in my mind, heart and behaviour.
Because I am full of God's light I am always reflecting this blessing on to others.

Finally, it is important that we are not too upset or disturbed by our excesses, our temptations, our addictions or our tendencies towards them. For those within whom the forces of life are pulsing strongly, there is no guaranteeing the nature of the final directions of such forces. The heart of creativity is often an ambiguous, bloody place. The *passion for the possible* within us is never self-adjusting, never self-regulating, never safely tamed. The mystery of our being is always open-ended, unpredictable. Even the best of our kind were seduced by false beauties. This disorientation is a 'given' in our originally sinful nature. Nobody escapes the human condition. Jesus certainly did not.

We ex-addicts are in good company.

What love can do

We are not strangers to the destructive forces within us. We are well aware of their fatal attraction. It is also true that in its essential nature, love too is awesome in its power. Human love tends toward totality – the totality of the freedom of the beloved. In its essence it is ordered toward non-possessiveness and the welfare of the person, community or cause that is loved. Because all life is seen as intrinsically valuable beyond description, one dies repeatedly in trying to love unconditionally. We have the perfect model for such a fundamental option. In Christ's human love, with his many small deaths before his final letting go into the love that he trusted, we have a tangible paradigm for unconditional love. There is a sharp edge to the reality of unconditional love. It is filled with separation, loneliness and hints of death.

We are here at the heart of mystery. It would appear that for unconditional love to be redemptive, to continue burning brightly and surely, it must be daily fuelled by a thousand sacrificial deaths. While we have our litanies of great martyrs and hallowed lists of saints – men and women whose courage and endurance in testifying to a limitless kind of loving inspire us again and again to look within at our own potential – yet, in hidden crucibles of pain all over the world, there are silent sacrifices lived every night and every day, where deep in the human heart there happen victories of love that are celebrated forever in heaven. *In A Time for Love*, Eugene Kennedy writes,

> Life is filled with impossible loves, with people who have had to reach across chasms of separation to support and sustain each other. Some of the deepest and most responsible love that I have seen in this life has been mysteriously present outside of marriage ... I have seen it in people kept apart by illness or other obligations of caring for sick relatives – lovers who have had to face unexpected sacrifices for the sake of others. And I have seen, in the complexities of real life, men and women reach across the boundaries of marriage itself to give support and strength to others without breaking the vows of either marriage. I have seen love like this, a love seldom written or spoken about, but a love whose source is in the Spirit, and it is a love that gives life as it gives everything and can take nothing in return. (Image Books, 1987, p141)

Not many have had the experience of being loved unconditionally. In childhood particularly, where growing is synony-
mous with adapting, imitating and adjusting, the love of our
parents often seems dependent on our capacity to conform to
their expectations of our development. As children we are ready
to change ourselves in all kinds of ways to merit and hold
parental love. And here, somewhere, is the beginning of a long
and tragic story, because we learn to suppress our anger, our
sexuality and our innate sense of justice in the desperate effort to
deserve the most important love in our young lives. We are
loved, it seems to us as children, conditionally. We, in our turn,
continue to love conditionally. Conditional on change: 'I will
love you if ...' 'I will love you more when ...' We grow up in a
world of reward and punishment, of comparisons and competition, of judging and criticising, of merited love.

Here lies the reason for the strange difficulty many people
have in accepting the concept, and certainly the reality, of unconditional love. On two occasions recently when I was reflecting aloud on the universality of divine unconditional forgiveness, I was forcefully taken to task for spreading false rumours.
Such speculation was dangerous. It sinned against the positive
persuasion of fear, the justice of God and revealed truth. More
often than not the aggression comes from adults who were
never hugged by their parents, who never experienced much in
the way of freely bestowed forgiveness and who, as children,
were never asked to forgive their often manipulative parents.

It is almost impossible to experience a person without evaluating that person, or to evaluate without judging, or to judge
without condemning. A brief, honest look into our own hearts
will convince us of that state of affairs. There is much projection
going on here. We still carry around with us the parental tape of
fault-finding and critical evaluation of our behaviour. When we
play it, and we always do, we deal with this crippling voice of
blame by blaming in return. It becomes a destructive habit of
mind, making growth impossible. We are the ones who suffer.
Our confidence is killed. Everything we send out comes back to
us.

The experience of being loved unconditionally is a rare gift. It
works wonders for our self-image, our confidence and our self-
esteem. We know we can only claim it for our own by blessing
others with the same grace: to love without judging; to forgive
without desiring improvement; to pledge friendship forever

with no strings attached; to regard each encountered person as either extending love generously or as fearful, and silently pleading for acceptance with no conditions. We find it hard to believe that this is the only way for our own spirit to become truly rich and passionate. We only keep what we give away. It was pointed out during the famous banquet in *Babette's Feast* that our beauty in heaven will be created by what we have let go of here.

Like an early spring day entices the small flowers to wake up and the new life to venture forth, so too our fundamental option for unconditional love is full of gentle power. Nobody describes this awakening better that e.e.cummings in his famous image:

... your slightest look easily will unclose me
though I have closed myself as fingers,
you open always petal by petal myself as Spring opens
(touching skillfully, mysteriously) her first rose ...

In the current of unconditional love we become creative and powerful. These are the waters of inspiration and healing. The more we abandon ourselves to them, the more grace-filled we become. They will support us, enrapture us and bring us to an exhilaration we never knew before. We are flowing with and floating in the underground tide of love. 'If you trust the river of life,' Krishnamurti was fond of saying, 'the river of life has an astonishing way of taking care of you.' Loving unconditionally is to our hearts what air, food and exercise are to our bodies and minds. The only goal that is recognised as worthwhile by the spirit within is that of achieving a condition of free-flowering forgiveness always and for everything. A lived trust in love and in our capacity to become that same divine love, is the sun and the soil of our spiritual growth. This is the climate for which we were created. This is the only becoming that is worthy of our life's commitment. Everything else is flawed, or misleading, or severely destructive of that sacred but fragile desire to be perfect as God is perfect, to continue saving the world by dying for it.

While our aim is to be continually testing the limits of the infinite sea of our hearts, it is often in small decisions and spontaneous moments that progress is made or lost. Our innate allurement is toward unconditional trust in unconditional love so that by virtue of the incarnation we become that love, actualising and realising what we already are. This vision is incarnated slowly. Even in seemingly insignificant daily reactions and decisions there will often be a wild kind of extravagance, a refusal to calculate our generosity, to place conditions on our loving. What one strives for is a condition of openness that transcends our closedness, an interiorised option for trusting and letting go. There are those who acquire a second-nature predisposition, continuously nourished by a regular communion with beauty, for unerring accuracy in cutting through the fog of hidden prejudice, false self-justification, insecurity and fear. After a while, doing the loving thing comes naturally.

Our deepest longing is for unconditional love. Merited or 'deserved' love has a serious uncertainty about it. That is why unconditional love is more than a deep emotion, a humanitarian feeling. Unconditional loving is based on a commitment – a decision. It is not dependent on changing conditions. The marriage vows, for instance, express in accurate words this vision of the potential of human nature. Such love is transforming. There is no greater power. The beloved become confident of their worth and are set free to be themselves more and more completely. Unconditional love graces the other person with the gift of herself. When I am loved unconditionally I can see myself as valuable in the eyes of the lover; in the stillness of such a changeless love my own beauty is mirrored so that I can truly love myself for the first time in my life. And then I am free to empower the world with my own precious love. This is when the network of salvation is extended, when the conspiracy of redeemers surfaces in a new location, when the epidemic of a crazy kind of loving breaks out all over the place. Christians speak about the building of the kingdom.

There is a deep resistance to the possibility of unconditional love, in both the giving and receiving. There are false fears, of losing one's identity, one's freedom. That is to confuse love with fusion. 'Love consists in this,' wrote Rainer Maria Rilke, 'that two solitudes protect and touch and greet each other.' True love offers roots (for a sense of belonging) and wings (for a sense of independence and freedom). There is a space between that must remain empty. It is across this space that the encouragement happens, the empowering of the other to believe in the self, the challenging toward transcendence, the call to explore the rich delights of the promised land of one's own heart, the reminding of each one's responsibility to save, heal and redeem the other.

The most explosive truth that I believe in seems so ordinary. It is that love is all. Most of us will have learned this along the way, with our heads. But there are rare moments of disclosure when our hearts light up and the world is changed forever. Victor Frankl, that compassionate student of human nature, captures once such vivid moment.

And, as we stumbled along for miles, slipping on icy spots, supporting each other time and again, dragging one another up and onward, nothing was said, but we both knew; each of us was thinking of his wife. Occasionally I looked at the sky, where the stars were fading and the pink light of the morning was beginning to spread behind a dark bank of clouds. But my mind clung to my wife's image, imagining it with an uncanny acuteness. I heard her answering me, saw her smile, her frank and encouraging look.

A thought transfixed me: for the first time in my life I saw the truth as it is set into song by so many poets, proclaimed as the final wisdom by so many thinkers. The truth – that love is the ultimate and the highest goal to which humans can aspire. Then I grasped the meaning of the greatest secret that human poetry and human thought and belief have to impart: the salvation of humanity is through love and in love. (Quoted in Alan McGinnis, *The Friendship Factor*, Augsburg Publishing House, 1979, p 96)

PART II

The Way of Darkness and Emptiness

Revisiting the Cross

It will, I'm afraid, take more than one theologian's glimpse of revelation to clarify the confusion that has sprung up for so many of us around the mystery of the cross. As with all four central themes of this book, a theological reflection is vitally necessary here. It is so easy to lose our way in the land of the cross. This land is an intense place with which most of us are familiar. Our confusion and fears are often linked to the inadequacy of the maps and compasses we are given. My hopes for this section of the book are modest enough – simply to establish a few reliable landmarks for my fellow travellers, until more accurate maps for our battered hearts become available. I ask the reader to persevere with the following few paragraphs. They offer a few sign-posts for those who admit to being lost from time to time in their journey to holiness and wholeness.

There are, then, conflicting notions about the place of suffering and darkness in our lives, so many theories and models of Christian salvation. What follows here is my own attempt to find more love and meaning, more relevance to my life, in the dynamic 'moment' of the passion of Christ. This demands, for me, a breakthrough from the rather incomplete and inadequate model of salvation I grew up with, into another neglected but deeply traditional doctrine that now enriches my life immensely.

In his book, *The Liturgy of the World*, Fr Michael Skelley outlines the thoughts of Karl Rahner, on these two theories of the place of the cross in our salvation. 'Western theology adopted a juridical interpretation of the redemption. This approach presupposed that we could only be saved if God received the satisfaction due for the offence caused by our sin ... the incarnation brought a divine-human person who could render this satisfaction (death) for our sin.' In my early theology courses the resurrection was scarcely mentioned. It seemed to have no direct relevance to our salvation, no impact on our redeemed lives.

Everything hinged on the cross and the death. 'Nor does the humanity of Jesus, in this view, have any salvific function after the resurrection. It is as if the death of Christ would have saved us even if the resurrection had never happened.'[1]

The inadequacy of this kind of legalistic theorising is the manner in which the death and resurrection of Jesus are separated, the one following the other almost as a kind of private reward for the previous sacrifice of death. While most of us may agree about the poverty of such an explanation, few of us have escaped its powerful and misleading influence. At the level of many popular devotions and in all strains of fundamentalist evangelical drives we find endless variations on the themes of fear and guilt that are often associated with such time-bound, legalistic and satisfaction-centred theories of retribution and redemption.

The Cross: Sacrament of Darkness and Light
Without probing too deeply into theology here, I want to establish the intrinsic connection between the death and resurrection of Jesus Christ. A true Christian spirituality is based on the indissoluble unity between the two aspects of the one mystery. Without an understanding of resurrection as being the essential and final summing up of the life and death of Jesus, this book could not be written. Neither could we believe that at the heart of our personal and communal night of pain we can hope for a sure and certain dawn. The cross explodes into glory. The raising up of Jesus is the completion of his life and death in brightest joy; it is the confirmation and validation of the claim of Jesus that in his humanity he was always revealing the face of God; it establishes that for all time, the liberating grace of God can transform every human situation no matter how hopeless. Throughout his incarnational theology, Karl Rahner is anxious to clarify indisputably the inextricable intertwining of the death and resurrection of Jesus. In the same breath he insists that the cross-resurrection moment was a once-for-all achievement for Jesus and for humanity, and that therefore, all our deaths – both our little daily ones as well as our final one – will emerge in our earthly or heavenly experience of resurrection, if we but open ourselves to the mystery.

This kind of theology makes for rich and exciting reading. It is readily available. I have just been reading a remarkable little paperback, *Christ at the Centre*, by Fr Dermot Lane. In it, he gives the busy reader a marvellous overview of the theology we are discussing, with particular reference to a theology of darkness. 'Only by attending to the cross in the light of the resurrection and to the resurrection in the shadow of the cross can we begin to grasp the unified meaning of the saving death and resurrection of Jesus Christ.' Fr Lane then extracts the essence of St Paul's theology of the cross in a masterly way. When we meditate on this mystery, many questions emerge. One of them concerns the inescapable fact that God is not remote from Calvary; that God, too, suffered in that dark hour.

> Surely a God who takes the suffering of humanity into God's own heart is more credible than a God who exists outside the stream of human suffering? Can we not appeal here to the soteriological principle of the early Fathers of the Church who pointed out that 'what is not assumed is not redeemed'? Does this principle not imply that God as saviour in Christ took on the suffering of the world? Is not this part of the meaning of Dietrich Bonhoeffer's compelling claim that 'only a suffering God can help us'?[2]

In one of his later books, *The Trinity and the Kingdom of God*, Jurgen Moltmann writes about the self-limitation and humiliation of God that begins in creation: 'the divine *kenosis* (self-emptying) which begins with the creation of the world reaches its perfected and completed form in the incarnation of the Son. . . The cross is the mystery of creation.' Even a blurred glimpse of this amazing revelation will help us enormously in our grappling with the ever-present problem of pain. It will stretch our minds and imagination as they were made to be stretched. 'If we acknowledge,' writes Lane, 'the full gift of human freedom given by God to human beings in the act of creation, then we must also recognise that this implies some form of freely chosen self-limitation by God in creation. The divine act of creation is itself a divine act of self-emptying love (*kenosis*) in virtue of the gift of human freedom endowed upon humanity.' John Macquarrie puts it this way:

> In creating an existence other than himself, and in granting to that existence a measure of freedom and autonomy, God surrendered any unclouded bliss that might have belonged to him had he remained simply wrapped up in his own perfection. In creating, he consents to know the pain and frustration of the world.[3]

The cross, then, reveals the self-emptying love of God from the beginning. By the same token, it reveals that there is suffering at the heart of the universe from its creation. 'What Virgil once called "the tears of things", which lie at the centre of the world, have been disclosed in the agony of the cross. The historic cross therefore lays bare something of the flawed character of the cosmic process as well as the sinful condition of humanity.'[4]

Before we leave these musings on the intimacy of a Love that is intensely present in all our experiences, here is a remarkable story told by Elie Wiesel, a Jewish survivor of the Holocaust, in his book *Night*:

> The SS hung two Jewish men and a boy before the assembled inhabitants of the camp. The men died quickly but the death-struggle of the boy lasted half an hour. 'Where is God? Where is he?' a man behind me asked. I heard the man cry again, 'Where is God now?' and I heard a voice within me answer, 'Here he is – he is hanging here on the gallows.'

The silence of God in the face of suffering is not a silence of absence, or rejection or withdrawal in the same way that the silence of God surrounding the last desperate cries of Jesus on the cross was not a silence of absence or rejection. In both instances we are faced and challenged by the silence of God that allows human freedom to run its deadly course and yet, as only divine love can do, that can bring forth a harvest even from an evil cradling.

There is no suggestion here of an impotent or useless God. There is a power in surrender and weakness. We are dealing with paradox and mystery, as revealed in the cross and resurrection. There are many references to the strength of surrender in our Eucharistic Prayers and Prefaces. '(The martyr's) death shows forth your strength shining through our human weakness. You choose the weak and make them strong... (Preface of Martyrs). 'I, if I be lifted up, will draw all thing to Myself.'

The darkness of the cross of Christ is the only way, for the Christian, to see the light. The depths to which humanity can descend in its orientation towards destruction can lead to the heights to which God can soar in God's capacity to redeem. 'It was this struggle with darkness that prompted Martin Luther to say that the Christian is someone who, in the face of darkness and death, goes into the garden of life to plant a tree and knows that he or she does not plant in vain.'[5] The cross, therefore, in the life of Jesus and in our own, is never to be understood as an ex-cuse for passive, fatalistic acceptance of unjust situations, but as a creative moment on the way to newness of life. 'Behold, I will make all things new.'

The scandal of particularity

Let me try to explain what I mean by this strange phrase. I only refer to it in the interests of clarity, by providing a further theo-logical underpinning to the central claims of the last few pages and, indeed, of the whole book. This is how I see it. Many people are more comfortable with a generalised cosmic kind of medita-tion on the forces of darkness, on the conflict between good and evil, between light and shadow, than with a unique event in time, where the spotlight of destiny falls on one identifiable per-son, fixed in a historical context of time and space. This is what I mean by 'the scandal of particularity'. It focuses our collective intimations and universal intuitions on to a particular man, who carried a particular cross, for a particular purpose. So many peo-ple find this phenomenon to be an impossible option for their faith, an invitation too difficult to be taken up, a participation that is clearly too costly in its implications.

The Christian cross as a sign of contradiction confronts everyone with the glaring and awesome paradox that only in giving one's life does one keep it; only in dying to the lesser are we born to the greater. In embracing the cross, Jesus trans-formed it from a sign of shame to a triumphant signal of victory. When on the horizontal bar he is nailed to the vertical, heaven and earth meet in a burst of infinite love. And at that moment the human condition, with all its complexity, goes into God in Christ and is forever saved.

But what does it mean 'to be saved'? We hear it and celebrate it at every Christian liturgy. When cashed into the currency of daily, human experience, what does redemption mean? From what am I redeemed? If Christ's successful encounter with dark-ness has won light for the world, what are the implications of this historical happening for me? Does it mean that in some strange way my wounds and the wounds of the world, whether glaringly open or deeply hidden, can in fact be healed? And not just healed, but can become the source of new and life-giving growth for myself and others?

Paradox carries a complexity and a simplicity. For now, I offer two broad approaches to the mystery. These will be ex-

plored many times in the following pages. The first is about confronting the cross in our lives with great courage. There is no
denying our resistance to this invitation. It is with varying degrees of fear that we examine our cross in life, assuming that we
know it – because most of us deny it, suppress it, bury it. The
Christian is called to face it, to take it up daily. And not only face
it, but befriend and accept it. This is, indeed, a tall order! Kipling
must have struggled with the challenge:

> I have known Shadow
> I have known Sun;
> And now I know
> These two are one.

The second approach is different, but connected, and no less demanding. Just as Jesus embraced his darkness and in so doing
became the Light of the World, we too are invited to believe that
this transformation is ours for the asking. Because he freely accepted his death, and all the previous little deaths of his life, in a
willing sacrifice, but not without much struggle, doubt and effort, an explosion of healing light and love reverberated around
the world. We are asked to believe that such a miracle is waiting
to happen in our hearts once we surrender our distress in undis-
puted solidarity with the death and life of Jesus.

What is important to remember here is that the healing and
reconciliation that happened on that fateful weekend in
Jerusalem have universal and even cosmic consequences.
Salvation was not just for our own broken heart, but for a broken
human race, a broken world and a broken creation. It is of great
importance not to confine the once-for-all achievement of the
Saviour to the salvation of my individual soul. It was the making
whole of *everything* that is fractured, isolated and alienated in *all*
aspects of life that was secured for ever when Christ was raised
on the cross. That is when he drew all things to him, 'all things
whether on earth or in heaven'. (Cor 1:20)

Perennial Paradox
In matters of the faith-mystery, paradox is never far away. If we
are to rise with Christ we must first die with him. It is one thing
to have died symbolically in the baptismal font and quite another
to die daily to all that would prevent us from rising to ever higher
places with the Risen Lord. We struggle with meaning and symbolic language. 'If anyone wants to be a follower of mine, let him

renounce himself, take up his cross and follow me.' What is Mark revealing about suffering here? Nor does Luke's observation satisfy us. 'For anyone who wants to save his life will lose it; but anyone who loses his life for my sake will save it.'

It would be easy to miss, in the pretty piece of jewellery we carry somewhere on our person, the frightening totality of renunciation hidden within the familiar Christian cross-symbol. The very preservation of my own person is achieved only when I let go entirely into the Other. This is the final risk. It is the death that has to be taken if we are ever to enjoy the new age of Jesus Christ. It requires no less than a total surrender if we are to discover our true selves before God. Only if the seed in the ground dies will it bring forth the rich harvest. If we never care for the caterpillar there will be no new butterfly. The fresh and green springtime shoots can only begin to grow in the winter womb of last year's tree. George Herbert's serene and unwavering trust in the seasons of salvation and the redemptive power of God, is beautifully expressed here:

Who would have thought my shrivel'd heart
Could have recovered greenness? It was gone
Quite underground; as flowers depart
To see their mother-root, when they have blown;
Where they together
All the hard weather,
Dead to the world, keep house unknown.

We can reject the cross and it remains a stark instrument of torture. We can embrace it in trust and it becomes the source of our growth. The more we resist the cross, the stronger the fear inside us. The more we befriend it, the swifter the healing. It is as though in our acceptance of it we drain out and purify the energy of the cross. As the cross is disempowered, our spirits become delightfully empowered. Our pain becomes the fuel for the journey; our suffering the guarantee of a wondrous harvest. The visionary Teilhard de Chardin said that if we could but truly befriend the energies of suffering and fear, our world, in an instant, would be transformed.

The dance of light and darkness

Thomas Aquinas clarified and succinctly summed up a world of debate when he wrote that revelation is bound in two volumes – the book of nature and the book of the scriptures. When, in our doubt and desperation, we search for reasons to believe that death is not the end, that suffering is not all bad, that the cross has a positive dimension to it, we find not just scraps of hope, mere clues, in both of these books. We find convincing evidence for head, heart and soul when we observe how breakthrough happens in the natural order even before we read the story of the young Man who reconciled all things in himself. In the historical development of the universe, for instance, and in very general terms, through the stages of evolution and of every living cell, there is a clearly discernible pattern of growth that involves a straining, a conflict, a breaking, a disintegrating, a reforming and a transformation. It was from such phenomena that Jesus, and many other great spiritual leaders, drew their symbols, images and metaphors for the breakthrough of darkness into the light of redeemed life.

There is no area of life now that falls outside the presence and activity of God. In the cross, God is found to be active and present in the midst of extraordinary evil, suffering and death – drawing good out of evil, salvation out of suffering, and new life out of death … In its own way the cross of Christ captures the paradox of life that those moments in which God seems most absent can be recognised as moments in which God is most present … Instead, silence and signs, darkness and light, suffering and joy are now equally the location of God's creative presence and activity.[6]

When the Word became flesh, that same Word became all human experience, across the vast range of almost limitless human emotion. Such orthodox, incarnational theology holds that all human experience is potentially redemptive because Jesus, in his humanity, and by virtue of his divinity, has revealed the sacred nature of all creation. This is Christian belief. From the profound experience of the world of his childhood with its unique moments of wonder and surprised learning, of his turbulent teenage years of self-discovery, of the intense and almost unbearable awareness of his true identity, from the transcendence of his transfiguration to the depths of his despair on the cross, and the ocean of feelings in-between, of hurts and joys, of anger and compassion, of doubt and temptation – there can be very little of what the human heart can feel that Jesus did not experience. That is one of the reasons why we can know with certainty, that all our experiences of negativity, diminishment and emptiness need never be wasted because 'all, in the end, is harvest'. Remember the belief of the Church Fathers, quoted above, 'what is not assumed is not redeemed'.

What transformations would happen in our lives if we could but believe in such divine alchemy. We might even come to love our wounds and go freely to our appointed destinies as Jesus went to his death, 'a death he freely accepted'. We might even celebrate our scars because they are the essential openings to the abundant life. Maybe that is why we're told that those perfect bodies of ours in heaven will still proudly carry the signs of the cross that graced us here on earth. What a hard lesson it is to learn – that the place of our pain is the holy place, that the point of our hurt is the point of our growth, that it was in the darkness of Calvary that the bright dawn of Easter began, that there is no Sunday joy without the ever-present Good Friday shadow.

It seems that there is no short-cut to happiness, no cheap grace to salvation. But we are still trying to redraw the maps of our lives, without the jungles of confusion; to reroute the traffic of our rushing hearts, so as to avoid the rush-hour of painful encounter, to reset the compasses of our souls, creating diversions around the deserts of empty and arid places. If we only knew that in so doing we are resisting the disguised highway to our deepest wishes. Scott Peck reminds us that most of our neuroses arise from the avoidance of necessary pain. Ernest Hemingway observes that while life breaks all of us, some people grow at the broken places. It is not the experience of hurt and hate and envy that destroy us, but the refusal to acknowledge them, to accept them, to encounter and dismantle them. St Paul writes about taking care of the hidden self, about setting it free by bringing the suppressed emotions to the surface, about realising that what we thought was dead and buried was, in fact, only buried, but not dead. All of our buried emotions are buried alive.

And how we resist the call to come out into the light! How strong the attraction of the darkness! What fascination we carry for the destructive forces that are rampant in our deepest centre! I see it in myself all the time: and I see it too in those who participate in the workshops we offer.

The Exploding Cross
St Benedict's parish is the gateway out of East Leeds into the beckoning plains that show off the proud City of York. Its big fields creep trustingly up to the increasing network of highways

that run like the lines across an open palm, its finger pointing to the freedom of the Northern dales. The new and final twenty-mile stretch of the M1, for instance, will join the ancient Great North Roman Road – the A1 – within our Yorkshire parish just in time for the year 2000 AD.

We are in an interim period between the demolition of our old church building and the completion of a new one. A strong thread that holds us together in this wilderness of waiting is a beautiful bronze design specially commissioned to mark the opening of St Benedict's in 1967. It has an evocative motif recreated in its many imaginative presentations throughout the original building. The most striking of these is a strange-looking cross over which we often meditate. It lets the light in through a big gash at its centre so we call it 'the cross of light'. It has cavernous spaces in its design, so we call it 'the empty cross'. But most of all, it is full of jagged pieces of flying splinters, so we call it 'the exploding cross'. It is as though the energy at its centre can contain itself no longer and must break free from its prison. Hence its power. In our farewell to our beloved place of worship, I wrote this meditation:

> It is at the point of pain that grace gathers at its highest intensity. Suffering has truly been called fuel for the spirit. This we know from the passion of Jesus. His Calvary darkness exploded into Easter light. Therefore all our suffering is redemptive too. When we unite our pain with his, small miracles happen.

> The tabernacle door (which carries the same motif,) opens along the vertical line of the cross. Just as once in history, and far away, the stone was rolled from a certain tomb, to open the way for the saving Christ to come forth, so too, each Sunday morning, and in this very church, the opening Tabernacle door splits the cross at its centre, to reveal within its shadow, the bright Bread of Heaven.

I remember one Good Friday afternoon watching our parishioners remove their shoes and file slowly towards this very cross. One by one, young and old, they reverently pressed their lips, in a gesture of almost ultimate intimacy, against the cold comfort of this bronze symbol of pain. I was so moved at the mystery happening before me. I was astonished at the depth of a faith that could draw people into such a rich and profound ritual. How could they embrace this symbol of death? How could they kiss the very source of destruction? On this dark day, how amazing it was, how full of terror and beauty, of graced insight, of a trust that swept far beyond the boundaries of our earth-bound experiences, that we publicly and deliberately, mostly blindly yet hopefully, knelt down in adoration before the gaping wounds that destroyed him, and that are undoubtedly, at first perception, also destroying us. In *Oh God Why?* Gerard Hughes writes,

> Suffering, in itself, is an evil to be avoided ... But if we let God into our pain (even though this pain may well be self-inflicted, when our bruised ego is threatened by criticism, failure, rejection, etc.) and acknowledge its origin in our own expectations, and pray to be delivered from our own false securities, then the pain can become curative, leading us to freedom from our false attachments, and to the knowledge that He really is our rock, our refuge and strength, and that we have no other.

> ... Because if we are to be healed and transformed, we have to enter with Him, the pain of things. It is in our woundedness, not in our power, that we find Him. He is a God who weeps in our hearts, but His tears are healing tears, springs of everlasting life, cleansing, sustaining, giving hope when everything seems hopeless ...[7]

Crucifixion and resurrection are at one in the heart of the Paschal mystery. This risen body of Jesus is glorious not in spite of, but because of the wounds and disfigurations. Margaret Spufford, in an article for *The Independent* during Holy Week, reminds us that 'because the Lord God incarnate was glorious through his acceptance of his wounds, not in spite of them, we may also have hope that we ourselves in our malformations and damage, may be redeemed and become, in some small fashion, icons of glory. Blurred icons, indeed, but like Moses, or, if you prefer, like St Paul's translucent earthenware pots, we are intended ultimately to shine, as mirrors reflecting God's glory, each uniquely in his or her own fashion.'

The *Triduum* – the Three Days of Holy Week – is a time for our hearts to burst, a time to trust our own instincts that in this breaking there is new life, new power, new energy. The road to freedom and light is through God's passion. Yet we refuse to believe this. We domesticate the cross and try to tame it. Unless we can get back in touch with that passion and that pain, we are already good as dead. Because God is at the heart of this passion and pain. The passion story strikes chords deep within us and plays a music we must strain to hear.

When we look at the empty figure on the cross we see the finality of total surrender. The poignant figure at the centre of crucifixion is full of a letting go, a handing over. There is something ultimate about the last goodbye. None of us are strangers to it. In his lovely book *Passion for Pilgrimage*, Alan Jones wonders what it would be like to obey a God who is revealed as self-giving love.

We know something of this kind of love, which steps aside to allow others to be, in our everyday experience. The poet C. Day Lewis wrote these words about his son growing up. The scene is a sporting event at the boy's school during which the son turns from his father and goes off with his friends:

I have had worse partings, but none that so
Gnaws my mind still. Perhaps it is roughly
Saying what God alone could perfectly show –
How self-hood begins with walking away,
And how love is proved in the letting go.[8]

The Calvary of unmasking

The central theme of this part of the book is about personal transformation before its emergence into social transformation. It is about the new life that follows on our discovery and re-claiming of our true selves. This life-giving awareness is not easily won. This condition of simplicity costs not less than everything. That is why I now want to focus on the dying that happens when we risk the inner journey to the authentic self. This is a courageous journey of unmasking many false selves, of disentangling the web of defences carefully and subconsciously fashioned since childhood, of dismantling the scaffolding of pretence and projection built into our psyches quite simply by the fact of living in a world such as ours.

I am indebted to Gregory Baum, a *peritus* at the Vatican Council, for much of what follows. He, in turn, acknowledges the insights of a great religious philosopher, Maurice Blondel, who lived at the turn of this century. They both draw attention to the cross-dimension as a key element in creation theology and creation spirituality – that of embarking on the quest of self-realisation, of building self-esteem, and of discerning the potential mistakes along the way in achieving this task. Our self-realisation, our self-making which is God's redemptive work in us, is a *via negativa*, a process demanding sacrifice, discipline, and tough work.

It does not happen easily and spontaneously, by simply following our 'natural' impulses and instincts. We are all children of original sin. Discovering the 'hidden self' referred to by St Paul, is a complex process. 'Depth psychology has clearly established that hidden in man are angers, hostilities and other destructive trends that may not reveal themselves in his conscious mind, and yet have a profound influence on his behaviour.'[9] We are full of counter-productive and hidden games that may serve only to perpetuate our powerlessness, our self-hatred and ultimately our self-destruction. Those who push themselves into the centre of every conversation and every human situation have, on the unconscious level, the greatest doubts about their own self-identity.

What is present at the root of self-elevation is a hidden self-hatred. What is wrong with us, and what causes the awful things we do, is not simply that we love ourselves too much but also that, on a deeper level, we do not love ourselves at all. We are often impelled by an unconscious desire to keep mistrusting, to be betrayed or badly treated, to be punished. There is a long list of self-inflicted miseries. I labour this aspect of the mystery of our being only because it is the hardest nut of all to crack. So many of our attitudes and actions are smoke-screens, frantically erected, preventing us from knowing who we really are and what we really feel. To abandon these screens seems like death. We have so much invested in our defences. We fear that if these defences are let down, our whole house might fall apart.

It is only when we allow ourselves to be firmly grounded in the land of grace, and realise the *spirituality* of our nature, that growth and healing and freedom happen. And they happen only when we are open to the voice of the Spirit. This openness is a gift. It must be a gift because we do not naturally accept the painful truth about the games we play, the attachments we hold to destructive habits of heart and mind. Entry into self-knowledge is always a conversion. The *via negativa* is about the felt pain of such conversion.

> There are special moments when such a call comes to a man, or even to a community; the scriptures speak of them as *kairoi* ... It is always a response to a summons. It is never self-initiated. And it is always painful. There is in it an element of letting go, of falling into darkness, of wondering whether de-

struction awaits us; and yet there is also an element of hope
that we are not totally alone, that protection is available, that
something new will emerge in us, and as we fall into the
darkness that there will be safe place to land ...[10]

Since our destiny is divine, it is God's Word that reveals to us
who we are. And this is going on all the time. The Word, who
became incarnate in Jesus Christ, is in some way present at every
moment of our lives, in every conversation and encounter, even
where there is no explicit reference or awareness of such a presence. I feel sure it can be said that every entrance into self-
knowledge is divine revelation. To be well and whole is the
work of grace. This condition of sound health is not about a
naïve happiness.

The *via negativa* must always be travelled. To be well includes
the freedom to be unhappy in the face of human misery, injustice and war. To be incapable of grief at the evidence of our daily
inhumanity to each other is to be spiritually sick. To be well
means to be in touch with reality and to respond to it in a fully
human way. We celebrate the joy; we mourn the evil. On the one
hand, we see that the suffering in our lives, so often concerned
with insignificant issues when considered *sub specie eternitatis*,
soon lose their hold over us for a while. On the other hand, a
person must have been deeply transformed by grace to be free to
suffer the real sin in the world and not deny a personal involvement in it. It is so important to be able to distinguish necessary
from avoidable pain.

To be true to Baum and Blondel, in their many books and ar-
ticles, their chief concern lies with social transformation. To this
concern we will turn our attention in the fourth 'Moment' of this
book, the *via transformativa*.

In order to realise himself, man must face the evil on two
fronts, in himself and in the society to which he belongs, and
unless he wrestles with evil on both these fronts, he cannot
move far on the way to growth and reconciliation. If he con-
fines his struggle to the evil within himself, he will not be
able to discern how much his own spiritual values and his
ideals for the community are hidden ways of protecting his
social and political (and church-given) privileges. In order to
become himself, a man must be politicised ... Conversely, if a
man only wrestles with the evil in society and refuses to look
at the destructive trends in his own life, he takes the risk that

his social and political (and church-oriented) efforts will be
inspired by an unresolved personal conflict. The man involved in political struggle, who refuses to seek self-knowledge, may end up in total blindness, be out of touch even
with the social reality, and undo the work to which he dedi-
cates his life ... Man can enter into his self-realisation only as
he is willing to wrestle with the enemy within and without.[11]

God in the negative

In this second 'Moment' of the book, we are touching on what is
known as the *apophatic* approach – the way of denial, the *via neg-*
ativa. Without getting too heavy about it (and yet I feel it is important for the reader to know), this approach is based on the
presumption that really we can know nothing about God. It
holds that just about anything we say about the Source of Being
is misleading. In the face of transcendent mystery, our safest and
best response is silence. God is beyond all knowledge. Apart
from the clues given to us by God's creation, God's own essence
is unknowable. God is the mystery behind all mystery; the darkness behind all darkness. There is a sense in which we must let
go even of God. 'I pray to God,' wrote Meister Eckhart, 'to rid
me of God.' Hence the attraction of our Celtic ancestors for the
celebration of emptiness in the desert. There is a cautionary lesson here for those who claim 'to know the mind of God'.

From our reflections on the *via positiva*, we can see how positive happenings in our lives can be understood as experiences of
God. The *via negativa*, also, with its moments of pain and loss, of
limitation and emptiness, is potentially an even deeper experience of the divine mystery. Karl Rahner writes that the experience of God is perceived most clearly 'where the definable limits
of our everyday realities break down and are dissolved, when
lights shining over the tiny island of our ordinary life are extinguished and the question becomes inescapable, whether the
night that surrounds us is the void of absurdity and death that
engulfs us or the blessed holy night already shining within us is
the promise of eternal day.'[12]

He refers to loneliness with a fine sensitivity. We carry within
us a deep and insatiable longing for completion, for intimacy.
We ache for the eternal but are frustrated in time. We reach out
for the whole world but our arms are not long enough to embrace it. Our lives can be hounded and driven by a great restlessness until we accept the fact that here on earth all symphonies

remain unfinished. This acceptance brings freedom from the tyranny of the temporal, the relentless need for instant results, the primoridal imperative to eat of the fruit of the tree of knowledge *now*. But we continue to expect too much from life. We demand to hear the last bars of the finished symphony. This kind of expectation can do much violence to our uncertain hearts and our uncertain lives.

There is always the temptation to run away from the cross. There are many ways of running away. Most of us become adept at escaping. And yet, the wise people tell us, if we do not take up our cross, we will never discover the truth about ourselves. We will miss the moment – the moment of disclosure. Because such are the times for our 'hidden self' to emerge; such are the dance-floors for light and shadow to create something new; such are the only challenges where human transcendence can happen. When the running has to stop, when we are cornered by our fear, when our bluff is finally called, then we come face to face with the reality of self and God. These encounters are experiences of limitation – our personal limits, those of one another, of our relationships, of our family, of our church, of life itself. But because they are such intense feelings of limitation, they can be equally powerful experiences of transcendence and of God. To know that we have limits, but that we are not the victims of those limits, is already to be free. To sense that the black wall of the prison might just possibly be a kind of horizon instead, to suspect that there is a 'beyond' to that horizon, provides a glimpse of the nature of God's immanence. And this glimpse can only be experienced from the vantage-point of what we call the 'place of limit'.

Not everyone allows their shadow to draw near enough to be recognised. Among examples of that inter-face of disclosure, those moments of transcendence, the following could be mentioned. Whenever we consciously face loneliness and rejection, when we accept responsibility for our sins and destructive drives, when we refuse to give up despite immense pressure to call it a day, when we stay faithful to our vocations in spite of failure or betrayal by ourselves or others, when we are falsely accused and refrain from blaming, when we are struck down by failure, disgrace or diminishment and still trust, when we continue to believe in beauty in the face of ugliness and lies, when we forgive those who try to destroy us and seek reconciliation, when our broken hearts find new power – when any of these things happen to us, there, and there only, is the moment of truth. This is the timeless time when the saints are made. It is called the *via negativa* to God.

The paradox of God's ways, written into the hearts of God's people, is often best captured by those who combine good theology with good poetry. For instance, the poet R. S. Thomas, whose poetry is full of theology, when he wrote 'Via Negativa'.

Why no! I never thought other than
That God is that great absence
In our lives, the empty silence
Within, the place where we go
Seeking, not in hope to
Arrive or find. He keeps the interstices
In our knowledge, the darkness
Between stars. His are the echoes
We follow, the footprints he has just
Left. We put our hands in
His side hoping to find
It warm. We look at people
And places as though he had looked
At them too; but miss the reflection.

Then there is our theologian Karl Rahner, whose theology is full of poetry when he reflects on the implications of the incarnation for the deeper meaning of our daily experiences. Human beings, he says, 'are forever occupied with the grains of sand along the shore where they dwell at the edge of the infinite ocean of mystery'. Each moment of our lives is like a grain of sand lying just by the side of the sea of infinity. Every event, no matter how negative or sinful even, is a potential experience of God. God is not tied down to the overtly religious or sacred. In fact, the experience of God does not normally take place at 'holy' times. Referring to the sacraments and to liturgical celebrations, he holds that we can recognise the presence of the absolute mystery in church events, only if we have already greeted it and welcomed that presence in the happenings of each day, particularly in the hurtful and negative ones.

The promise within emptiness
The cross has many shapes. If emptiness has a shape it must be cruciform. I write these paragraphs after our Christmas reflections on the extraordinary phenomenon of God's self-emptying

into the tiny body of a baby. I have always found it extremely difficult to believe that the wild power of an almighty Deity would risk the weakness and vulnerability of a defenceless infant. But that, we are told, is what Love does.

Love is forever surrendering itself but only to be reborn more intensely. The Eternal Word of God took on the fragility of a precarious existence, pulsed only by a small human heart, in darkness and danger, and in a strange place.

> Be the same as Jesus Christ who, though his state was divine, still did not cling to his equality with God, but emptied himself to take the state of a slave. He became as people are and, being as all people are, he was humbler yet: he even accepted death, death on a cross. (Phil 2:5-8)

And as with Jesus, so with us. Each one carries a perennial cross, consciously or subconsciously known. This condition may have to do with waiting, letting go, experiencing darkness or emptiness in some form or another. The mystics remind us about the process of freedom that happens in our acceptance, not avoidance, of our worlds of suffering. The Book of Life encourages us to take up the cross. This will entail the need to love our enemies, embrace our fears, enter the shadows and risk the encounters that follow. The amazing revelation in the mystery of incarnation, death and resurrection, is that in the acknowledgement and acceptance of our vulnerable emptiness we are saved and healed. It is as though the wound that crucifies us provides the opening for grace to enter in. Too much armour, too heavy defences, too many thick walls of protection and projection prevent the vulnerability that lets grace through.

> We sin against the *via negativa* by refusing to develop our capacities, in this instance our capacities for endurance, our strength for the journey, our ability to endure pain. The strength called for in the *via negativa* is not a stoical strength of gritting the teeth nor a macho strength of controlling the situation; it is a vulnerable strength, the strength to absorb, to receive the dark with the light, the pain with pleasure, a strength to keep on falling and rising. It is a strength born of sensitivity, a refusal to live with insensitivity, with coldness of heart, with the god of protection, the idol of invulnerability. To be able to undergo what Gandhi calls the 'mountains of suffering' is to discover a new source and new level of energy – the strength of emptiness, nothingness, the zero point.

This strength shatters our very definitions and projections of
what it means to be strong.[13]

At the end of the day, when the darkness comes too soon, or the
emptiness is like a sinking feeling, we can only trust. 'Go your
way, your trust has saved you.' Trust makes whole. But it is so
desperately difficult to trust in the light when the darkness is as
thick as a wall around your head. Yet the refusal to trust, to trust
the buoyancy of the water, the hidden dawn at midnight, the invincible spring in our winter, is to despair. Trust invites us to
taste and explore the mystery of darkness. It drives out fear, and
when we let go of fear we gradually become ready to live again,
to love again, to be channels of healing and salvation. We let go
of the fear of death itself. This is part of that salvific gift of
strength that the *Via Negativa* has carved into our spirit. This
strength is a letting go of weakness, of self-pity, of puerile shame
and guilt, of fear to be different or to be ourselves. In the theological notes of the next section on the *via creativa*, the central
place of the extraordinary powerful grace of trusting and believing will be looked at again.

Risking the abyss

In a brave and ambitious book, *An Expanding Theology* (E. J.
Dwyer, 1993), Tony Kelly pushes traditional theology into making unfamiliar personal, global and even cosmic connections in a
rapidly and radically changing world. At the very end of this
work (pp 213-216), he uses a meditation of the scientist, poet and
theologian Teilhard de Chardin, to gather up some central
strands of his explorations. I reflect on these passages here because they remind me of the breakthroughs that happen when
we commit ourselves to the *via negativa*. They are about the mystery of the shadow and light, of the fear and trust that we encounter once we risk the journey of faith.

In *The Divine Milieu*, de Chardin describes the confusion and
imbalance he felt when he began to pursue the call of the heart.
When he moves deeper into his 'inmost self' and away from the
clear and practical occupations of each day, he refers to a sense
of sinking into an abyss. He feels he is losing contact with the ordinary and the routine.

At each step of the descent, a new person was disclosed within me of whose name I was no longer sure, and who no
longer obeyed me. And when I had to stop my exploration

because the path faded from beneath my steps, I found a bot-
tomless abyss at my feet, and out of it came, arising from I
know not where, the current I dare call my life.

When we allow ourselves to become vulnerable to mystery, a
profound anxiety or panic tends to happen. We are dismantling
our house of meaning before we have a clear plan for its replace-
ment. We are in the nameless desert between two cities, in the
uncharted wasteland between two cultivated places. It is not a
pleasant address to live at. The edge of mystery, the borders of
what both transcends and yet enfolds us, is not a comfortable
lodging. Teilhard de Chardin agrees.

I then wanted to return to the light of day and to forget the
disturbing enigma in the comforting surroundings of familiar things – to begin living again at the surface without im-
prudently plumbing the depths of the abyss.

But a point arrives when the attraction towards continuing onwards grows stronger. Despite the huge temptation to return to
where one was before, the relentless call to explore is stronger.
Then this divine imperative for clearer vision is nourished by
special glimpses.

But then beneath this very spectacle of the turmoil of life,
there reappeared before my new-opened eyes, the unknown
that I wanted to escape. This time it was not hiding in the bottom of the abyss; it disguised its presence in the innumerable
strands which form the web of chance, the very stuff of
which the universe and my own small individuality are
woven. Yet it was the same mystery without a doubt: I recognised it.

Creation theology and creation-centred spirituality carry a deep
wonder at the miracle of creation and existence. They are always
infused with a sense of the mysterious intimacy between the
inner and outer strands of being. There is an interplay of energies and forces in the unfolding of our lives. Tony Kelly reminds
us that the mystery hidden in the depths of our experience
emerges in the length and breadth of the history that has
brought us forth. We live in a world of connections. And the pattern is very unclear. In fact there is no pattern. Each is unique.
This turns the *via negativa* into a very daunting prospect. The
sense of such intimate yet elusive inter-dependence is unfamiliar and frightening.

Our mind is disturbed when we try to plumb the depth of the world beneath us. But it reels still more when we try to number the favourable chances which must coincide at every moment if the least of living things is to survive and to succeed in its enterprises. After the consciousness of being something other and greater than myself – a second thing made me dizzy; namely the supreme improbability, the tremendous unlikelihood of finding myself existing in the heart of the world which has survived and succeeded in being a world.

Such immense themes are never far from any of our journeys along the four paths of creation-spirituality. They are heavy with wonder, struggle, creativity and transformation. Kelly reflects about how the fifteen billion years of cosmic emergence, the miracle of life that has occurred on this tiny planet, have given each of us, as a supreme improbability, to ourselves and to one another. Our existence becomes a calling, to relate to the mystery which has given us into being, and to make connections of care with everyone and everything that is already part of our identity. Compassion is the name for this connecting love. It is only possible when one's own true self is understood in terms of shared, universal life.

This understanding does not come easy. In fact, like wisdom, it makes 'a bloody entrance'. But, as the *via negativa* reassures us, this is when the healing happens and the hope becomes more real. We have to trust that this is so. In the presence of mystery it is better to be humble and to remain silent.

At that moment, as anyone will find who cares to make this same interior experiment, I felt the distress characteristic of a particle adrift in the universe, the distress which makes human wills founder daily under the crushing number of living things and of stars. And if something saved me, it was hearing the voice of the gospel, guaranteed by divine successes, speaking to me from the depths of the night, 'It is I. Be not afraid.'

Fields of waiting

Only yesterday, or so it seems, the trees outside my window were thin and empty, their arthritic branches stabbing into the low sky. They were black and stark against grey mists. Today, clad in lush and green splendour, and waving luxuriously in the April winds, they obscure the beloved fields that stretch between my window and the dreamy mountains. 'The Valley Speaks' is the title of the last chapter in Gerard Hughes' evergreen *God of Surprises*. In it he is conversing with the Vale of Clwyd about the horrors of the nuclear threat. Recently, I too have been fretfully asking the same 'pastoral forehead of Wales' for glimpses of wisdom and understanding. My searching soul was heavy. 'What is really the key to attaining peace and joy? How do I achieve the abundant life here and now? Why can I not *feel* my soul? From where comes that invisible barrier between me and my heart-centre, between me and nature, between me and humanity, between me and my God.'

I look at the valley lying open to weather and sky, playing host to a variety of two-legged and four-legged creatures, to a million tiny insects, and obedient to the quarterly visitation of the seasons. Nor does it cling to any one of them. Even the harvest, the fruit of its body, it gracefully releases in due time, becoming empty again, like the trees outside my window. The valley, in fact, holds nothing for itself. It is always letting go. It moves between fullness and emptiness, holding and releasing, yet always expecting and trustfully waiting. But this morning, in the precious stillness, before we all rejoin the frenetic kind of life-style from which we have temporarily disengaged, it is the overwhelming awareness of letting go that reaches me from the valley. Her fields cling neither to their offspring nor to the changes in the weather. Her multitude of guests come and go just as they are and just as they please. The cows drop their dung, the sheep their lambs, lovers their guard. The tractors leave their wheel-marks, the walkers their footprints, the hedges their shadows and the farmers their blessing. They are cut open in the spring for the seed which is cut down in the autumn for the harvest. You don't have to tell the fields of the valley anything about letting go.

To what extent, I ask myself, do the fields of my controlling heart reflect the wisdom of the valley? How do I attain to self-forgetfulness, like the fields do, resisting the conditioning that presses in from all sides. How do I come fresh to each new season, each new morning, unblinkered by prejudgements? The more 'learning' I carry with me from moment to moment, from lesson to lesson, from caution to caution, the less ready I am to live fully the next encounter, the more encumbered I am by yesterday's baggage. It is not easy to be completely present to reality while you are evaluating it. It is difficult to drink in the richness of the experience while you are even subconsciously passing judgement on it. Can you really savour the flavour while you are wondering if it is good for you? I looked again through the window. The open, waiting fields were a green and silent sermon. 'Let go,' they sang, 'Just let go.'

Something important was dawning on me – a new understanding. I had certainly been well instructed in other so-called priorities – information about being successful, for instance, and short-cuts to knowledge and virtue. Also I had always 'known' about letting go; but I had yet to become it. I had been travelling along 'the way of acquiring' rather than 'the way of letting go' – of skills, possessions and even grace. The *via negativa* is a shaky and scary journey. It is about trust in delayed gratification. There is no immediate satisfaction. It often seems as though there is no satisfaction at all. Nothing seems to happen in this unfamiliar place. 'How,' I ask the fields, 'can I grow from emptiness, from not wanting, from staying detached?' I waited. Only silence. And there, of course, was the answer.

So now, at least for once, I will stop marshalling my thoughts and organising my prayer. I will close my eyes and let go into the abyss. I will let my mind be dark and empty, full of silence, unfocused and free. Why should I try to strain for new words – anyway I have no more to say. God is well aware of my needs, my pride, my deceit, my loves, my shadow, my light. I am tired of trying to be good, tired of falling, tired of struggling. Today I will simply let go, give up, give in, give over. I have exhausted my incarnational theology, my creation spirituality, my Celtic mythology, my ancient mantras, my new age meditations. I have reached today, the end of a strand of my spiritual tether.

Maybe the mystics are right. Maybe we do grow by letting go. I need to trust the paradox. Perhaps this is the great and daunting invitation. Can I accept it? Was it like this with the dis-

ciples after Easter? A passage from *The God of Surprises* comes
back to me now. Fr Hughes is tracing some of the features common to the resurrection appearances and how this mystery affects our own lives today. This is what he writes:

> The first common feature is that those to whom Christ ap-
> pears are portrayed as being in a negative mood of some
> kind or other. . . and that we too can only come to know the
> risen Lord when we have experienced some kind of death,
> some disillusionment with ourselves and others, some loss,
> some bereavement, sense of fear, hopelessness or meaning-
> lessness and have not tried to anaesthetise ourselves against
> it. The answer is in the pain, which is revealing to us our
> poverty and our need of God. If we can acknowledge and be
> still in our poverty, Christ will show himself to us in his
> glory. (Darton, Longman and Todd, 1985, p 134)

Like the fields of the valley we accept the pain and then let go of
it. Even the best of our efforts changes little. The fields do not try
to control their tomorrows. They are in peace because they have
learned to trust. And we are so slow to learn. Fr Hughes continues:

> A second feature common to the gospels' resurrection ac-
> counts is the slowness of his friends to recognise the risen
> Jesus Christ. This is also true for us in the slow dawning of
> the truth that he is a living presence in every detail of our
> lives. Slowly, if our faith is developing, we come to know the
> resurrection as something that is happening now. The risen
> Christ is continuously coming through the closed doors of
> our minds, closed through fear of ourselves and our fear of
> other people, and says to us 'Peace be to you.' The power of
> his resurrection gives us hope in a situation where before we
> felt hopeless, gives us courage to face a task when before we
> wanted to run away, gives us the ability and strength to be
> open and vulnerable when before we could think of nothing
> but our own protection and security. (pp134, 135)

Those waiting fields, that inspired these musings about being
open to God's grace, seem to echo the statements of St Paul. In
their emptiness is their fullness. In their surrender to nature lies
their power to generate. In their letting go of control they co-
create with God, like Jesus did.

> His state was divine
> yet he did not cling

to his equality with God
but emptied himself
to assume the condition
of a slave.

He became humbler yet,
even to accepting death
– death on a cross.

But God raised him high … (Phil 2:6-8)

High heeled shoes

From my eyrie perched half-way up the hill, I can see the A55 snaking its way through the fields and over the rivers of North Wales, into and out of the valleys, until it disappears on both sides, over a ridge on my left, and into distant woods on my right. On this Bank Holiday morning it is a busy motorway, as people are going in all directions in search of change. Some cars have boats secured on top, some have skis, others bicycles, prams, boxes and all kinds of provisions for long or short excursions away from home. But on this Easter Monday I do not envy these happy travellers their precious freedom from the daily pressures of routine chores. I only hope that the sun will shine for them.

As for myself, my attention is somewhere else. I had hoped, this day, with the help of grace, to recapture the Paschal excitement of the early Christians, of the two Marys, of the Apostles and of Jesus himself. But I find my mind is full of a dream I had last night. The dream was about a young priest, handsome and dynamic, singing in church to a large group of teenagers who were clearly enjoying the performance. As I moved around behind the lectern where he stood, I noticed that his legs did not really match the rest of his body. Unlike his top half, which was liturgically and attractively dressed, his legs were thin and stilted, clad in badly-fitting blue corduroys. These ended well above his two spindly ankles supported by a pair of awkward-looking, precariously-structured high-heeled shoes.

One possible interpretation of this dream is occupying my mind. Am I that priest, performing at a surface level, attending only to my shallow act and public persona, 'playing to the gallery' of my visible image and popular acceptability? But underneath the veneer of confidence, is there a pathetic clinging to a transitory pursuit of empty popularity? Below the seemingly impressive but insubstantial exterior, are the hidden feet of clay really wobbly and insecure? Out of sight of the people in front lies the fear of my own superficiality, that inner weakness which will not be acknowledged, the hollow legs that tell the whole sorry story. The dream seemed to mock my constant efforts these days, to be firmly grounded, to be centred like a rock, to be planted like a tree.

My thoughts and feelings are coming quickly now, as I try to process the dream. More clearly than before, I am aware of a great deal of fear in my life. But fear of what? Is it a fear of others, of rejection, of failure, of not being successful? What am I afraid of losing? Is it popularity, youthfulness, attractiveness, masculinity? Or am I afraid of being found out, found empty or wimpish, found wanting in some way? In short, is my dream telling me that I am in a prison of pride?

The painful questioning goes on. In some way, linked to the self-centred obsession with my image, and lurking in the shadows of my suspected narcissism, another constant and almost subconscious habit of my mind is emerging. Not immediately connected to the dream, but flowing within my present 'stream of consciousness', is a new awareness of a tediously negative and critical attitude towards a great deal of those people who happen to be in my environment. Maybe this is the point of the dream. Maybe this is the Achilles heel within my high-heeled shoes.

I found it quite disturbing to discover within me a cynical and running commentary of obverse observations about the way people are behaving and expressing themselves in my company. Such a presence to others only distills bad vibes into the atmosphere, polluting the channels of love. It is difficult for potentially graced relationships to grow with such destructive elements floating around. And yet it was such a relief to uncover this dis-ease within me. Now it was out. The fault did not lie with the focus of my judging. It was within me all the time. This was a liberating realisation. Maybe this is what they mean by facing your 'bad bits', by befriending your shadow, by staying in the dark until, through a moment of disclosure, self-knowledge emerges.

So let me review how the Spirit of the Risen Christ this morning is working with my dream. A dream is sometimes referred to as the 'whisper of God'. If anything is clear about the resurrection it is the triumph of love and the transcendence of fear. Today's Easter gospel reminds us of the first words of the victorious Jesus, 'Do not be afraid.' Over and over again, it is the message of our risen Lord. And just as he looked at Mary then, he looks at me now. 'Let me be your rock,' he is saying, 'and ground yourself in me. You are ready now to understand this life-giving truth. That is why you had your dream on Easter Sunday night. *I* am your centre, your balance, your confidence. *I* am your strong new shoes. Trust in me and your will know no fear. I will drive you like a peg into a firm place. My perfect love casts out all fear.' And into my mind came the grounding, centring words of St Paul to the Ephesians:

> Out of his infinite glory, may he give you the power through his Spirit for your hidden self to grow strong, so that Christ may live in your hearts, and then, planted in love and built on love, you will, with all the saints, have strength to grasp the breadth and the length, the height and the depth; until, knowing the love of Christ, which is beyond all knowledge, you are filled with the utter fullness of God. (Eph 3:16-19)

And so I hand over to God this 'bad habit' of relentless judging, (and therefore condemning) of others – this long-playing tape currented by personal ambition, pointless rivalry and comparisons, stemming perhaps from wounds of childhood, or later, from a subtle and very real insecurity. It is time to stop picking at the scabs. Having forgiven Peter, still shamed to the core for his human weakness and carrying to his death this now life-giving scar, the risen Christ now turns toward me. 'You are created,' he is saying, 'in the image of my Father. His glory is your glory. You are his son, flesh of his flesh, blood of his blood. You must not be less. This glory is your inheritance now, your Easter treasure. From now on, these frail threads of sin that bind you to your fallenness, are transformed. Like an eagle, you are free. Last night, I was the dreamer of your dream. Today it has come true. Nothing can take away from you your passion for the possible. Because I will always love you, your strong legs will carry you safely through the world like a fearless giant.'

I peel an orange and look out again over the Clwyd valley. Like a bright stream of light flowing into the horizon, the A55 is now clear and open, inviting and waiting, full of courtesy and full of promise. Maybe I should join the others after all!

Slow dawn

Like tall, silent strangers slowly moving out of the shadows, the chestnut trees outside my bedroom window gradually grow closer and clearer, as the early, misty light spreads across the grey vale of Clwyd. It is four o'clock on the morning of Holy Saturday. I try to imagine the thoughts of those closest to Jesus as the first dawn without him breaks over the Hill of Killing. Watching for daybreak, how profound and inexpressible, for instance, must be the depths of lost love and anguish that flow in and out and over the broken hearts of the two Marys.

This is a very peculiar hour of day. It is easy to feel alone – too alone – at this strange time; to be too silent at this dead moment of in-between, when the restless world turns over in its sleep. The watching, waiting heart needs caution now, because this is the time when all that is hidden in its deep waters rises unexpectedly to the surface, breaking before it with ominous ripples. Now is the time when what the busyness of the day keeps safely at bay in the wings of the soul, silently and swiftly slips free into centre-stage. And now is the timeless time when for once, in each turning of the world, the sentry of the heart betrays its trust, and the cold reality that we cannot or will not face in the light of day, confronts us with a stark intensity in that thin and defenceless moment.

So, while the watchman sleeps, the grey procession of ghosts begins to cross the threshold of our unprotected, inner sanctuary, to haunt, to mock, to accuse, to remind, to torment. The chances we have missed, the dreams we have suppressed, the false beauty we have pursued, the deadly choices we have made, the secret sins we have never truly owned up to – they are all there, relentlessly queuing up and waiting to be acknowledged.

In the shadow of the shrouded hill, the two Marys, mingling their different love for the same man, continue their heavy vigil. In spite of their numb bewilderment, their blessed and bruised hearts of anguish must keep on beating. Having dared to love, are they prepared to grieve? With him, yesterday, they had lived a day of death: today, without him, they would live another, and another … In that sharp-soft embrace of sorrow, more felt, I think, by women than by men, they sit, confused and bereft, at their window of slow dawn.

For as long as I can remember, I have always felt a sudden pang of compassion welling up within me at the sight of an old person, frail and undecided, one hand half-held out for help, waiting, fearful, lost. It may be at a pedestrian crossing, getting on or off a bus, in a gust of wind, on the bottom of a step going up, at the top of a step coming down, or looking out of a hospital waiting-room window on to a windswept parking-lot – the feeling I get is close to pathos.

My heart also twists with an indefinable ache whenever I think of the same mute look of apprehension on my brother Joseph's face on many an occasion. (Joseph, a Downs Syndrome diabetic, died a few years ago.) He always trusted us implicitly and risked coming with us on an outing, even though he was often surprised by pain at the end of the journey. 'Please come with us, Joseph,' we would say and, being unable to speak, his lovely eyes would anxiously scan our faces and hands for some sign of what we had in mind. Was it to Cork (and yet more suffering for him in the City Hospital) or to Killarney for his beloved cup of tea at the Arbutus Hotel and afterwards, a (very) small ice-cream? But there was always that moment – how long is a moment? – of waiting.

Why does that vulnerable glance of indecision, that mingling of trust, fear and pleading, touch us so? Is it because we are made by God to know, to be confident, to be sure; to celebrate always the first gifts of the Spirit – wisdom, knowledge and understanding – all graces of groundedness, centredness and assurance? Maybe there is an elemental fear that we carry around within us – the unbearableness of being helpless, disoriented and dependent. These human conditions assume a particular pathos when they are mirrored in the eyes of those who are seriously ill or handicapped, who are very young or very old, because, perhaps, in our heart of hearts, we know it is ourselves that we are watching.

What do I mean by that? People often say that things beautiful disturb them. We do not have to be a Blake or a Wordsworth to be moved by the divinity within the ordinary, to experience a wave of loneliness, or of a longing and a yearning that ebb and flow somewhere within us in the presence of beauty, obvious or hidden, perfect or seemingly damaged. By 'beautiful' I do not mean the latest in art-forms, designer-styles or current fashions.

It has, I think, something to do with the absence of embellishments rather than with their presence, with innocence rather than with what is contrived, with subtraction rather than with addition or multiplication. It has to do with a condition of simplicity where something is stripped to bareness without pretence or pretentiousness. It is a state of nakedness. The make-up is wiped clean, the masks and facades are gone, there is no more to be taken away.

At such times there are no defences, no ambiguous self-consciousness, no misleading posing or posturing. It is, I think, the vulnerability in all such moments that is truly beautiful – and especially the vulnerability that is revealed in waiting. The waiting person has no more control. Only hope and trust remain. This is the raw material of our humanness at the pure point of a possible self-transcendence. There is nothing superfluous here, no alloys, no impurities. Maybe we are moved because we sense something of God's own nature in those unlikely moments of grace. The divine in us is stirred. Deep calls to deep and, in one of the most startling paradoxes of God's affairs with humans, the moment of resurrection happens in the vulnerability and emptiness of waiting.

It is in the light of, and by virtue of the mystery of the incarnation, that power is sensed and revealed, in such vulnerability. How strange it is that there is so much frailty in the noblest souls that grace our world – frailty and not knowing, anxiety and even desperation. Every version of the ageless myth about the *Hero's Journey* exposes such a basic condition. Only yesterday the two Marys watched their young God as he staggered, stumbled and crawled his humiliating way up a wretched hill, waiting for crumbs of comfort from the confused watchers. He who was a child and dependent on his parents' care, who was later a young man and needy for Lazarus's friendship and Mary's love, continues his earthly journey in total dependency. He is the sacrament of a waiting God.

Like our Joseph, he waits, wondering what will be done to him next. Will a Veronica wipe his face, or will yesterday's friend throw another stone? Will he see a face of compassion or of hatred during his last crowded climb? Will he be forever betrayed or proclaimed, executed or reprieved? Is all of this for an absent Father or is it a horrible mistake? He can only wait, and wait; and hopeless, helpless, keep stumbling on – the next step, the next second, the next fall, the next doubt …

Sometimes I think I know why Jesus peered at the two Marys through blood-shot eyes with that heart-rending look of a child lost in a crowd. I have seen that glance of utter bewilderment in the face of once-strong people, suddenly struck down in mid-life, being wheeled swiftly down corridors of anxiety, under cold-white tubes of indifferent light, to the operating-table at the end. I saw that same fearfully distressed and pleading look in the face of our own Joseph, through the rear window of the neighbour's car that carried him on what was to be his last journey on this earth.

Jesus, having freely chosen to share our finite condition, looked that way, I think, so as to transform all those desperate times when we find ourselves at the cross-roads of indecision and panic-filled waiting. He looked that way, out of his self-emptying solidarity with humanity, so that the ache we all feel when we are present to the pain of hopelessness will not go on forever but will become, for us, a source of healing, a passover moment to redemption. Jesus looked that way then so that everyone who looks that way now can share in his saving passion. Such 'weakness' is now strength.

We cannot see it clearly yet, except in glimpses, and through a glass, darkly – glimpses of a God who waits anxiously in our every anxious waiting; glimpses of every empty look as a small sacrament of a deeper emptiness that only God can fill; glimpses that ultimately every twisting of our heart and every contraction of our spirit, whether for ourselves or for another, is the call of our divine parent, beckoning to her eternal child, from the door of light, to be home before the dark.

Here at St Beuno's, all is still silent. This will be a slow morning. Holy Saturday is the longest day. Before the seventh day of God's rest, this is God's day of solitude and waiting. Even nature is quiet. Creation broods. The divine energy is dead, buried in a tomb of earth-darkness. Without the sustaining arms of God, the temple shatters and the sun searches for her light.

But, unlike Jesus, we know the whole story. In the turning of the mystery, the tomb becomes the womb. Today's silence is the most fruitful silence the world has ever known. For it carries the harvest of all the quiet and anxious waiting since the first creation. In this womb, new love and new meaning blesses every mother's waiting, every baby's cry at night, every groaning of the world for completion, every watching face at every window of waiting, along the corridors of our lives.

It is always Holy Saturday in the one who silently and patiently hopes against hope, and stays trusting against all the odds. It is always the eve of Easter in the heart that endures in the face of the forces of death. It is the moment of resurrection when what seems like a useless life of boring routine is resumed again because someone believes that nothing goes to waste. And again, and again, the stone is rolled away when, after long, lonely nights of heart-ache, the graced watcher greets the dawn like a child with a new look in her eyes.

The bell is ringing now, for prayer. The first light, no longer shy and reserved, is flooding the room.

You, O striking Christ of brightness, you give a stature to our waiting.

Blazing with your Father's glory, you wait no longer here.

And you, O Mary of his body, and you, O Mary of his heart,

who still linger in the half-light of your waiting-room,

pale prisoners of his beauty,

you do not know it yet,

but your hours of waiting are almost over.

Fold, fallow and plough

There is little doubt that the view I have through the window this morning covers the actual landscape that inspired Gerard Manley Hopkins to write *Pied Beauty*. It is March in Wales. I sit here in 'the College' as it used to be known, where Hopkins studied for the priesthood, practised his sermons and wrote almost half his poetry. A most beautiful valley sweeps down to the sea behind me and up to the low sky in front. The fields are spread like a giant green-brown tablecloth over the hills and hollows, lying open to the nights and to the days. There is a perceptible hush these mornings, an atmosphere of expectancy, as everything outdoors seems to be waiting for spring to come and sit at table. The hard, wintered ground will soon endure the relentless but vital plough-share and then the thin rivers of dark furrows will run like a music-score across the fenced and silent pages of the countryside. It must have been on such a morning that Isaiah wrote 'The mountains and the hills will burst into singing and the trees will shout for joy.' (Is 55:12b)

As I sit here meditating on the futility of our own efforts to acquire holiness no matter how hard we try, the image of those patient fields stays with me. Soon enough they will be triumphantly waving their precious harvest of grain. But now they wait. How astonishing it is, that at this moment, before the perennial miracle of explosive growth and transformation takes place, the only evidence of that mysterious power is hidden in waiting. In the annual cycle of the renewal of the face of the earth, this morning's hush is the inescapable and timeless dynamic of trusting hope.

Like the field, still and silent, waiting for the seed, I too wait for my Lover's presence. My own most brilliant efforts will add nothing to the process. Yet urgency fills me. But waiting, they say, is not negative or diminishing. Expectant waiting, I'm told, is somehow already fulfilled. Pacing the floor in a kind of vacuum just now, it is nothingness that I'm aware of, not imminent surprise. It seems more like desperation to me than expectancy, futility rather than hope.

I look at my watch. Nine o'clock. I think of the morning busyness of workers in the towns and small cities around here. Everyone living at the limit. Drivers willing the lights from red to green, others feeling distress at the slow bus, so many holding down the panic as time runs out. Have we lost control? Are we taken over by some pseudo life-imperative? Why the frenzy to make it to the top, to be successful and wealthier, to be the best in the business, the smartest dresser with the right connections? How high on the tree is the top banana?

Most people lack the time or the desire to explore such questions. Why do I still think that these are important issues? Why do I wonder about hidden values that underpin the way so many of us live our lives? Between dropping and collecting her children at school and for leisure, a busy mother spends six or seven hours at work outside the home. Her salary is needed to meet the heavy mortgage. The house may be small but finds itself in an expensive area. For twelve years of my life, after teaching-time, I would head off to sundry venues, near or far, to offer courses in adult education. There would be no time to eat with my temporary community. Very often weekends were no different. There was no space in my life, no rhythm or timing. The only waiting was at the filling stations.

Here I am, a few years later, looking out a window, watching traffic hurtle along the new A55 – a motorway that was once a pathway for saints and scholars and vagabonds to stride and shuffle their way between Ireland and the cities of Europe from the time of Columbanus and John Scotus Eriugena. Am I simply dodging work or have I found something new? Are all those people out there, many of them desperately on the breadline, somehow misguided? Have I, comfortable and privileged here on my long retreat, seen a light that they have not? Without a spouse or family, house or car, salary or personal profession, am I projecting my own emptiness and subtle delusion with life on to others, deviously trying to undermine the authenticity of their valuable lives? Maybe there's a hint of 'sour grapes' in my reflecting today, vainly trying to pass off plain old-fashioned laziness under a fancy spiritual disguise called 'expectant waiting'!

Before I convince myself that this may well be the case, let me bring this meditation to a close! In my heart of hearts what do I really believe now about this issue? What is the most important thing in my life? If love is, then how do I discern the loving thing to do a hundred times a day? I don't know the answers to these questions but at least they sound like the right kind of question.

Of one thing I am sure. In those busy decades of my life up to now, a certain inner voice was silent. Maybe not so much a silent voice as one to which I never paused to listen. I didn't need to really, I presumed. And I had good reasons for this presumption. Wasn't it the Lord's work I was carrying out, morning and evening? Like Jesus, wasn't I only about his business? Hadn't I even 'discovered' a new approach to spreading the Word and was extremely busy in marketing my exciting product?

So what am I saying? I certainly mean to judge nobody in this reflection – neither those involved people out there getting on with raising a family and working hard to keep the wolf from the door, nor those involved people in here, busy about satisfying a more specifically personal hunger in their own hearts. Both quests may, or may not, be spiritual. Only a fool would judge. But I do know that during certain years of my life I could not see the forest for the trees. I was trying to direct Hamlet without the Prince of Denmark. I had lost sight of Jesus in my urgency to spread the gospel. This has come with a kind of shock to me. I seemed to be meeting him now as if for the first time. I was, in fact, quite embarrassed before this 'stranger' Jesus. And yet, maybe the timing is right after all. Maybe it's all happening as it was meant to – the tilling, the sowing, the waiting, the harvest – with the perfect timing of the divine Farmer who 'drenches the furrows of the earth, levels it, softens it with showers and blesses its growth.' (Ps 64)

Now the green blade rises from the buried grain,
Wheat that in the dark earth many days has lain;
Love lives again that with the dead has been:
Love is come again, like wheat that springs up green ...

When our hearts are wintry, grieving or in pain,
Your touch can call us back to life again,
Fields of our hearts that dead and bare have been:
Love is come again, like wheat that springs up green.
(*Hymns Old and New*, Kevin Mayhew Ltd, no 376)

The point of pain

When listening to people's stories I am often intrigued by the number of places in which their Achilles heel may be found. For instance, what really frightens one person will leave another unmoved. Or I find myself able to laugh off what holds my friend in the grip of irrational panic. Close friends and lovers know the location of each other's point of pain. During the intimacy that mutually and trustingly reveals the well-guarded vulnerabilities of the heart and the raw, but deeply-hidden, terrors of the soul, the maps of these points of pain are exchanged. So later, when the battle-lines are drawn, the missiles of destruction are swift, accurate and deadly.

And thus it is with God. Or so, in my anger and distress, it seems. I pray for transformation – that my heart and soul belong to God in total conversion. (That this can only happen through the process of suffering, I somehow, at the time, choose to ignore.) Our Tremendous Lover listens to me and slowly reaches for the divine quiver. With unerring aim and superb delivery the pain-tipped arrow is dispatched into my carefully-camouflaged Achilles heel. How did my Sacred Archer know the precise and protected place in my inmost being where the maximum havoc could be wreaked in the briefest time? For how long did God examine my most secret fears, my most sensitive soul-nerves, before taking perfect aim? Oh the mastery and timing of the thing! If it were not for my distress and anger with God just now I would probably admire the efficiency of the process – the painful process necessary for my prayer to be answered.

But today I ask – *is* conversion happening, or is it all a pathetic delusion? What do I learn, if anything, during this wrestling-time of the spirit? In my drowning, when I surface for breath, what, if anything, is becoming clearer? In the moments of respite, what transformation is taking place in my bleeding soul? Please be patient while I try to work it out. For one thing, I must stop struggling. This only deepens the pit I'm in. Nor will my wound heal while I'm picking the scab. Several times a day I must pause for a moment – to simply trust. How difficult this is! To let go of the control, to risk handing over the steering-wheel, to place my destiny in the hands of God and others. Such surrender never becomes a habit. Something inside us cries out against

111

it. When the black whisperings of panic are upon me I have a choice – to run or to stand, to doubt or to believe, to fear or to trust, to commit myself to suicide or to intensified life. When my imagination runs amok with wild exaggerations and my heart begins to pound I can either self-destruct or self-create. What do I mean by that?

I have choices here. Trusting and letting go can only truly happen when we face the source of our disquiet. This disquiet has to do with our own evil. Peace only comes when our evil is acknowledged. We are trapped by our conditioning into the illusion that we should be perfect. (As applied to human behaviour, the word 'perfect' is seriously misinterpreted in popular versions of the Christian scriptures.) Our expectations of ourselves are ridiculously unreal. Because of our basically flawed nature, this programming from childhood leads to relentless denial within ourselves, leading to a deadly pattern of projection on to others. There is a rather hard-hitting paragraph in Sheldon Kopp's thoughtful book *If You Meet The Buddha On The Road, Kill Him!* He is writing about the necessity of laying claim to the evil in ourselves so as to avoid its power over us. He gives an example.

> A patient comes into therapy complaining that he does not get along well with other people; somehow he always says the wrong thing and hurts their feelings. He is really a nice guy, just has this uncontrollable, neurotic problem. What he does *not* want to know is that his 'unconscious hostility' is not his *problem*, it's his *solution*. He is really not a nice guy who wants to be good; he's a bastard who wants to hurt other people while still thinking of himself as a nice guy. If the therapist can guide him into the pit of his own ugly soul, then there may be hope for him. Once this pilgrim can see how angry and vindictive he is, he can trace his story and bring it to the light, instead of being doomed to relive it without awareness. Nothing about ourselves can be changed until it is first accepted. Jung points out that 'the sick man has not to learn how to get rid of his neurosis but how to bear it. For the illness is not a superfluous and senseless burden, it is himself; he himself is that 'other' which we were always trying to shut out. (Sheldon Press, 1974, p 78)

I sensed something of immense importance for my spiritual growth as I reflected on such insights. At this moment in my life

I was being visited by my shadow. I could try to avoid the encounter or I could befriend the darkness within. Something told
me that if I tried to run from the perceived evil in myself it
would only increase my diminishment and negativity. Maybe
all evil is only potential vitality in need of transformation. 'To
live without the creative potential of our own destructiveness is
to be a cardboard angel.' Why, I wondered, did Dante have to
visit the Abyss of Evil before he could ascend to be illumined by
the Divine Light? Why, too, did Jesus descend into Hell before
he rose to sit at the right hand of God? And what about me,
Daniel? Does Daniel think that he is to be the glorious exception
to all other mortals, human and divine? Can Daniel grow in the
white light of a shadowless land where no mountains give
meaning to valleys, where no darkness supports the splendour
of the stars, where fear can never give birth to a heroine, nor sin
to forgiveness? Does Daniel hope to assume his graced divinity
without wrestling with the dragon that in turn empowers him,
without experiencing the prison before he can be ecstatically
free of it, without knowing the deadly confusion of being hopelessly lost before waiting to be found forever, without feeling
the emptiness of despair before being filled by a driving passion
for the possible?

Exquisite is the brief peace when the warring factions pause.
The light is true at those times of ceasefire. What is important is
that the enemy has been confronted and engaged. The point of
the battle is not that the enemy be routed or destroyed. The
whole exercise is about *befriending* the dark warriors of the
night. They carry the gift that I need. They are my rescuers in
disguise. Because if I yearn for the true light, if I call out for total
transformation and conversion of my wayward heart, how else
can this happen except through the encounter with the dragons
of my fear and the spectres of my darkness? Where else can the
ghosts of my terrors be exposed to reality except in the dark corridors of my hauntings? Until I meet them I cannot greet them;
until I greet them I cannot be free of them; and until I'm free of
them I cannot enlist their power and energy to liberate my
world. This whole experience is an extraordinary process. One
moment I'm cringing in fear; the next I feel as fearlessly safe as
God. One morning I find myself at the bottom of a suffocating
pit; by eveningtime I'm raised on high in something little short
of ecstacy. Is it any wonder that sometimes I fear for my sanity!

Today, September 14th, is the Christian feast of 'The

Exaltation of the Cross.' The paradox here, as in the preceding paragraphs, is very obvious. How can we celebrate our vulnerability? What does St Paul mean by declaring that his weakness made him strong? 'How great the cross,' enthuses St Andrew this morning, in the Office of Readings, 'what blessings it holds! Whoever possesses it possesses a treasure. Without it we would not be free, we could not enjoy the tree of life, paradise would not have been opened and *the underworld would not have yielded up its spoils*. Listen to the words of the exalted Christ, "And I, when I am lifted up (on the cross), I will draw all people to myself".' The feeling I have from such reflections is centred around power – the sense of being empowered. From my own journey these days I begin to understand more vividly the images used by Jesus about the transformation that happens when deaf people start hearing the music of life, when the miracle of sight is restored to those who are denied the beauty of the visible world, when the exhilarating power of movement flows through still and restless limbs. Fleetingly as these glimpses come and go, (and who would blame me for hoping that one day their visits will be longer and more reliable), they bring an attitude of gratitude and humility to my shell-shocked soul.

So what am I learning these days? That divine healing will limitlessly take possession of my life only to the extent that I cease to rely on my own efforts. We are swimming in a sea of God. 'In God we live and move and have our being.' I must empty myself of all trust in my own run-down batteries. What is called for is a simple and honest (but strongly resisted) awareness of what is going on within me from moment to moment, action to action, reaction to reaction, thought to thought, feeling to feeling. To seek the source of the negative emotion. To waste no time in remorse, regret, shame or guilt. Nothing can bind me except myself. Life is not binding me, only calling me into the flow that carries me to the ocean of freedom. Jesus has assured us that the entire power of the Universe lies within us. Therefore, each morning I say,

I unleash God's spiritual force within me. I am unfettered and unbound. There are no real limitations in my life, no false condition has any power over me. I am free in the spirit of Christ within me and by this spirit I will live my life today.

Soul-friend

Yesterday I was on retreat and the topic I was asked to reflect upon was the intimacy of my friendship with the human Jesus Christ. I was provided with a passage from the gospel to help concentrate and guide my wandering thoughts. The whole exercise did not particularly excite me because of my uneasiness regarding a certain sentimentality in popular devotions to Jesus, and also, since childhood, I have reacted against an over-domesticated piosity directed at a very unscriptural understanding of the Messiah. With time to think, I ambled around the hallowed walls of St Beuno's, a retreat-centre whose spirituality is based on the Exercises of St Ignatius.

I recalled how, in my pursuit of holiness, in the journey of my soul, I had plunged into the study of exciting theologies of revelation (especially those with a liberation and feminist emphasis), creation spirituality (and its Celtic connections), pastoral renewal (particularly the notion of collaborative ministry), and issues of justice and peace, now that the new millennium was fast approaching. All of these pursuits and areas of meditation and study, are still among the strongest desires of my heart. I hope, in fact, to spend the rest of my days in further exploring their endless richness. Nevertheless, yesterday's few hours of prayer revealed to me something that quite surprised me in its obviousness, something that was missing from the centre of all my efforts.

The gospel passage I was given to mull over was Jn 21:15-17. It records the triple question of Jesus about the depth of Peter's personal love for the Risen Christ. There is no doubt here about the nature of the relationship that Jesus had in mind; it was the intimate commitment of human friendship. Jesus does not ask Peter about the orthodoxy of his incarnational theology, the validity of his mystical experiences, or his latest insights into the cosmology of the time. He simply asked 'Do you love me?' It was the same vulnerable question I felt he was addressing to me at that moment. In the imaginative scenario recommended by proponents of Ignatian spirituality, I felt suddenly challenged and confused. Under the level, intense look of a young, brown Jesus, I had to look away. Because I could not say 'Yes'.

It occurred to me with something like shock that I had never pursued, or accepted (and probably sub-consciously rejected), the offer of a man-to-man love-relationship with Jesus. In my attempts to avoid the exclusive and seemingly claustrophobic 'fix' on Jesus that I had as a child, I had, inadvertently, closed the door to a maturing of that love into my later life. Having spent decades probing the implications of the fleshing of the Word for our world, reflecting on the meaning of the incarnation for all humanity, and searching for the most appropriate model of revelation for a swiftly-changing universe, I had somehow missed the central point that the whole Christian mystery celebrated – the tangible immediacy of God's own self in the warm, human presence of a man called Jesus, now pleading with me simply to love him!

It was like working for the kingdom without knowing or loving the King; like explaining to others what it is like to be in love without ever loving anybody oneself. The Jesus I had written and preached about was more of a world-shattering cosmic event than a human friend; more of a universal revelation about the meaning of life than a very ordinary heart searching for love; more of a risen spirit powering its way throughout all creation setting everything free and on fire, than a sensitive, needy brother looking for the reassurance that I loved him.

Some of my books are on sale here at St Beuno's. They are neatly stacked, with many others, by Mary, in little piles of 3 or 4, on trestle-tables along the corridor, and replaced with new ones, as they are bought by the retreatants or casual visitors. During some of those long, rainy, silent evenings of the Exercises, we walk, at a measured pace, up and down inside the building. On occasion, as I had done this, practising and perfecting my humility, my spiritual discernment, my *custos oculorum* ('custody of the eyes'), and trying to reach what St Ignatius called 'the third degree of indifference to the esteem of others', I became aware that every now and then my hooded eyes would rake along the rows of books to see whether 'my pile' was diminishing or not. I was hopeful that my ratings in the opinion of others would be boosted up as the pile went down, that more affirmation for me would emerge, as the depth of my writings sank in! (I even bought one or two copies of my own books to make it look as though they were all the rage! 'Oh how perverse is the human heart, how deceitful; and who can know its ways,' wrote Jeremias, 17:9).

Anyway, to get back to my embarrassing confrontation with Jesus. The episode about the books in the preceding paragraph clarified something very important for me. As I flicked through them from time to time that evening, I found little fault with them. They were all, quite obviously, Christ-centred. They were full of my conviction about God's unconditional love for every living creature as revealed in the life of Jesus Christ; they were underpinned by a theology of celebration of our undoubted God-given beauty, once and for all established in the wonder-filled humanity of God's own son; they carried messages of hope for those who, in their silent suffering, battle with the forces of darkness and emptiness – a priceless message revealed in the passion, death and resurrection of our Saviour. So, the personal and universal transformation, which is the prayer and hope of all true believers, is totally and unmistakably the work of the blessed fruit of Mary's womb. So where is my problem about the place of Jesus in my life, in my writing, in my preaching? Why all the fuss? I must love him very much indeed, if he is at the heart of my energy, if he is at the core of everything in which I believe.

Yet, why am I so unsure, so bothered, so restless? Yesterday there was a simple question addressed to me by Jesus, 'Do you love me?' Why do I still feel awkward and uncertain about the unrivalled role of Jesus as my 'soul-friend', my *anam-chara*? While not wishing to make too much of a distinction between head-knowledge and heart-wisdom, I feel that the beginning of an answer to my distress lies somewhere there. I am well aware of the importance, even the necessity of having a 'soul-friend' – someone to trust implicitly and love disinterestedly, someone to walk alongside in troubled times and calm, someone with whom you can be totally yourself, an intimate friend who is willing to reflect back to yourself the state of your soul. And yet, why do I find it so hard to call Jesus my *anam-chara*? Ironically, while being the inspiration of everything good in my life, of everything that I have grown to be, of every grace I have ever experienced, of every redeeming word I have written or said, something tells me I love my Saviour with my head. But do I know him by heart?

Knowing by heart

When something as bewildering and as exciting as yesterday's encounter with Jesus happens, you do not forget it in a hurry. It stays with you through the nights. Today, I'm still turning over in my head and heart, the discomfort I felt when asked that hard, profound, yet simple question 'Do you love me?' Let me go through it again.

A hundred times I must have explained with diagrams, poetry, short films, symbols of the expressive arts and stories, that God is known only through the humanity of Jesus Christ; that because God's Son thought with a human mind, loved with a human heart and related through his human body, then all human experiences are potential revelations of God's essential being. (There are many theological references throughout this book in support of such a statement.) Every personal encounter with the man Jesus, during his life on earth, was a meeting with God. Because such is the case, we can now say that every true interpersonal relationship in our lives is also, even though we may not know it, a communion with divinity. In Christ, a new window is opened up on God, a new meaning emerges, and our understanding of our daily experience is changed forever.

Christ, according to Karl Rahner, completed and perfected what God began in creation. He was, at once, the way *forward* for the final and irrevocable break-through of humanity into God, and the way *in* for the ever-approaching, self-emptying love of God for us. Another theologian of beauty, Hans Urs von Balthasar, captures this insight into revelation, with echoes of Teilhard de Chardin's 'Mass on the World', in an enchanting note about the mystery of the eucharist:

> It is here that the two flames fall upon each other: the holiness of heaven falling down like fire on the earth, devouring the earthly prayers and sacrifices, and the holiness rising up to heaven of the man who obeys and offers himself and is devoured for the sake of all men, on whom God's pleasure rests and whom God transfigures on the mountain into his uncreated light. It is not possible to conceive of anything more intensive, more devouring, more compelling than this encounter of the two fires which fuse into one. For what is happening here to man? 'This is my body which is given to you.

This cup is the New Covenant in my blood, which is shed for you.' This man is fanned into countless sparks by the fire of God, he is in the state of such abandonment to God that God can distribute him indefinitely, inexhaustibly through all time and space. (*The Tablet*, Sept 20 1997)

Put more simply, God and God's creation are lovingly united forever in one human person, Jesus. The implications of this revelation for each one of us, and for the whole world as well, are pursued, as best I can, throughout these pages. I only mention them here, in the context of this reflection, to indicate the centrality of Jesus in the work that I do.

Now, in all of this, here is what I feel I failed to grasp. It is all too easy to miss the essential meaning in the proclamation of Jesus as the Word made flesh, the Way to the Father, the Incarnate Love of God. There are many levels of assent to this mystery, many ways of believing it to be true. But whatever way we grapple with it, whatever personal insights we may be blessed with, we are faced with a human person who is more than just a moment in history, even a unique one, more than a vital evolutionary leap forward in the life-story of the universe, more than a Messianic finger pointing to heaven. The face of God was revealed to those around Jesus during his time on earth, to the extent that they had entered into a trusting, human relationship with him. Jesus was not just a sign-post; in his very humanity he *was* Divine Love. It was *in* his humanness, *in* his lovableness and in all the other qualities that we predicate of a human being, that the true nature of God was revealed. In the economy of salvation, as applied to his followers, those who were closest to the human heart of Jesus were also closest to the Father.

What is becoming ever clearer to me during these special days of silence is the need of Jesus for a friendship such as mine, a friendship I had never really shared with him. As I tried to be true to the imaginative structure of the Ignatian method of meditation, I continued to visualise the prescribed passage from scripture. I was surprised by the touching aspects of Jesus' personality that came across with such intensity. Especially, as I have mentioned, his desire for friendship. He certainly was a person who needed others. His relationships were so important to him. His sense of unity with a close group of followers came across to me so strongly. I became aware of a mutual dependence, a sense of intimate conversation, a sense of play, an un-spoken loyalty.

I then attempted to be a companion for Jesus during the awful Holy Week trials that we were just then re-living at St Beuno's. (Even as I promised him my support and love, I was aware too that even now, long after his own personal, historical trauma, there is a sense in which he still wants us to watch with him, as his Body today – all humanity and all creation – continues to be persecuted and destroyed.) In imagination I kept trying to feel what Jesus felt during those fate-filled hours before his death. How shattering his terrible experiences must have been to his trusting heart and failing body. How his heart must have kept breaking as he was betrayed by Judas and denied by Peter, and when he heard the howls for his blood from a people he had only loved and healed throughout the land. And at the end, he must surely have thought that even his beloved Father, up to now the light of his life and the constant companion of his short and strange career, had also abandoned him.

It is so easy, on this day, in one way, to reach out and hold Jesus in my arms as, blinded by his own sweat and blood, he stumbled and blundered into people and pillars – it was easy until I began to realise, in a more striking way than I had ever suspected, the implications for my life of such a dangerous promise. As with everyone, Jesus, too, deeply desired to love and to know others; to be loved and known by others. He wished with all his heart to entrust himself to another, to find his true self in such a surrender.

This is what I was missing out on. I had fallen in love with an *idea* of Christ's humanity. My relationship was with an incredible revelation about the meaning of creation, with all its life and people – that everyone, flawed and beautiful, is saved for heaven. Yet somewhere in the middle of this, I had missed the essence of the mystery, the vulnerability that lies at the heart of all humanity, and the humanity of Jesus in particular, the lonesome, complaining figure who sadly said 'Could you not watch one hour with me?' It is somewhere here that the terrible significance of the self-emptying of our Saviour begins to hit home to our hearts. (Phil 2:6) In *The Practice of Faith*, Karl Rahner writes:

> Only when Jesus himself is accepted and loved in himself, over and above one's own knowledge about him – Jesus himself, and not our mere idea of Christ – only then does a true relationship to him, the relationship of an absolute self-abandonment to him, begin. (SCM Press, 1985, p 116)

But then the questions begin again. How can you love someone so far away, so distant in terms of time, history and culture? In a different context, the question was endlessly asked during the massive outpouring of national emotion when Princess Diana died. How could people who never met her grieve her death so intensely? Even though we believe that Jesus is risen and alive with God, can we realistically hold a truly human love-relationship with him? Countless millions have no doubt about it. It is almost universally accepted that a love between two people is absolutely possible, even though separated by time and space, until death and beyond. In his spiritual writings, Karl Rahner explores this question in his painstaking but clarifying way. He goes to great lengths in his efforts to unravel the difficulties that those of us, who can only admire and envy what is often called the 'simple faith of our fathers and mothers', struggle with. Towards the end of his reflection on love for Jesus in *The Practice of Faith*, he movingly writes:

> At this point in our considerations we have only sought to make it in some measure clear that the spatial, cultural and temporal distance between Jesus and us need present no insuperable obstacle to our really loving him – loving Jesus himself, the concrete person who, only through his seeming disappearance into the incomprehensibility of God, can come right up close to us as the real, historical person he is – on condition that we *want* to love him, that we have the courage to throw our arms around him. (p 120)

There are two further and very consoling reassurances in his final paragraph. The first concerns the mutuality of our love for Jesus and our love for each other. In no way is either relationship constricted or diminished by the other. Rather do they complement and enrich each other. And for the Christian, this must be so. He also comforts us by the very human observation that our love of Jesus is not a 'given' from the start.

> It must grow and ripen. The tender interiority of this love, a tenderness it need not be afraid to admit, is the fruit of patience, prayer and an ever renewed immersion in scripture. It is the gift of God's Spirit. We cannot commandeer it, we cannot seize it violently and without discretion. *But we may always know that the very aspiration to such love is already its beginning, and that we have a promise of its fulfilment.* (p 120)

Dangerous Liaison

To arrive at Easter Sunday without having first travelled by way of Holy Thursday and Good Friday could lead one to a very false destination. To try to befriend only the Risen Lord, once again in proud possession of his surrendered glory, could be a dangerous liaison for the urgent neophyte. To overhear only the post-resurrection words of power and authority addressed to the barely-recovering disciples by the triumphant Christ, would be to miss the full story. Because the truth is that the paschal road is one of the bloodiest journeys of history, strewn with broken promises and fallen idols, littered with betrayals and denials, marked by raw flesh and angry tears. This road is crowded with very human beings, some of whom had reached the ultimate levels of brutality and soullessness, while others, at one with their Beloved in his empty desperation, were transcending their fallenness into a more hopeful way of travelling. This is the hard apprenticeship for all disciples: there are no free passes to the end of the marathon, no 'byes' to the final victory.

Loving Jesus (like praying the 'Our Father' or receiving Holy Communion) is a dangerous business. But it is only dangerous if we are aware of what we are doing. Such involvements, when they are heart-felt and true, are always sacrificial. True worship and the love of Jesus, without sacrifice, are worthless. Would we celebrate the eucharist so casually, often giving but a notional assent to its prayers and readings, if we realised the implications for our very lives of what we are engaged in? We would rather be viewers than victims.

It was not so easy for Peter, either before or after his triple vow of love when Jesus warned him that the price of such a commitment was death. And sure enough, his hard life had a hard ending. So too had Paul's. And Stephen's, and countless others. Even poor old Lazarus, who was given a second shot at life on earth because of his friendship with Jesus, walked right into a heap of trouble. 'The chief priests planned to put Lazarus to death because on account of him many of the Jews were going away and believing in Jesus.' (Jn 12:10) Such high-risk loving carries too much voltage for the normal human wiring. The sparks fly, the fuses blow and, in the explosion, something or someone usually dies. *If you dare to love ,be prepared to grieve.*

'Am I,' asks Gerald O'Collins, in *Finding Jesus*, 'a dead Lazarus, bound and quietly corrupting in a sealed tomb – someone over whom people can only shake their heads and say "Poor O'Collins [O'Leary!] there's no helping him now?" Or am I a Lazarus already shuffling my way toward the door and the light? Or have I been fully awakened, raised and freed, so that I can genuinely stand at Jesus's side?' (Paulist, 1983, p 37)

What is becoming clear to me at this time of grace, is that to stand at the side of the risen Jesus, to experience the joy of salvation, to delight in the presence of God, there are no short-circuits around the dying of the seed, no inside tracks to instant birth. This is the whole message of the mystery of incarnation and passover. It is not as though Jesus had opened a door out there somewhere and said, 'Go through this into the house of my Father'. What he made so clear was that *he himself was the door*. Only 'he who knows me knows the Father'. And knowing Jesus entails being acquainted with, and living through, all the seasons of his life – its winters as well as its summers.

What is so noticeable about the current searching of our society for a deeper meaning to life, for a spirituality that nourishes its soul, is the 'quick-fix' philosophies and some of the 'instant' New Age remedies that are offered to our hungry people. While the suggested ways of affirmation to promote a worthy sense of self-esteem have much to commend them, the glaring omission is the necessity of the way of the cross. Only to the extent that I accept, identify with, and love the 'total Jesus' – his desert-time as well as his transfiguration-time, his temptation-time as well as his glorification-time, his Good Friday experiences as well as his Easter Sunday brightness – can I ever hope for heaven, in this life or in the next.

There are no hot-lines, ring-roads or short-cuts to present or future redemption and fulfilment. If there were, there would be no need for the Word to become flesh; incarnation would be superfluous; Calvary a one-off and disposable event. God became human so as to be known in the only possible way by other human beings – through God's humanity in Jesus. And in this humanity we find, like we discern in the life-story of a diamond, the darkness and lightness of being, the long pressures and new releases of growing, the many little deaths and the many more beginnings that make up the health and wholeness of what we call the abundant life in the here and now.

But not only do we discern this pattern of death and life in the humanity of Jesus as though we were regarding it from a distance, as though it were a notional acknowledgment we might give when 'making the Stations of the Cross', we are called to identify with it from our innermost experiences, to see the vicissitudes of our lives as a vital part of the living-out of the passion of Jesus, so as to grow through his passover into sharing in his unending delight. The invitation is to read the story of Jesus, and of our love-affair with him, in terms of the totality of life's experiences as well as in terms of its final end. I have found much blessing in the following, rather lengthy reflection of Karl Rahner about the nature of our human efforts to stay in love with Jesus and to understand something of its mysterious meaning about dying:

> ...death, in a theological sense, does not in the last resort co-incide chronologically with the medical exitus, but occurs throughout the whole of life and reaches its completion only at the end. Hence, from the nature of the case, it was legitimate for Christian piety in its entire history to seek to realise the following of the Crucified in Christian *life*, in the acceptance of everything that Christian usage, even up to the present time, described as the 'cross': the experiences of human frailty, of sickness, of disappointments, of the non-fulfilment of our expectations ... What occurs in all of this is part of man's dying, of the destruction of life's tangible goods. In all these brief moments of *dying in installments* we are faced with the question of how we are to cope with them: whether we merely protest, merely despair (even for brief moments), become cynical and cling all the more desperately and absolutely to what has not yet been taken from us, or whether we abandon with resignation what is taken from us, accept *twilight* as the promise of an eternal Christmas full of light, regard lesser breakdowns as events of grace. If we take the cross on ourselves daily, we are accomplishing part of the following of the Crucified, we are practising faith and loving hope in which death is accepted as the advent of eternal life, and then the following of Jesus, the Crucified, reaches its completion. (*The Practice of Faith*, p 129)

What has been missing, I feel, in my personal relationship with the man Jesus, was an understanding of the desperate neediness of every human being. Here was a man who needed his close friend John to lean against his body, who needed another close friend Mary, to bathe and wipe his feet, who needed others to weep for him, who needed Lazarus by his side, who needed Peter to tell him that he was loved more than all the rest, who needed his group of followers around him for security and companionship, who needed his three chosen ones to watch him while he suffered during his last, long night.

What was coming together in my *via negativa* of Holy Week, this *Moment of Darkness and Emptiness*, was my head and my heart; the cosmic Omega-centre of my mind and the weeping, smiling Friend of my soul. They are both essential dimensions of the Lord and Saviour of my life. This is the intimate balance I was hoping for when I wrote:

Just as spring each year finds,
as if for the first time, the empty tree
and persuades from within its winter womb
the buds, the leaves and blossoms,
so too do you, Jesus, the everlasting spring.
You easter your way into our hearts,
drawing out in ever deeper richness
our moisture, our freshness, our greenness,
our beauty. You are the invincible summer
at the heart of our dying.

Dan's cardigan

Something startled me from my dozing. Across the ward a man is turning purple. His tortured body is writhing in a chair, his misshapen arthritic leg is kicking in uncontrollable spasms against the nearby cubicle curtains. Sweat edges down the furrows of his face. His pained eyes are pleading for my help. Taut and strained with the intense effort, he makes one last violent twist. And before a passing nurse can reach him, he utters a hoarse cry of triumph. The vital struggle is over. Proud as can be, he begins the long and complicated manoeuvre of buttoning his cardigan. The cardigan that Dan had just managed to put on.

I felt very moved. At that moment I tried to become more aware of the nature of my emotions. First there was a feeling of helplessness. I wanted so much to leap the few yards across the ward and help Dan with his cardigan. But I could not. My own movements were very limited. Up to last week I had jogged and exercised for an hour each day. I was so proud of my fitness. And today, after a sudden operation, and for some time to come, my fluency will be reduced to an embarrassed, stilted hobble.

But Dan seemed to understand. It was a moment of shared weakness, an experience of frustrating impotence. I reflected on the precariousness of life and the futility of making plans. A favourite phrase of my Mom's came to mind. 'How do you make God laugh?,' she would interrupt me whenever I outlined, in detail, the course of my life over the next decade. 'Tell him,' she would smile, 'your plans for yourself.' So today I resolved to lighten up a little, to hang that bit looser to my projects, to leave room for surprise, to allow more space for the inevitability of the unforeseen in my tight life. I decided, in fact, to whole-heatedly commit all my energies to collaborate with the unpredictable! I wrote a poem 'Incognito' many years ago on this theme. Here are a few verses:

Lest human beauty be the norm
that cages God's own face and form
the baby weak, with tears and cries
reveals the depth of God's surprise.

While God writes straight with crooked lines,
makes melodies with rhymeless rhymes,
in powerless poor God's strength is waiting
God's night is ever dawn-creating.

So if we're wise, we'll be aware
of those with lumps and humps who stare
and stammer and twitch, and can not marry –
they hide and show the God they carry.

A little later in the day, as I tuned into my feelings again, I noticed now within me a sense of Dan's creativity. Michaelangelo's shout of victory as he stepped off the Sistine ladder for the last time had nothing on Dan's quiet smile of satisfaction as he finally pushed his severely arthritic hand through his impossible second sleeve. There was something beautiful about the simplicity of what happened this morning. It was beautiful because it was neither contrived nor pretentious. It was honest and it was real. Here, according to D. H. Lawrence, was a man 'in his wholeness wholly attending'. And for some reason, the title of Soren Kierkegaard's little classic came into my mind – *Purity of Heart is to Will One Thing*. There was no distraction in Dan's single eye as he struggled with his unco-operative cardigan. If beauty is 'the product of honest attention to the particular', then we witnessed a small epiphany of beauty today.

In the unpredictable way that our angels have, I had been unknowingly prepared to notice this moment. The link between creativity, beauty and concentration was being forged in my mind just before Dan's civil war with his cardigan broke out. I had just been reading a book by Richard Harries, the Bishop of Oxford, on art and beauty. In it he discusses contemporary images of beauty. By a strange synchronicity, a very popular celebration of beauty is about to happen tonight, within sight of these very hospital windows. Here in this lovely, southern peninsula, sometimes referred to as *Heaven's Reflex*, a huge crowd gathers each autumn to salute 22 of the world's most beautiful women. I refer to the Kerry Festival when, in the Dome of Tralee, a Rose is picked to grace our days for another year.

Is there any link between the ritual of Dan and his cardigan this morning and the pageant of the Roses this evening? Without straining its meaning, can we apply the word 'beauty' to both moments? Was one spiritual, the other physical? Is beauty the naked simplicity that is left when all the additions are once again subtracted? These questions are taking me on a roller-coaster ride of theological thoughts and physical feelings, of memories and experiences.

The bishop's book catches my eye again. It is called *Art and the Beauty of God – a Christian Understanding*. Expectantly, I flick through it. The author tries to place beauty at the centre of our lives. Without an affirmation of it, there can be no faith, no God worth loving. 'Late have I loved you, O beauty, ever-ancient, ever-new.' The gradual disappearance of people from the mainstream churches of contemporary Christianity is due, in no small part, to the almost total neglect of beauty. R. S. Thomas is deadly accurate, as usual, with these words from *The Minister*:

Protestantism – the adroit castrator
Of art; the bitter negation
Of song and dance and the heart's innocent joy –
You have botched our flesh and left us only the soul's
Terrible impotence in a warm world.
(*Collected Poems*, Phoenix, 1993)

There was a sense of beauty among the pagans. Plato believed that pure beauty was experienced by the soul before birth and the soul still remembers and recognises this on earth. The early Christians had a strong sense of the beauty of a God whose love spilled over in incarnation. Generally speaking, this sense was soon lost. St Thomas Aquinas was one of the few theologians who kept the notion of beauty alive. He saw wholeness, harmony and radiance as its qualities. The Orthodox churches have maintained a fine awareness of the beauty of God. Today, in the Roman Catholic Church, Karl Rahner and Hans Urs von Balthasar are among the few who can be called theologians of beauty.

This is such a pity when so many of our poets and artists would agree with Dostoyevski's belief, in *The Idiot*, that 'only beauty will save the world'. Tony Blair eulogises John Macmurray, one of today's most famous philosophers and quotes from his *Freedom in the Modern World*:

I am inclined to think that the worst feature of modern life is its failure to believe in beauty. For human life, beauty is as important as truth – even more important – and beauty in life is the product of real feeling. The strongest condemnation of modern industrial life is not that it is cruel, materialistic, wearisome and false, but simply that it is ugly and has no sense of beauty. Moral conduct is beautiful conduct. If we want to make the world better, the main thing we have to do is to make it more beautiful. Nothing that is not inherently beautiful is really good. We have to recapture the sense of beauty if we are not to lose our freedom ... There are signs – small signs – of a revival in and reverence for beauty amongst us. I for one would pin my hopes to it rather than to anything else. (p 218)

A truly incarnational theology of revelation tries to restore the balance between created beauty and God. This balance has been knocked out of kilter by the many virulent strains of Gnosticism and Manichaeism that still distort our Christian perspective on the meaning of incarnation. This lost balance needs immediate redressing. *For damaged beauty needs a new design.* Those with vision come to our aid here. They point out the underlying divine beauty in almost everything around us. The true beauty of the world is the radiance of the divinely created order and pattern of all things. *It will flame out, like shook foil,* according to Gerard Manley Hopkins. Being so intimately present in and through all things, the world becomes a sign and sacrament of God's beauty. In *Waiting on God,* the French religious thinker Simone Weil wrote:

The beauty of the world is Christ's tender smile for us coming through matter. He is really present in the universal beauty. The love of this beauty proceeds from God dwelling in our souls and goes out to God present in the universe. It is also like a sacrament. (Fontana, 1959, p 120)

St Augustine, much maligned by many for his so-called dualistic doctrines, is nevertheless a great defender of *the human face of God,* the very title of one of his books. In his search for truth, he asked all the elements and objects in his experience for an answer. Each replied that it was not God.

And I said to all these things in my external environment: 'Tell me of my God who you are not, tell me something about him.' And with a great voice they cried out: 'He made us.' (Ps 99) My question was the attention I gave them; their response was their beauty.

Augustine had a passion for beauty, yet remained very aware of its dangers. Frightened by its potential seductive powers, he was still drawn by its attraction for his soul. And so, in his

Confessions (OUP, 1992) we read the passage that has become so
popular with so many of us:

> Late have I loved you, beauty so old and so new; late have I
> loved you. And see, you were within and I was in the exter-
> nal world and sought you there, and in my unlovely state I
> plunged into those lovely created things that you made. You
> were with me and I was not with you ... You called and cried
> out loud and shattered my deafness. You were radiant and
> resplendent, you put to flight my blindness. You were frag-
> rant, and I drew in my breath and now pant after you. I tasted
> you, and I feel that hunger and thirst for you. You touched
> me, and I am set on fire to attain the peace which is yours. (p 201)

Our best theologians agree with Augustine about the allurement
of false beauty. Whether we read Teilhard de Chardin, Thomas
Aquinas, Hans Urs von Balthasar or Karl Rahner, we find an
emphasis on the need for a graced discernment, a reminder
about our gullibility and naïvete when it comes to finding a worthy focus for the aspirations of our soul. They warn us about the
pitfalls that await our uncertain searching; the deadly disguise
that deludes our untutored and our radically flawed hearts. But
true to their trade, they never fall into that other tempting trap of
dualism. They never hold the one form of beauty as essentially
over against the other; they never endow the competing beauties with totally separate origins. In the end, all real beauty, no
matter what its shape, comes from God.

> One of the strengths of the Christian faith is the way it can
> hold together in one vision, the physical and the spiritual.
> The world has been created good and beautiful by God.
> Christ has claimed it as his own and will raise it to eternal
> light and life. This means that the material and the immaterial,
> the visible and the invisible, the physical and the spiritual in-
> terpenetrate one another. The physical world becomes radi-
> ant with eternity and eternity is seen in terms of a transfig-
> ured physical world. This means that all everyday experi-
> ences have a sacramental character. (Harries, p 87)

Theologians of the true meaning of the incarnation ask for a concentration of the soul's eye. They counsel a faith-filled attention
to the pursuit of the ultimate, a persistence in a following-
through that is risky, but free from fear, a total attention to the
work in hand. Which brings us back to Dan and the strange stir-

ring of beauty I felt as he doggedly persisted in completing his
task of the moment. There was nothing luke-warm about his
commitment. I only hope he doesn't mind sharing in this reflection with the theologians and philosophers of beauty!

As Simone Weil and Dietrich Bonhoeffer both emphasised,
we should give ourselves wholly and without thought of
anything else to the beautiful, with a single eye. God is implicit when we do this and in doing so we are saved from
half-heartedness and semi-attentiveness ... Beauty has the
strange effect of at once beckoning us to itself and pointing
beyond itself to that which seems tantalisingly unattainable.
Augustine and Hopkins both exulted in the beauties of the
world and saw them irradiated by the light of eternal beauty ...
The special insight of Christianity, as opposed to Platonism, is
that the divine beauty is to be seen in and through the particular, of which the incarnation is the supreme expression ... It
was the special genius of Hopkins, drawing on the influence
of Duns Scotus, to see the particular and the universal, the
human and the divine, together. (Harries, pp 42, 43)

A final chord must be struck in this desperately inadequate reflection about beauty. Beauty is so often ambiguous, elusive and
unpredictable. It is not always immediately obvious. It lives in
the most unexpected places. Remember the two moments of
beauty at the beginning of this reflection – the private saga of
Dan's lonely duel, at dawn, with his reluctant cardigan and that
same evening, the spot-lit pageant next door, in a Festival Dome
full of the beautiful people.

God's glory is revealed in humble, self-effacing lives of faith
and love. It can be fully present in failure and ignominy. It is
almost entirely a glory that is veiled ... In the light of this,
many of our standard notions of success and failure are radically reversed. Christ, the King of Glory, reigns from the tree
... He reveals the divine glory because he is the truth of God
and the love of God in human terms ... As human beings we
will always stand in a profound, puzzling, tensionful relationship to all forms of beauty. For the full glory of the world
about us will be largely hidden in lives of secret self-sacrifice,
of unceasing inner prayer, of profound artistic achievement
that goes unrecognised in its own time. On the other hand, all
that is fine and flourishing, all that is beautiful and radiant as
God intends it to be, has its place in that transformed world

which belongs first and foremost and finally to the poor and humble. (Harries, p 62)

One final thought. When a lover says to the beloved, 'You are beautiful', the grateful reply, 'You have made me so', is often made. To be sure, there is a sense in which this is true. But it is not the whole truth. What happens, I think, is that we draw out and reveal the beauty already there within another. We create the circumstances for the shy and frightened loveliness in the other to emerge. We are catalysts of transcendence. When we are awake to our own beauty, we open the eyes of the sleeping beauty in another. Our hearts design a sacred space of trust into which, tentatively, the first small steps of another's self-belief are taken. This is the most sacred moment. If birthdays are celebrated in heaven, if the Lord of Life calls creation to attention, if ever the angels bow down in adoration, it must surely be at such threshold incarnations of our Tremendous Lover.

But how do we know this? Are we not falling into a hundred heresies of Pantheism, Pelagianism, Monism and many others by making such wild and extravagant claims? A theology of creation is sure-footed and fearless in affirming these assertions. I hope it is already clear from the *theological glimpses* at the beginning of each *Moment* of this book, that we are only applying to our earthly existence what our Lord and Saviour has revealed through his incarnation. Jesus Christ is our reason for never denying the divine beauty in every created being. His birth is our birth-right. Every baby is born to divinity – to inherit the fullness of the glory of God. The revelation of incarnation is the revelation that all that was true of Jesus is true of us. The transfiguration, to take one instance, should set our minds at rest. This major feast in the Orthodox churches is strangely neglected in the West. John of Damascus, in *On the Divine Images*, writes:

Christ is transfigured, not by putting on some quality he did not possess previously, nor by changing into something he never was before, but by revealing to his disciples what he truly was, in opening their eyes and in giving sight to those who were blind. For while remaining identical to what he had been before, he appeared to his disciples in his true splendour ...

I want to add to this lovely passage of John of Damascus, the suggestion that the main impact of the transfiguration was on Jesus himself. Like the lover who finds a new confidence and power, a sense of self-worth, self value and self-respect in being acknowledged and cherished, so too with Jesus. For most of us, most of the time, like it often was for Jesus, the curtain is tightly drawn. Life is drab, routine and ordinary. Maybe even worse, like it was for Jesus too. But occasionally, perhaps just for a magical once, we see the shining in our souls, the weaving of the woven light of which we and all things are made.

There is one more aspect of our helpless fascination with beauty. It is more than the realisation and experience of our own beauty. It is even greater than our longing to be forever in its presence, to build our tabernacle on the mountain-top of transfiguration. It has something to do with the desire that we ourselves might be so changed that this beauty becomes a part of us, that we become what we behold. St Paul was lost in this fascination. 'And we, with our unveiled faces, reflecting like mirrors the brightness of the Lord, all grow brighter and brighter as we are turned into the image that we reflect; this is the work of the Lord who is Spirit.' (2 Cor 3:17, 18)

Beauty beckons everything to itself. The yearning aroused by experiences of beauty is a longing for God's own self, for communion with divine beauty. Bishop Harries reminds us that this desire for communion with the inexpressibly lovely is only a part of the reason for the intensity of longing that we experience in the presence of beauty. 'We do not merely want to see beauty,' wrote C.S. Lewis in *The Weight of Glory*, 'We want something else that can hardly be put into words – to be united with the beauty we see, to pass into it, to receive it into ourselves, to bathe in it, to become part of it.'

Sometimes when I find myself in places of peace and light, I'm often filled with a strange longing for something or someone well out of reach, unclear and uncertain. It is a disturbing feeling that has something to do with time and eternity, with our restlessness to be reunited with the source of that beauty from whence we came. 'The beauty of the world has made me sad,' wrote the poet-soldier Pádraig Pearse, 'this beauty that will pass.' Maybe the longing is for some kind of permanence in a life that is held hostage to the relentless, death-dealing ageing of our finite condition. And so we long that we ourselves might become all beauty, all light, all glory, in and through the glory of God shining in the face of Jesus Christ.

There is a supreme confidence in the prayers and readings of the Requiem Mass about the nature of the human soul. Through

the grace of God in Christ we are to be totally changed, to become like God. We are to take on God's beauty; to become light
as God is light. This transformation, to my mind, does not happen at, or after, the moment of death. It begins a long time before. And this is the liberating revelation; this is the meeting-
point between creation and incarnation; this *theiosis*, this divini-
sation, is always happening. The beauty seen in Christ at the
transfiguration is already irradiating all creation. If it's not happening now, it will not happen later. The perfect union of love,
human and divine, in Jesus, became an explosive power for
transfiguring all creatures and all creation into its own likeness.

> If beauty delights you, the dust shall shine as the sun. If you
> enjoy that speed, strength and freedom of the body, they
> shall be like the angels of God ... If you drink in any pleasure
> that is not impure but pure, they shall drink from the torrent
> of the pleasures of God. (*The Prayers and Meditations of St
> Anselm*, Benedicta Ward ed., Penguin, 1973, p 260. Quoted in
> Harries, p 136)

A most significant threshold to be crossed in our own transformation into the beauty that affects us so deeply, is to be present
to it in a way that is not dualistic or divisive. Because so many of
the tedious debates about the respective values of human and
divine beauty take place outside the context of the incarnation,
they get us nowhere. A respect for the mystery of God-made-
human will urge us to see earthly beauty as the moment of disclosure of divine beauty too. We need to learn the holy skill of
reading the events of life in this way.

When a father's heart leaps with joy at the smile on his baby's
face, there is no 'space' in the father's understanding of the moment between the smile and the baby; they are immediately and
intimately one. And this shared presence, in turn, creates a profound bond between baby and parent. Likewise with our life-experiences. Are we comfortably and confidently aware, for example, of the pleasures of the senses as theophanies? Do we hear
the beauty of God in the sounds of music that bless our ears?
Does the father see, without straining and theologising, the
smile of God and the baby's smile in the same wonderful moment? C.S. Lewis has learned the answer. Referring to the distinction we make between our life-experience and then our later
interpretation of them in terms of revelation, he writes:

> The distinction ought to become impossible; to receive some-

thing and to recognise its divine source are a single experience. This heavenly fruit is instantly redolent of the orchard where it grew. This sweet air whispers of the country from whence it flows. It is a message. We know we are being touched by a finger of the right hand at which there are pleasures evermore. There need be no question of thanks or praise as a separate event, something done afterwards. To experience the tiny theophany is itself to adore ...
(Harries, pp 144, 145)

It was a dark, eerie afternoon at the end of March, 1970, outside a Sheffield Nursery school, overlooking the grimy rows of belching factories. The children were streaking to freedom towards the forlorn school-bus. Suddenly a little girl noticed the magnificent rainbow. There it was, a bow of beauty, elegant as a ballet-dancer, encircling the blood-shot sky over the silhouetted city. Her companions gathered around her. Fine-tuned as they were to the play of light and shade, to the dance of colours, from their Lenten class-preparation for the Feast of Brightness, they missed nothing in the miracle of the ring of surprise that hung, like a silent blessing, over their homes and streets. Their teacher joined them. I knew what she was thinking. Would she talk about God, about Easter, about a prayer of thanks? She didn't. Instinctively she knew that the still wonder of the children was already an act of adoration – there was nothing more, just then, to add. And maybe that timeless moment had more to do with the transformation of the world than we will ever know. In their awed silence they were doing and being something beautiful for God.

Awakening the dawn

The Celtic Otherworld felt near enough as I walked the wet, un-
even roads of Maigh Rua this heavy autumn evening. There was
little to lift the spirits as decay and death pressed in as relentlessly
as the silent mist along the Limerick-Tipperary border. It was
not easy, then, to believe in warm summer evenings and singing
birds. I felt the darkness. I grieved the loss of light. But the imminent *via negativa* that was about to touch my anxious mind, was
not about an outside threat. Robert Frost put it well.

They cannot scare me with their empty spaces
Between stars – on stars where no human race is.
I have it in me so much nearer home
To scare myself with my own desert places.

And then I began to reflect on the Christian revelation about
such conditions and visitations, cosmic or personal, brief or persistent. Is it possible that such moments are precious; that they
hold a treasure – a spiritual pearl that is only discovered inside
the shell of hard times? The words of Psalm 117 that I had sung
only yesterday with the monks of Glenstal Abbey came readily
to mind: *My only companion is darkness.* The mystics keep reminding us that this darkness must be embraced as an ally; it
can bring a fine blessing. Yet not many really believe this truth.
It goes against the grain of our experiences. We would rather
avoid the pain than explore it for its hidden graces. Not many of
us wish to be victims of sacrifice no matter what the promised
reward. When we find ourselves in the tunnel that is black and
empty, we find little consolation in the assurance that the stars
shine brighter because of it and that the darkest hour is before
the dawn. Such assurances seem pious and romantic; they do
not touch the fearful heart.

But the mystics were under no illusion about what they describe as *the dark night of the soul.* They wrote compellingly of the
mystical death of the spirit, that dreadful, inner annihilation that
brings despair. They have vivid images to portray the awfulness
of the lonely and silent emptiness that numbs the spirit. There is
no beauty now, no hope or wonder. Spiritual poverty they call
it, deadly in the extreme.

Many of us are familiar with something akin to what they describe – something distasteful, frightening, ugly and blank. We may not wish to flatter ourselves in believing that our own undignified and ignoble moments of desperation are a part of the deep, enriching and profound kind of dying that the saints and mystics experience. We may feel unworthy to call our anguished depression or despair by the lofty title of a 'dark night of the soul', especially when so much of our sorry plight is self-induced and is the consequence of our sin. But I do believe it to be true. No matter what kind of human suffering we go through it is, from the beginning, indivisible in terms of 'sacred' or 'profane'. Because Jesus took on himself the totality of humanity, because no loss, no grief, no suicidal thought, no sin was left outside the all-embracing compass of God's compassion-made-flesh, then all of us, in all our petty hurts and habits, are heirs to the Christian faith regarding the fruits of the passion and resurrection of Jesus, as applied to each one of us, in all the mundane and unique details of our lives.

The 'classic' understanding of the *via negativa* tradition is an amazing one. It holds that the condition of alienation from God and from life, of emptiness and inner despair, of a loss of faith and meaning in the very reasons for living, can be the nearest we ever get to experiencing God. It seems like a strange contradiction, a meaningless paradox. In fact it is contradictory and paradoxical. But held up against the mystery of incarnation it is also true. The *via negativa* is 'the way of unknowing'; it is about divine presence through humanly perceived absence. The reality of God is so far removed from anything we can know or feel, the holy and wise ones tell us, that *the dark night of the soul*, in its countless forms, is actually the nearness of God.

Those terrible trials that especially beset those who are seriously committed to an intimacy with Infinite Love (and most of the readers of this book, I believe, belong to such adventurers) are the only way to purify and intensify our aspirations. The purification happens in the destruction of the stubborn self-reliance that is always dominant, or lurking, in our self-centredness. This self-centredness comes with our human condition: it is part of the ambiguous legacy of original sin, the *felix culpa* that is full of potential. In fact, so intrinsic to our very being is a dependence on the many faces and facets of our ego, that Karl Rahner holds that we cannot be sure of eternal grace until, almost with our last breath, we whisper the final *fiat*.

Naked trust in God alone is a rare, beautiful and final state of soul. It is promised to those who, along with Albert Camus, believe that in the depths of winter we finally learn that within us lies an invincible summer. 'In the middle of the night,' wrote Meister Eckhart, 'there was spoken to me a word, a secret word.'

Before morning light tomorrow, I will be praying, once again with the monks, paying special attention to the final shout, sometimes confident, sometimes desperate, of Psalm 56, '*I will awake the dawn.*'

Trusting the water

There is something about 'being grounded' that absorbs me. Maybe it is a reaction to the comments of my friends when they advise me to 'come out of the clouds', to 'get my body and my mind together', to 'stay in the present and join the human race'! I always resent these unsolicited remarks but I also feel that there is some truth in them.

This morning I feel grounded, but in a peculiar kind of way. For too long the quality of my life has been dependent upon the excitement, the achievements and the occasional thrills that are planned or that just happen along the ways of my days. Such rather ephemeral goals and moments are too often the anticipated bench-marks of my weeks, the keenly-awaited milestones and reassuring signposts of my happiness, the green oases of a desert life. At unguarded times, I find my energy coming from intervals such as the planning of another project, another article, a long week-end, a short break, a word of praise, an old addiction, a new relationship.

Common enough, I suppose, when perceived in proportion, when welcomed as a bonus-event, but alarming when the perspective is awry. During the rare and graced moments of disclosure about the meaning of my life, I see such a condition in terms of digging a grave, of weaving a deadly web. And yet, there is always some whisper, some barely perceptible intimation, that there is another way of being, that there are parts of me, maybe the most powerful and beautiful parts, still undamaged though sound asleep, waiting to be woken.

Anyway, as I sit here with the monks, after Sunday matins, peering through the abbey windows at the cracks in the dying night, feeling, against the panes, the silver rain sheeting across the flat fields of Limerick, I hear another word about the ordering of my life. There are new risks to take if I am to purify my vision of the horizons to which I feel called. And the word that is being made flesh in my mind is about the withdrawing of my attention from the fatal fears and attractions of tomorrow so that I can live today, explore this hour, this perfect moment, this breath I draw, this sound I hear, this touch I feel, this fine pleasure of living within my body with all its wonderful sensations.

And yet, so quickly, the anxiety returns. My mind is full of
terror. The risk is too great. Trusting the present moment means
letting go of the safety of planning the future, the security of
controlling tomorrow, the anticipation of longed-for successes.
Without these, the prospects are bleak, the frame is empty. Is
there really enough music in the present moment to fill the infinite soul to its fullness? If I dive into the unexamined waters of
the now, will they hold me, sustain and nourish me in a safe and
complete way?

When I was 20, I remember my fear-filled attraction for surrendering all to God as a possible way of living 'the abundant
life'. In my seminary days it was called the art of 'self-abandon-
ment to divine providence'. The book, with a similar title, that
touched my life at that time was written by Jeanne-Pierre de
Caussade, an 18th century mystic. He saw each person as a kind
of statue in the making at the hands of the divine sculptor. I
must patiently allow myself to be worked on, to be crafted and
honed, by the creator-artist. Robert Llewelyn, in his *Daily
Readings Series*, from the mystic's writings, remembers another
image about learning to float:

> We shall at once say that we must abandon ourselves to the
> water, trusting it, welcoming it, giving it every opportunity
> to do its work. We shall know that as soon as we begin to
> struggle – it may be through anxiety, doubt or fear – every-
> thing will be lost and the water will engulf us. (p 27)

This surrender is a desperately difficult thing to do. It calls for a
suspension of the safety-net programming that is a given condition of our nature and of our up-bringing. But this self-emptying
is not a quietist passivity, a philosophy of not caring any more.
We are, when learning to float, as I have experienced in this
challenging process, making many almost unconscious mental
and physical adjustments within ourselves, adapting instinctively to our body-weight and balance, to the depth and movement of the water, struggling with all kinds of fear and doubt
about death and survival. There is intense energy of body and
soul in this kind of immediate surrender.

In the final analysis, maybe, at moments such as these, we experience the finest and most distilled energy of all. To change
the image again, the flame of divine love acts upon the raw material of our human nature, purifying and refining it, by strip-
ping and wounding it. With mystical words, de Caussade de-

scribes the holy process: 'But the time will surely come when the fire will lay hold on the wood; even so will the divine action seize upon the soul, making it as one with the living flame.'

One of the many blessings that follow on such a daily dying is a deeper awareness of the unfolding of God's compassion in the grounding grace of the sacrament of the present moment. It is only in the letting go of the anxieties and preoccupations of the past and future, that the attention is free to be present to the miracle of *the now*. It is only in the present time that God and the soul can meet, and bless each other, and play. The incarnation is about the immediacy of God, the 'scandal of particularity'. The present moment is the only address for the continuing incarnation of God, repeated every second, and forever.

Whether we image our grounding in terms of paying unceasing attention, with the mindfulness of the mystics, to the life-giving energy of our roots in the soil of life, or to a small immersion in calm waters, or to a whole-hearted plunge, a blind dive, into the dark abyss of the mystery of our complicated lives, we can be sure that there, and only there, will we find the unity and the intimacy with God, for which we were created.

PART III

The Moment of Creativity and Healing

Experiencing Resurrection

One day recently, I was sharing my thoughts about the *via creativa* – the moment of creativity, of reconciliation and healing – with my brother priest, Nicholas Plant. He serves the Church of England community in our sister parish, St Mary's, here in Garforth, Yorkshire. He prompted me to re-emphasise a crucial dimension of Christian doctrine so easily overlooked in the telling of the story of creation. This aspect of our tradition has to do with clarifying a truth already touched upon in the first *Moment* of the book. While creation happened first in time, it is only in the light of the later incarnation that the full meaning of God's initial dream for a gifted universe is finally and irrevocably revealed. Theologians refer to this as the christocentric principle of creation.

Nicholas was concerned that a vital and intense personal relationship with Jesus Christ, both our earthly brother and yet the pre-existing Logos of the Blessed Trinity, could be lost in the fog of a vague, cosmic and impersonal understanding of a mystery that has, at its centre, a human heart. The fire of his conviction was enkindled from his profound love for and study of the scriptures, particularly where Christ is depicted as the Agent of Creation.

> In the beginning was the Word, and the Word was with God, and the Word was God. He was in the beginning with God; all things came into being through him, and without him, not one thing came into being. What has come into being in him was life, and that life was the light of all people ... (Jn 1:1-4)

Our conversations, I remember, emphasised a neglected aspect of the mainstream tradition of the Christian Church – that of a christocentric theory of creation and its strong implications for any view of the relation between Christ and ourselves.

> He is the image of the invisible God, the first-born of all cre-

ation, for in him, all things in heaven and on earth were created
... He himself is before all things, and in him all things hold
together. (Col 1:15-17)

In a similar vein, we have the opening verses of the Letter to the
Hebrews (1:1-3):

Long ago God spoke to our ancestors in many and various
ways by the prophets, but in these last days he has spoken to
us by a Son, whom he appointed heir of all things, through
whom he also created the worlds. He is the reflection of
God's glory and the exact imprint of God's very being, and
he sustains all things by his powerful word.

In his book, *The Church in the Midst of Creation*, Vincent Donovan
reassures us that St Thomas Aquinas, a cornerstone of Western
Christianity, is very much at home with such an orthodox creation theology. He puts to us a profound and challenging question:

Is it possible that the true and ultimate meaning of the church
and the final meaning of the sacraments, can be found only
outside the church, in the area of the world, in the midst of
creation?

Is such a thought outlandish? Did not Thomas Aquinas say that
the Father has spoken only one time, and speaks that Word still.
It is just that we hear the Word twice. The first time we hear it, it
is the Son, the Word spoken from all eternity. The second time
we hear it (looking back), it is creation, our world of created
things.

Are these *two* words, or just one Word heard two times? If
our world issues from that same one Word spoken by God
which begets the Son of God, would it seem strange to find in
that world the final meaning of our church and our sacraments? The world is the body of God.[1]

Nicholas also suggested that we in the West might well look to
the Eastern tradition and its wonderful icons, for evidence of
Christ's involvement in creation. He mentioned a 17th century
icon from the Muscovite school, and quoted from Thomas
Kala's *Meditation on Icons*:

... what is stressed in this icon is the tenderness and inexhaustible mercy evinced in the facial expression – Christ is

the Lord who sustains all things and is the prototype of transfigured humanity.[2]

The other day, I, too, came across another 16th century icon of the Saviour from St Jovan's Church in Okrid, now in the art museum of Skopje, capital of Macedonia, and recently reproduced by Sister Aloysius McVeigh. Both of these icons belong to a tradition of portraying Christ as *Pantocrator* – the one who holds all things in being. In the latter, Jesus is drawing our attention in two directions, reminiscent of the insights of St Thomas to which we have just referred. One hand holds a book of the Hebrew and Christian scriptures, pointing to what is revealed in the Word-made-flesh in Jesus; the other points to his own sacred, human heart, to what is already revealed in the Word-made-flesh in creation.

I begin this *Moment* with these observations about the historical Jesus and the Cosmic Christ because they are central to our understanding of creativity and healing. At this point I would like to move into our 'theological glimpse' by touching into the mystery of the resurrection. Somewhere within it lies a window through which we can look at all I want to say about the *via creativa*.

Behold, I make all things new

The exploration of the mystery of the resurrection goes on forever. It is the evergreen forest of our often faltering hope, the ever-fresh spring of our often doubting belief. And it has infinite dimensions to it. That is why, in these few pages, we must leave aside for another time, some central aspects of centuries of doctrinal discussion and biblical exegesis about the physical resurrection of Jesus, about life after death, about the *four last things*, and many more.

Just now, I wish to concentrate on our own experience of resurrection each day. This experience is as real and true for us now as it was for the friends of Jesus as recounted in the Christian scriptures. Here, too, we enter into another theological debate. Put very simply, in the form of a question, it goes like this: Did revelation cease with the death of the last disciple? Or does it continue today with the same vibrancy in our human condition? Dermot Lane reminds us that one school of thought seems to suggest that what happened after the crucifixion is absolutely unique, quite specific to that period and those people, and there-

fore unrepeatable. There is therefore a break between the experience of the first disciples and the experiences of contemporary
Christians. Another school of thought suggests that there is no
such radical difference between then and now.

I mention this debate only because it concerns the whole
thrust of the theology that we are 'doing' in this book. At the end
of the day, what is sure is this. Whether we are talking about the
revelation accorded to the disciples, or the 'revelation' given to
us today, Jesus, after his death on the cross, is experienced by all
as a new presence and power, personally alive and active within
our lives, transforming the disciples and ourselves, creating a
new people, missioning them and us, and holding all together in
and through the one Spirit of Pentecost. This element of the personal presence of Jesus, dynamic and empowering, is forever
available to each and every open heart and mind.

> What does the message of resurrection have to say to con-
> temporary experience? What particular human experiences
> of life today does the resurrection of Jesus express? If we can
> tackle these questions we may be able to pave the way for a
> fusion of horizons between the Christian tradition of resur-
> rection and human experience. Otherwise the resurrection of
> Jesus will remain a dead dogma of the past.[3]

Once again, Lane helps us out. He writes about relevant dimensions of contemporary life such as the fragmentation of the individual and of society, our hopelessness in the face of injustice,
and our anxiety about a future life after death. Taking these in
order, he refers first to the breakdown of traditional values leading to a growing insecurity about the future. There is dualism
between spirit and matter, between individuals and community
that brings a new kind of human loneliness and isolation. The
mechanisation of nature and the technological control of society
are contributing to a completely new sense of personal insecurity.

In his address to the Conference of Major Superiors in
Virginia, USA, (1966) Fr Timothy Radcliffe, the Dominican
Master General, spoke about the context of a society in which
most people suffer from a crisis of identity. 'The global market,'
he said, 'wipes out all sense of vocation, whether you are a doctor, a priest or a bus driver ... To be a musician, a lawyer, a
teacher, a nurse, a carpenter, a plumber, a farmer, a priest, was
not just to have a job; it was to be someone; one belonged to a
body of people with institutions that defined appropriate con-

duct, that shared a wisdom, a history and a solidarity. What we have seen over the last years is the corrosive effect of a new model of society…'[4]

In the autumn of the same year, the Bishops of England and Wales issued a pre-election document *The Common Good*. In it they acknowledge the critical rift between the individual and society. The focus for the thrust of their discussion is the dignity of each person 'made in God's image'. In a broken and divided world, we constitute one single human family in which no one should be excluded. There are 'structures of sin' within a society that treats people only as economic units.[5]

Healing the rift

There is also a disturbing divorce between the spiritual and material realities of our lives that has brought an emptiness and sense of loss that often lies just below the surface of our existence. The list is long. Millions feel cut off from the natural environment of mother earth. There is an intense sense of disconnectedness between women and men, between the rich and the poor, between the young and the old, between the endless differences in the human race. Those who can read the signs of the times agree on the urgent need for a sense of solidarity to heal the destructive splits across the face of humanity; a sense of interdependence and intimacy to create a safe journey for our universe into a new millennium. Without such a personal and planetary transformation the future of the human family is bleak indeed. But we are not without hope.

Is there not a case to be made that the ultimate source of human solidarity is to be found in God's solidarity with the human enterprise? Can we not say that the resurrection of Jesus is the ultimate act of divine solidarity with humanity and with the whole world? In the resurrection, we have God's personal acceptance and adoption of the human condition. A new kind of unity is forged in the resurrection of Jesus between God and world, between spirit and matter … The doctrine of the resurrection is a symbol uniting in solidarity God and the world, humanity and nature, matter and spirit in a way that enables us to see beyond the immediate experiences of fragmentation and isolation. In and through the resurrection of Jesus, God has entered into a new oneness with the human race that is the basis of the contemporary call to a universal solidarity embracing past, present and future.[6]

We all carry within us, too, a sense of both personal and global injustice. We carry living memories of childhood times when we were wrongly blamed, and later when we suffered as victims of unjust or misguided regimes whether of society or religion. And in a wider context, as we read and watch the media's daily presentation of the cruelty and inhumanity that is rampant in our world, our souls revolt in helpless outrage. As human beings, as baptised Christians, to what or to whom do we turn?

> In recognising the jagged edges of human existence and the awful ambiguity of living and dying, we begin to understand what it means to hope against hope. Human hopes arise out of a stubborn refusal to give way in the face of so much evil and suffering, out of the extraordinary ability to begin again and again after being touched by tragedy, out of momentary human glimpses of transcendence in the midst of pain and joy. These hopes, though fragile, are a persistent and universal experience of the human spirit.[7]

This is the key point of connection with the meaning of the first Easter. The resurrection of Jesus reveals and empowers the human heart's capacity to trust in its God-implanted graces. It makes clear, in spite of all evidence to the contrary, that we are an Easter people, in whose breasts hope springs eternal. Even though our nature is radically flawed, even though our vision is perennially distorted by our sinful condition, we persistently carry a relentless belief in the light. Maybe this hope in not just in spite of, but because of our original sinfulness. How else can we explain the triumphant cry of the Easter *Exultet*, 'O happy fault; O *necessary* sin of Adam...'

> The symbol of resurrection is an assurance that evil and suffering do not have the last word, that injustice and inequality do not finally endure, that death is not in truth the end. Resurrection reverses the outward appearances of living and dying, and reminds us that invisible realities deep down do count in the long run. Put more positively, the resurrection of Jesus from the dead is a statement that good triumphs over evil, that suffering can be transformed into new life, that justice will take over from injustice, that death itself is a point of entry into new life.[8]

Most of us understand the resurrection of Jesus in terms of the divine guarantee that after death, and after the purification of purgatory, we will, one day, enjoy the delights of heaven where we will become like God's own self. As anyone who has felt the sorrow and loss of mourners will know, this is our greatest comfort and consolation at the moments of bereavement in our communities. The purpose, however, of the present theological reflections in this *Moment* of the book is to highlight the transforming power of Easter grace in our human circumstances today. This particular perspective of resurrection stands out in opposition to a world interpreted and understood in terms of conditioned individualism, dualism and fragmentation. The resurrection is not only something that happens after death; it is also something that affects the character of daily life and living *before* death.

Easter: Yesterday and today

Because, to my mind, the theological basis for the vision outlined in *Passion for the Possible* is so radical, let me summarise it again at this point of the third *Moment*. The implications of the incarnation are quite staggering and, according to Karl Rahner, as yet unexplored by most Christians. A very inadequate theory of redemption has limited its importance to the historical lifespan of Jesus, as though a once-for-all and deadly transaction had been negotiated between Father and Son. A truly incarnational understanding of the mystery of God's humanity discloses an incredible truth. It reveals that, as the Body of Christ, which the Christian scriptures assure us we are, his power is now ours – the power to create, to heal, to complete, and even more. (Jn 14:12) We have within us what Jesus Christ had within him – a unique capacity for compassion, forgiveness, redemption. We are, in fact, the continuing incarnation.

Just as Jesus, in his human relationships, drew out from people their own creativity, convincing them of the 'kingdom within', so too with us and our relationships. We are now the anointed ones of Christ.

The mystery of the incarnation is incredibly extensive. It is not just the institutional churches that carry the mystery of God in human flesh. All love that is in grace is the Word made flesh. What has God given in the incarnation? The power, literally, to block death and hell. If we love someone, she cannot go to hell because Christ is loving her. If we forgive someone, he is forgiven because Christ is forgiving him. They continue to touch the hem of Christ's garment as surely

as did the woman in the gospels who suffered with haemor-
rhage.[9]

What is important to believe always, yet so difficult to remember at any particular moment of personal, communitarian or
global crisis, is that the cross and the glory are forever intertwined. My gut feeling is that no matter how spiritually sophis-
ticated or advanced a person may be, this link is always a difficult and elusive one. It is almost impossible to find an exception
in our lives to the rule of this inevitable and all-pervasive paradox. And stranger still, not only are life and death connected,
not only must death come first before life can follow, but the
seeds of new life are contained within, and only *within*, the
dying. It is not like the demolition of the old before the new; it is
not as though winter is the space between the fall of autumn and
the rise of spring; it is only *in* the process of suffering and death
that the birth of new life happens.

As our more recent RE guides and catechetical material
abundantly illustrate, the Good Friday/Easter Sunday pattern is
worked out and lived out in countless natural phenomena. The
natural cycle and rhythm of all evolutionary processes is inter-
woven with some kind of force and counter-force. The living cell
must divide to regenerate in itself; it must die to grow. The egg
of the tarantula is fertilised in the decaying body of the mother.
The caterpillar enters the death-like cocoon stage before its
multi-coloured metamorphosis. The baby is torn between the
safe sanctuary of its mother's womb or arms and the imperative
to risk itself in birth or in taking its first step. At another level,
there is usually profound reluctance and resistance before we
finally shift our deep-seated attitudes to someone or something.

In his delightful *True Resurrection*, Harry Williams looks towards critical moments in people's lives for evidence of this
perennial and paradoxical truth.

An artist, at first only painfully aware of an utter emptiness
and impotence, finds his imagination gradually stirred into
life and discovers a vision which takes control of him and
which he feels not only able but compelled to express. That is
resurrection ... A married couple find their old relationship,
once rich and fulfilling, slowly drying up into no more than
an external observance, to the point where it seems impossible that these dry bones should ever live again. Then a new
phase emerges, one that is deeper, more stable, more satisfy-

ing than the old one, with a new quality of life that is inexhaustible because it does not depend on the constant recharging of emotional batteries. That is resurrection ... People, we say, are never the same again after a severe illness or the premature death of someone deeply loved. Sometimes they do shrivel up and atrophy. But appearances can be deceptive. Under the devastation of their ordeal, which leaves its deep and permanent traces, one can be aware that they are in touch with a new dimension of reality. They have somehow penetrated to the centre of things. They are greater people. They are more deeply alive. That is resurrection ... [10]

Readers of the work of Teilhard de Chardin will find his synthesis of the evolutionary stages from first creation to present-day life deeply satisfying and truly amazing. Combining poetry, science and theology, he offers a magnificent panorama of the 'spheres' that mark the critical breakthroughs in the evolution of the world. It is not surprising that his mystic soul saw the mystery of the incarnation, with its birth, death and resurrection, as the paradigm of life's unfolding. What remains to be accomplished finally, in the evolutionary process, according to de Chardin, is the ultimate breakthrough of the human spirit into what Rahner calls 'the cosmic Easter', that graced sphere of full unity when God will be 'all in all'.

Every Sunday the eucharistic assembly proclaims in the *Credo*, '...he descended into hell (the lower regions, the dead)...'. Karl Rahner seizes on this moment and reveals breathtaking graces within it:

Jesus said he would descend into the heart of the world (Mt 12:40), into the heart of all earthly things where everything is linked together and is one, where death and futility hold sway. Down into death he has penetrated. He let himself be conquered by death so that death would gulp him down into the innermost depths of the world. In this way, having descended to the very womb of the earth, to the radical unity of the world, he could give the earth his divine life forever. In death he has become the divine heart in the innermost heart of the world. And the earth, behind and beyond her continual development in space and time, sinks her roots into the power of the almighty God.

Christ has risen from this one heart of all earthly things ... in his body. He has forever taken the world to himself; he is

born anew as a child of this earth. But now it is an earth transfigured, an earth that is set free, that is untwisted ... His resurrection is like the first eruption of a volcano which shows
that God's fire already burns in the innermost depths of the
earth, and that everything shall be brought to a holy glow in
his light. The new creation, prefigured from the beginning,
has already started; the new power of a transfigured earth is
already being formed from the world's innermost heart ...[11]

There are times when many of us will need some convincing of
such claims (even though we assent to them at a cerebral level).
It is so hard to believe in the light while it is still dark; to believe
that love is holding us close when all we feel is pain. Because the
waters of grief and guilt still flow on the surface where we stand,
we think that their source in the depths has not yet dried up.
Because evil still carves new lines into the face of the earth, we
conclude that in the deepest core of reality, love has gone dead.

Yet Rahner insists that the negative and sacrificial experiences of limitation and loss can be even more explicitly potential
disclosure-moments of the power of God in creation and in the
resurrection. The experience of God is perceived most clearly,
Rahner believes, 'where the definable limits of our everyday
realities break down and are dissolved, where the decline of
these realities is perceived, when lights shining over the tiny island of our ordinary life are extinguished, and then the following question becomes inescapable: whether the night that surrounds us is the void of absurdity and death that engulfs us or
the blessed holy night already shining within us as the promise
of eternal day?'[12]

Graced nature

When all of this sinks in to our bewildered and anxious hearts
there is only one response. We fall silent. And then we bless and
praise and thank. It is all so unbelievable. Yet the eyes of our
soul are coded from all time to glimpse the vague outline of a
love and a meaning running through our own lives and the history of the universe. This glimpse does not impose on us an in-
tolerable choice between the goodness and beauty of this world
and of God. Christ is already in the centre of the earth, our
beloved mother. He is with us like the light of the sun, which we
do not notice; like the beating of our hearts, that we take for
granted; like the air in our lungs, that demands no attention. He

is the mysterious law and innermost essence of the unfolding of the universe and of everyone and everything in it and on it.

> He is in the history of the world, whose blind course, with all its victories and all its crashing defeats, steers with uncanny precision towards the day when his splendour, transforming everything, will erupt out of the earth's own depths. He is in all the tears as hidden joy, and in every death as the life that overcomes all by seeming to die. He is in our weakness, as the strength that dares to let itself seem weak, because it is invincible. He himself is even right in the midst of sin, as the mercy of everlasting life that is prepared to wait until the end ...[13]

From beginning to end, this book is trying to explain how grace builds on nature, how our destructive dualisms can be reconciled, how our divided loyalties between heaven and earth can be centralised in one source of being. The blurred nature of this glimpsed possibility, the incompleteness of this vision of a basic and compassionate unity, is due to the twin instincts within us towards trust on the one hand, and doubt on the other. How welcome then are those brief and blessed moments when our prophets pull open, even for a moment, for the straining eyes of our souls, the curtains that conceal the revelation.

We are children of the universe and we are children of God. Only the eyes of faith can dissolve the anxious ambiguity that grips us when we struggle to hold these seemingly opposites together. We cannot deny our loving origins in the womb of our mother earth and in the heart of our Father God. How do we avoid betraying the one even as we embrace the other? The answer lies in our faith in the revelation of incarnation. Along with de Chardin, and many other visionaries and mystics throughout the centuries, Rahner, too, lifts our hearts:

> This is the faith that offers blessed consolation to all that we experience in life, the faith that can love the earth because she is, or is in the process of becoming, the body of the risen One. We do not need to leave her, for the life of God dwells in her. When we want both the God of infinity and the familiar earth, as it is, and as it shall become, when we want both for our eternally free homeland, *there is one path to both!* For in the resurrection of the Lord, God has shown that he has accepted the earth for all time. 'Caro cardo salutis', said one of the Fathers of the Church – the flesh is the hinge of salvation ... (Jesus) has transformed the *flesh*. Ever since that moment, mother earth bears only transformed children.[14]

The impossible dream

The resurrection, for me, is the assurance that the revelation outlined in the last few paragraphs is true. What the pagan heart
suspected, what a Celtic spirituality glimpsed, what the Hebrew
scripture writers hoped for, what Jesus during his life on earth
promised, was guaranteed and confirmed by God at the first
Easter. There was always the intuitive hunch in the human spirit about the possibility of its own divine origin – the hint of the
infinity within. The resurrection affirmed the truth of that
hunch: it validated the authenticity of that hint. For Christians
today, therefore, it is no longer an intuition. Since the first
Easter, it is a revealed truth. But we have the utmost difficulty in
accepting it as true. In fact, I doubt if most of us believe it at all.

Why do we find it so difficult to welcome these inspiring
truths about ourselves? Maybe it is because we have lost the
sense of transcendence that would delight in such good news.
Our hearts no longer recognise their liberation. The traces of a
beautiful and wild element in each of us have long since been
tamed. The small flame of creative vision has been slowly but
surely blown out. In so many people, the sacred imagination is
asleep or has died through neglect, rejection or suspicion. Yet
the God within, the God of surprises, is essentially creative, as
the wonder of the Word reveals. God is a wild artist and extravagant lover of the complexity and simplicity, the colours, tex-
tures and shapes, of galaxies and insects, of stars and pebbles, of
varieties and species of life, that daily and nightly flow down the
mountains of mystery from the divine source.

The same creative intensity burned in Jesus Christ. He had
the fire of a new vision, a new age, raging inside him. By virtue
of our shared humanity, we now know that what was true of
Jesus is true of us. Because we are sisters and brothers of his in
the solidarity of the flesh, we too have God's creative power at
our centre. The resurrection of Jesus set free forever what was
promised at his birth and, long before that, the dream that was
sealed into the heart of Adam (and therefore into our own) in the
Garden of Eden.

We are God's work of art and we are called to co-create other
works of art with God. 'We are co-workers with God; we are
God's farm.' (1 Cor 3:9) Thomas Aquinas points out that 'although a created being tends to the divine likeness in many
ways, this one whereby it seeks the divine likeness by being the
cause of other beings and things takes the ultimate place. Hence

Dionysius says that of all things, it is more divine to become a co-worker with God.' (*Contra Gentiles*, 21:8) This most orthodox of theologians writes with passion about the human role in continuously co-creating with God. He sees the 'dignity of causality' as an original blessing whereby we are irresistibly drawn to imitate the creativity of God. 'Human virtue,' he insists, 'is a participation in the divine power.' (*Summa Theologiae*, q 129, a1)

The imperative to create
There is much excitement in the way Thomas writes about the human imperative to create. If you think about it, we are always creating in one way or another. From the baby's tentative explorations of its mother's face and its own body, from the billions of examples in our unconscious doodlings to this world's masterpieces of art and architecture, through the daily musings and planning that we are all engaged in every day when we add a touch of this or that to a recipe, or try to surprise a friend with an unusual present, or lovingly agree to incarnate our love in the birth of a baby, what else are we doing but creating something new? Think of the fascinating drawings of a child at school, or of a pupil's own schedule for work and play, or of a student's imaginative scenario for a free-flowing essay: think of the ways that unemployed people find work to do, of the ways that oppressed people manage to survive, of the passionate imperative that leads to the music and poetry that nourishes our souls when nothing else can touch us: think of the way that in our darkness we still reach for the light, for the courage to be – in all of these moments, and many, many more, we are participating in the incarnate energy of God.

St Thomas chooses evocative words to describe the gift of enabling and bringing forth. 'The creature approaches more perfectly to God's likeness if it is not only good, but can also act for the good of other beings, than if it were good only in itself. That which both shines and casts light is more like the sun than that which only shines. Matthew prescribes that we should let our light shine before people...' (*Contra Gentiles*, 45, 4) It is for those who are closed, who hide their light under a bushel, who bury the talent, that Thomas reserves the term 'sinful'. He is aware of the power of fear in human beings, the fear of change, the fear of risk, the fear of the new. But he has little time for the timid, referring to them as 'pusillanimous': they are 'the small-souled people who refuse to strive after great accomplishments and aim at certain petty undertakings when they are truly capable of what is great'. (*Com. on Aristotle's Ethics* IV, L8) Without courage there is literally no hope. Fear and insecurity hold people helpless. Great danger stimulates a great fear 'which shrinks or contracts the heart'. 'Magnificence,' on the other hand, 'belongs to divine power'.

Aquinas sees all of life as resulting from the ever-new and ever-changing outpouring of divine energy into the world each day. He sees this mystery as the activating of the seeds of growth already placed by God at creation in the deepest spirit of all creatures. The Angelic Doctor, as Thomas was known, compares the process of creativity to the manner in which a doctor stimulates self-healing in a patient or to the way in which a teacher draws forth the wisdom already within the spirit of the student. God is in the human heart, he insisted, and God's presence tends to spread from heart to heart as fire spreads over a field of stubble. We most resemble God when we are busy setting fire to each other's hearts.

One can catch Thomas's excitement. He uses words like wonder, beauty, wisdom with great frequency. 'God's love sets a person on fire from gazing on the divine beauty.' (*Summa Theologiae*, 11-11, 180, 1) He writes about the delight of the imagination 'which is the image and offspring of the divine mind'. The generative thrust of human artistry is an essential dimension of God's creative essence. God's love and goodness and beauty are essentially self-expressive. They tend towards spreading and enkindling 'as the potter impresses beautiful form upon base matter'. (*Com. on Psalms*, 32) Once aware of the divine wisdom within us, we are eager to empower others with the gift. This happens when we help people to become more aware of the mystery of their own lives; aware of the potential for 'sheer joy' within them; aware of their power to heal and enrich others; aware of the pleasure that such generative commitment brings.

Our creative child

The poet-potter M. C. Richards, in her book, *Centering*, writes:

> The sin against the Holy Spirit is the sin against new life, against self-emergence, against the holy fecund innerness of each person. It can be committed quite as easily against oneself as against another.[15]

It is dangerous, for many reasons, to suppress, ignore or deny the divine imagination within us. Years of conditioning and pro-gramming about our inability to be artistic or co-creative cannot be changed without tears. There is a deadly conspiracy in soci-ety against the nurturing of the mystic, the prophet, the contem-plative; against the nourishing of that community of artists we carry within us who forever image the in-dwelling Blessed Trinity of each human soul. Our minds expand, our pettiness is transcended, our cynicism dries up and our insecurity is con-fronted when our divine power is acknowledged and the flow of our creativity is let run free.

When the marvellous gift of connecting begins to happen, when we risk revealing our vulnerability, when we explore our boredom and reclaim our sacred imagination, then there is an immense completing and healing followed by a deep personal delight that rings so true. There is a uniting energy that connects with the God within, that strikes at an all-embracing dualism, and reveals the superficiality of so many of our habitual preoc-cupations. Only then is sprung the fresh well of the exciting mystery that we are.

Despite that fear that surrounds it, the good news of our human divinity brings nothing but blessing to the human race. It restores us to God and creation. There is healing and wholeness in the revelation within incarnation, within the immanence of Emmanuel. The most destructive dualism of all is that which di-vides the sacred from the human, which denies that God's blood flows in our veins and that God's heart beats in ours. The divine child within us rejoices in the call of its Parent. It recognises the voice of its source and summit. It knows it by heart.

Creation theology is a theology of creativity, of imagination, of prophecy, of the present moment. It is a theology of begin-ning, of trusting and of healing. It springs from God's dream-made-flesh in Jesus Christ. The Messiah himself is the work of the divine imagination. And because of our shared ownership with this incarnated mystery, God's very being is always hap-pening in and through us. Much of Thomas Merton's spirituality can be summed up in the following passage from his essay in *The Sacred Land*:

The theology of creativity will necessarily be the theology of the Holy Spirit re-forming us in the likeness of Christ, raising us from death to life with the very same power of God which raised Christ from the dead. The theology of creativity will also be a theology of the image and likeness of God in humanity.

Incidentally, when we hold that we are completed as well as healed by the mystery of the incarnation of God in Christ, we touch on a huge theological debate. At the risk of over-simplification it can be put in the question of whether Jesus Christ came to perfect and finalise God's first creative act in making the world, or to redeem us after we got off to a disastrous start in the Garden of Eden? Was the incarnation a vital moment of revelation in line with God's initial wish for the completion of creation, or was it a desperate second-order rescue-plan when the first one went horribly wrong? The answer, of course, is not simple, as we realised when we touched on this debate at the beginning of the book. There are many strands of meaning in mystery. Many decades ago, the universally accepted scripture scholar Bernard Anderson wrote in his *Israel's Prophetic Heritage*, that 'Second Isaiah links creation and redemption so closely together that one is involved in the other. Yahweh's creative acts belong to the history of salvation … His redemptive acts are acts of creation; and his creative acts are acts of history.' Yahweh the Creator is also the Deliverer.

> Send justice like dew, you heavens,
> let the clouds rain it down.
> Let the earth open up
> so salvation will spring up.
> Let deliverance, too, bud forth
> which I, Yahweh, shall create. (Is 45:8)

The great contribution of creation theology is to renew the balance. The dualistic theology of past centuries has all but obliterated the essential truth of incarnation. Fall or no Fall, it was God's desire to become human as we are human, because of the passionate nature of divine loving. What we are about here is a redressing of this imbalance, so that the vital connection between creativity and healing can be seen in a new light. This insight, in turn, will profoundly inform our attitude towards the infinite value of every true aspiration of the human heart.

The dancer
Only a creative artist like Ben Okri could talk about creativity 'as the highest civilising faculty, as evidence of the transhuman, as growing out of humility and as full of suffering. Creativity of

any valuable kind is one of the fullest expressions of the human and the Godlike within us … It is a form of prayer, and the expression of a profound gratitude for being alive.'

In *Birds of Heaven*, Okri tells a story. Because it is so good, and so relevant to this *Moment* of the book, forgive me for quoting it in full.

A flamenco dancer, lurking under a shadow, prepares for the terror of her dance. Somebody has wounded her in words, alluding to the fact that she has no fire in her any more. She knows she has to dance her way past her limitation, and that this may destroy her forever. She has to fail, or she has to die. I want to dwell for a little while on this dancer because, though a very secular example, she speaks very well for the power of human transcendence. I want you to imagine this frail woman. I want you to see her in deep shadow, and fear. When the music starts she begins her dance, with ritual slowness. Then she stamps out the dampness from her soul. Then she stamps fire into her loins. She takes on a strange enchanted glow. With a dark tragic rage, shouting, she hurls her hungers, her doubts, her terrors and her secular prayer for more light into the spaces around her. All fire and fate, she spins her enigma around us, and pulls us into the awesome risk of her dance.

She is taking herself apart before our sceptical gaze.

She is disintegrating, shouting and stamping and dissolving the boundaries of her body. Soon she becomes a wild unknown force, glowing in her death, dancing from her wound, dying in her dance.

And when she stops – strangely gigantic in her new fiery stature – she is like one who has survived the most dangerous journey of all. I can see her now as she stands shining in celebration of her own death. In the silence that follows, no one moves. The fact is that she has destroyed us all.

Why do I dwell on this dancer? I dwell on her because she represents for me the courage to go beyond ourselves. While she danced she became the dream of the freest and most creative people we had always wanted to be, in whatever it is we do. She was the sea we never ran away to, the spirit of wordless self-overcoming we never quite embrace. She destroyed us because we knew in our hearts that rarely do we rise to the higher challenges in our lives, or our work, or our humanity. She destroyed us because rarely do we love our tasks and our lives enough to die and thus be reborn into the divine gift of our hidden genius. We seldom try for that beautiful greatness brooding in the mystery of our blood.

You can say in her own way, and in that moment, that she too was a dancer to God. [And, I add, with respects to Okri, you could say that God was dancing in her.] ...If we could be pure dancers in spirit we would never be afraid to love, and we would love with strength and wisdom. We would not be afraid of speech, and we would be serene with silence ... Our smile, our silences would be sufficient. Our creations and the beauty of our functions would be enough. Our giving would be our perpetual (and healing) gift to the universe.[16]

Precarious life

On an autumn evening, 1991, I hear the news. Seven miles up the Clare coast from where I'm standing, four men set out in their fishing boat yesterday. Beneath them the periscope of a nuclear submarine slid silently into their nets. Within seconds, the fishermen were dead. All the necessary precautions were taken. Fishermen respect the whims of nature's elements, especially the power of water. They take nothing for granted. But destiny lies in the hands of Another.

While walking home I reflected on the way we are always trying to control the future, to name our destiny. So much of our energy goes into the charting of our course through the troubled seas ahead. To be sure, there is a kind of carefulness which is but a sensible effort to live responsibly, the honour, the accountability without which we culpably drift into chaos. But my thoughts, this black November evening, are about the tension and tightness of a control that can destroy the spontaneity and playfulness of life in the Spirit – the spirit of the divine child within us.

On the evening of Ash Wednesday, 1994, the bishop phoned. Would I evacuate our church building forever – next weekend. His reasons were sound. But the news was sudden. I examined my reactions. I tried to notice my emotions while they were happening. Have you ever done that? The 'sudden' tests our groundedness. It is a unique challenge to our integrity. It questions our roundedness and readiness for the vicissitudes of life. With no time to put the masks in place, the 'sudden' pierces straight through to the raw feelings. It is something like the times that we are unaware of being observed. Our faces are not in 'public mode'. We feel caught with our guard down. What are we like when this happens? What do people see? More importantly, if we can be brutally honest, how do we see ourselves?

One thing is for sure – we are not in charge. We do not know the day or the hour of the happening that will change our lives forever, especially the moment of the 'last call'. Each day is filled with a thousand precarious moments. The next letter, the next telephone call, the next knock on the door, the next second, a moment's hesitation, a rushed decision, and the course of our lives may be radically and irrevocably altered. The firm and cer-

tain plans are so swiftly confounded, as they were for the four
men in the boat and for our happy parish. The sea is so big and
powerful and our boat is so small and fragile.

My mother often reminds me that 'a breath can make thee as
a breath hath made'. 'Leave lots of room around the margins of
your plans,' she would advise; 'don't fill all the space, allow for
the unexpected.' A certain kind of flexibility, an awareness of
the unpredictable, a reverence for mystery is essential where the
future is concerned. On the one hand there must be a totality
about our commitment to the realisation of our ideals and principles, and yet, because of the precarious nature of our finite
lives, and the awful mystery of the unknown, we must hold ourselves in readiness for another possibility. 'How do you make
God laugh?' my mother often asks, when she observes my fever-
ish attempts to control and secure my future. I look at her and
wait. 'Tell him your plans for yourself!' she says.

This awareness, this readiness is not easily achieved. Most of
the time we miss the silent music, the divine whisper that beckons us to a different pace of living. It is so easy to stay oblivious
to the subtle axis on which the balance of our precarious existence turns. The mystics tell us that the silence of the heart is the
place of the hidden revelations about the shape of our destiny.
Unbidden, they rise to the surface of our consciousness from the
quiet depths of our open mindfulness. But there is a fine discipline about the watching and waiting for the often almost im-
perceptible moments of disclosure.

I have long since discovered that the intensity of the relent-
lessly-turning wheels in my head can block out the gentle voice
that forever tries to call attention to another way of being.
Reaching this level of awareness is a delicate and hard-won condition. If, blind and blinkered to the wisdom of my redeemed
heart, I persistently pursue only the product of my rational
thinking, then I am laying the foundations for sterile future. I
may well be successful on a number of fronts and to the eyes of
many, but these years I dread the possibility of a terrible emptiness at the end of my days.

There were many inappropriate themes to do with death, I
feel, during the years of my seminary 'training'. I remember the
times we were asked to meditate on a picture of St Alphonsus, I
think, holding a human skull in his right hand, above a caption
which asked '*Quid hoc ad aeternitatem?*' (What has what you are
doing, to do with eternity?) With hindsight, maybe it was not

such a bad question! There are rich attitudes and wise insights that last us into heaven and there are successes and achievements that are dead even as we reach them.

The pity is that, like the Lazarus and Dives story, we wake up too late. So often it is only the major shock, the sudden accident, the awful tragedy, the terrible experience, that, as with the prodigal son, 'brings us to our senses'. One way or another, our first destiny will be fulfilled. The resistance and blindness of our original sinfulness never leaves us. But neither, at whatever cost, does the relentless pursuit of our jealous and tremendous Lover.

This third *Moment of Creativity and Healing* has to do with the graced offer of trusting in God's providence and of an ultimate 'letting go' of our anxious and fearful resistance to that invitation. This reflection is to encourage faltering hearts to take a tiny step outside, to test the ground, to feel the difference, to sense the welcome. This tiny step is, in fact, a 'giant stride of soul', the triumph of light over darkness, of love over fear. Each one of us needs to repair our damaged sense of trust in the love that underpins all of life and in the possibility of transcendence. 'If you trust yourself to the river of life,' Krishnamurti promises, 'the river of life has an astonishing way of taking care of you.'

This reflection is to reawaken and rebuild a wounded childhood ability to trust, so that we can let go of compulsive attachments to past and present securities, of an understandable suspicion of the unknown. The future is a loving mother waiting for us with outstretched arms: the future belongs to an all-powerful father who is crazy about our freedom and our fulfilment, and who longs only for us to let him love us. 'Why is it that some people do not bear fruit?' asks Meister Eckhart. 'Because they have no trust either in God or in themselves. Love cannot distrust.'

Careful hands

'Speak to me of God,' I asked the cherry tree. And the cherry tree blossomed. That is what happens when we let God be God in our lives. God is the one who draws out of us our inner beauty. The spring sun really adds nothing to the trees. It simply makes it safe for them to bud forth what is already waiting within. What is in a germinal state is released into its true essence.

This, I believe, is true also of our human relationships. We are like mid-wives easing into birth the new wonder in the womb of our personality. At a recent wedding I asked the guests whether the focus of the sacrament lay in the mutual liberating by both parties of each other's truest and most creative self. What a soul-sized undertaking every deep friendship is! How quickly such an enterprise exposes the often-selfish nature of our commitment to either another person or within a small group!

A shy and hidden spirit is set free to blossom in these beautiful words of e. e. cummings.

…your slightest look easily will unclose me
though i have closed myself as fingers,
you open always petal by petal myself as Spring opens
(touching skilfully, mysteriously) her first rose…

… (i do not know what it is about you that closes
and opens; only something in me understands
the voice of your eyes is deeper than all roses)
nobody, not even the rain, has such small hands.

But even in nature it can go wrong. Misreading the signs outside their dark waiting rooms, the eager crocuses, during a fine week in winter, can be tempted to venture out too early into the ambiguous light from the rich womb of mother earth. So too between people. The mutual unfolding, fragile and special, can never be guaranteed. A shadow falls across every truly loving moment. When we wake up the angels in each other's hearts, the demons are aroused as well. When we unlock each other's prisons, we unchain the sinister forces too. In every light that is given space to shine, the shadows crowd around every edge.

Something negative is never far away every time we draw closer to each other in trust and love. Do I exaggerate when I say that our shining always happens in the company of darkness, our loving efforts stalked and infected by destructive viruses? So what do we do when suspicion and fear, jealousy and envy, possessiveness and greed, cynicism and doubt, meanness and closedness, blame and ridicule make their disturbing and diminishing effects felt in the most delicate part of our reaching out, our trusting, our loving desire for true belonging? What strategies enable us to encounter, befriend, dismantle, transform and harness these significant powers before they poison at their core the lovely but fragile flowers of the heart's garden?

At a recent homily, when I asked these questions, a number of points were made. This is how we saw a way forward. In the first place, there can be little hope for friendship and love to survive without the generosity of 'old-fashioned' forgiveness. The 'strong' one is challenged to overlook, to let go, to be bigger than the one who is, unwittingly perhaps, trying to destroy. The strong one will try to understand where the distressed one 'is coming from'. *To know all is to forgive all.* We are asked to walk a few miles in each other's shoes before we start to criticise. By 'strong' one I mean the one who is more open to grace at the time of challenge or conflict. And the roles may change with each new growth-point.

Another way forward is for the one who is caught in some negative reaction, unconsciously assuming some controlling role, held in some potentially diminishing emotion to find time and space for a little self-examination and self-awareness. In so many instances all we are doing in our aggressive and blaming mode is, in psychological terms, a matter of projection. Put very crudely, it means that what we cannot face in ourselves we project on to others. It often emerges that fear and insecurity form the root of such behaviour.

When we search for an explanation for these deep-seated emotions we may discover that they are connected with some unhealed wounds that have been suppressed, and, more often than not, for a long time. These days we hear talk of 'the wounded child'. This is a reference to the painful experiences of childhood when we force ourselves to adapt, adjust and pretend in order to survive. Sometimes we get away with it; more often than not, in later life, maybe around the mid-life years, we may realise, if we're lucky, that some work must be done to restore a healthy psychological balance in the way we act and react to life and to each other. It is true to say that it is not the emotions themselves that damage us but their denial and 'burial'. We may well think that we have 'dealt' with them, 'forgotten' them, exorcised them out of our lives. In fact, because they have never been truly confronted, their power has subtly increased. They make their presence felt in various modes of behaviour.

There are those who are driven by a seething and unacknowledged anger, by a desperate possessiveness, by unprocessed grief, by a deep-seated guilt. Others are rendered almost ineffectual by a crippling and constant feeling of inferiority, by debilitating anxiety, by an overwhelming sense of meaninglessness. The resulting behaviour patterns may well reveal a tendency towards negative attitudes, such as a tendency to judge and condemn, a reluctance to ask for help or to risk anything or to be positive about self-help, an exaggerated fear of failure, feelings of jealousy and envy, difficulties in trusting or in receiving thanks or praise or in letting go of possessions or ways of thinking and acting. All of this is by way of suggesting that when the negative attitudes that threaten the growth and love of a relationship between people comes out into the open, a condition of insecurity, unexplored fear, deep-seated anxiety and a sense of powerlessness may well be one of the root causes.

Immense graces emerge when we attend to our inner life and courageously encounter our shadow. The forces of original sin are part of the essence of our human condition. We ignore such elemental powers at our peril. The rewards for setting out on this journey into our dark places and risking unpleasant discoveries about ourselves are very great. What begins with the taking up of our cross may end with a new experience of resurrection. The potential breakdown of a friendship or a group's bonding may then become a real breakthrough into another stage of growing and healing. At this point in a talk I was sharing recently Liz raised her hand and spoke about a rowan-tree plant, her favourite, given her by her husband some time previously. She was distraught when some budding vandals broke it one Friday night. Soon she realised that wonderful new blossoms grew at the point of fracture. 'Life breaks all of us,' wrote Hemingway, 'but some people grow at the broken places.'

The life of Jesus, his particular friendships, his forming of a band of followers, were all punctuated by breakdowns and breakthroughs. There were turmoils and temptations in his tempestuous public life. The milestones of deaths and resurrections that marked the path of his ministry and signalled the progress of his archetypal journey to Jerusalem, were but a preparation for his final death and resurrection. This was the death 'he freely accepted' – the only way into the Land of the Ever-Young. That is why we kiss the cross every Good Friday. We embrace the suffering because, paradoxically, it sets us free. We even celebrate the crucifixions of life because the lifted-up figure of Christ destroyed draws all of us into pure joy.

Against the unbelievable backdrop of all of this, the brokenness, the conflicts, the diminishing and negative forces at work whenever people seek out a sense of belonging and intimacy, assume a renewed meaning. The imperfect becomes very important. It is at the point of our imperfection, as it is with the crystal at the point of its only flaw, that the healing, growing and liberating happens. The God in whom we live and move and have our intimate being has a surer touch, a sounder vision concerning the pattern of development of the human heart. God loves the imperfect in us. We, in turn, are challenged to accept and love the shadow-side of ourselves. This becomes possible only when we can trust another or others with those hidden places that need the light.

At this point we are back where we started. We began with the hope that friends will draw out the best in each other, that deep calls to deep and our true beauty is coaxed into the light. Only now we realise that it's not so easy; it takes that bit longer. Even Jesus could not find a short-cut. There is no cheap grace. It takes a clear vision, a vivid dream to sustain us on the mountain: and a certain amount of stubbornness, of head-down cussedness, of a digging-in of heels to survive the distractions, the obstacles and even the aggression that makes us doubt, afraid and confused. And this is where the powerful Spirit comes into her own, exploding into life in her element. Because she is always already there. 'It is in the faithful waiting for the loved one,' writes Henri Nouwen, 'that we know how much (s)he has filled our lives already.'

Almost seduced

Halfway between the Yorkshire villages of Wheldrake and Thorganby, safely secured on the dry verge of one of Englands's last great wetlands, Thicket Priory stands silent guard. This is a Carmelite monastery where holy women pray the world in tune. Here, suddenly, I find myself walking, in the middle of Lent, as an impatient summer day has broken ranks and stolen ahead into March, to renew our flagging winter spirits. As I pause by a river-bend in the lower Derwent valley, surrounded by wild-flowers, lapwings and kingfishers, I am drawn to something glinting and dazzling in the bottle-green water. Ever-expectant, I excitedly explore, poking around with a broken branch, probing for the sunken treasure of my imagination. Having finally dislodged the disappointingly ordinary Guinness can, my thoughts turn sober.

All my life I have been easily seduced. Led by my ever-susceptible nose, the bright and pretty have always distracted and attracted my gullible attention. The pattern was established early in my life. Even at four and a half, I remember being held high in my mother's arms, surrounded by glittering objects and silvery boxes, while I considered the question, 'Which of these do you want?' Without hesitation I greedily yelped, 'All of 'em; all of 'em.' Let me explain the context.

As the parish missions and missioners of my childhood came round every few years in our home village, a small army of souvenir-sellers followed them faithfully. A magic row of tent-shops full of multi-coloured rosary-beads, bejewelled statues, framed mirrors with saints' faces, golden cases containing all kinds of shiny, kitchy things tempted and distracted young and old alike on their way into and out from the roaring priests. Because we lived near the church, I was in a position to 'help' the tent-dwellers in a variety of menial ways. On this particular occasion, as the miserable day of their departure approached, one compassionate mission-nomad had the generosity to reward my unflagging interest in his holy business with the above offer. I tell this story only to indicate the pattern of allurement that would dominate my life.

I have often written about my propensity for being dazzled

by false beauty, about how green the faraway fields seem to be, about the exciting prospect of a 'quick killing'. I have never been strong on the tough wisdom that counsels prudence, the voice of experience that votes for delay. Impetuous, like the blustering Peter on the stormy lake, I have often leaped over the side of the boat too soon; unbalanced, like the complaining Judas at Mary's extravagant anointing of Jesus, I have often been too intense on a one-track ego-trip.

Even as an infant I was always after approval. I can still remember co-washing Miss Tobin's ugly dog on my fifth birthday, just to please the ravishing Miss Tobin. The following year Sr Concepta became the focus of my attention. I never forgot to mark her feast-day with my annual gift of a writing-pad and two dozen envelopes. I continued to ache for success and popularity. I wrote essays to win local newspaper competitions and I still remember my bursting heart when Fr Scanlon presented me with *The Best of John D. Sheridan* for imaginative composition. In my teenage years I had refined these pursuits with increasing sophistication; for instance my efforts were for the good of others, e.g. running for the school, winning for the team, preserving O'Leary pride. This kind of self-deception became easier still in the seminary. My deepening shadow-side was successfully disguised in a hopeless confusion of missionary zeal, personal sanctity, the pursuit of inner excellence for God and of universal acceptability for the kingdom.

And so my pre-scripted life-story unfolded. In my twenties I was hooked on naïve idealism, in my thirties it was mostly ambiguous pleasure, in my forties I was into awesome 'professionalism', and in my fifties I notice a creeping strain of a potentially dangerous, but in fact, quite harmless type of 'Messianic complex' virus. By the time you find yourself reading this rivetting resume of my life I'll be in my sixties, having entered, I suspect, a recycled and less spiritual version of my original Miss Tobin condition.

'Tis evening now and the last of the Arctic wildfowl that visit the winter lakes of the local wetlands are leaving for another year. The tufted ducks that live here throughout are silent as I leave the Carmel chapel. A phrase from the second Preface of Lent has stayed in my mind. 'Teach us so to live in this passing world with our hearts set on the world that never ends.' I suppose it is inevitable that we will be half-seduced from time to time in this rapturously wonderful world with its charms and

blandishments. Precisely because we are created for what is
lovely, and because our divine appetite for the beautiful is so intense, we will often be captivated by the less than perfect.

And yet, something else needs to be said. For many a year,
indeed for many a decade, and not excluding my tormented
menage à trois with Miss Tobin and her miserable mut, I have
been graced with a vision of wholeness – a condition of simplicity,
to quote the poet, costing not less than everything. It has to do
with total giving, with a refusal to compromise, with not settling
for less, with a relentless rising beyond all that holds us back,
holds us down and holds us stuck. *'… with our eyes set on the
world that never ends.'* There is such a temptation to say 'enough
is enough – after all we are only human'. And how many times
have I accepted such a reasonable-sounding argument and
called it a day?

Nevertheless, in the midst of my gullibility and addictions to
seduction, this beckoning God has challenged me daily to surrender further, to unpeel more layers, to cross more boundaries,
to die another death. To experience the true freedom of the children of God, I disregard my 'ifs and buts', no more bargaining, no
more reasonable and fair pleading, no more recourse to common sense and prudence. Sell everything, trust completely, leap
blindly, keep nothing, forgive all – there are no half measures
when drinking the full cup.

This vision of wholeness can only be sustained when it springs
from a persistent conviction of the power we carry within us. The
Christian is called to feel empowered by divine energy. There is
nothing, therefore, that cannot be achieved or overcome while
this awareness is high. Nothing can harm us in the presence of
this pulsating, life-giving flow. It is about 'staying tuned'. It is
about wild faith. It is about connecting without trying too hard.
It is about acquiring a habit of quiet discernment when it comes
to what is important.

That is why I have a skeleton hanging over my computer. It is
not a full skeleton. Just a head – a small, weird, shrunken, skin-
less, Hallowe'en-type death's face. Mary gave me this macabre
little gift as a joke. The joke became serious. Most of my
parochial, diocesan and personal desk-work happens around
the computer. That is why it is a good place to be reminded of
the grave. I have already mentioned my memory of a 'holy picture' of a pale and ascetic young man, holding a skull in his pale
hand and asking the question *'Quid hoc ad aeternitatem?'*

Roughly translated, it questions the relevance of whatever we happen to be doing just now in the passing world, to the world that never ends. As with so many other realities of my earlier years, this memory too was dispatched into the piled-high skip of meaningless baggage. And as happens so often now, I find myself, many decades later, rummaging around in that same skip for another look at what I once thought was useless junk. So why have I this daily spectacle of a dangling skeleton-head grinning at my best efforts in a most sinister and off-putting way?

I suppose it is because it points up for me a vital difference at the cross-roads of discernment – the difference between what lasts and what does not. The finest success and the most shattering disgrace are no longer a nine-days wonder – they are scarcely a nine-days news item either in the local media or in the parish bush-telegraph! So often we set our sights so tightly on a particular and temporary goal and block out a hundred gifts and blessings along the way in our tense tunnel-vision obsession with some perceived good. 'In a straight line no one goes very far,' the Little Prince reminds us. As a rule, our physical health, our relationships and our peace of mind do not improve in the intensity of our preoccupation with winning small races to the applause of a few fickle spectators in a very uncertain arena.

So when it comes to saving my soul, a pursuit which I'm reliably told has very long-term implications, I now find myself conserving my energies for the *'unum necessarium'*, the only goal that matters. Surprisingly enough, while we normally think of such spiritual concentration as having to do with things dim and distant in the eternal halls of heaven, nothing has more immediate implications for the balance of my complex self in the here and now. Any attention paid to the well-being of my spirit is like a natural and fairly immediate remedy for the ills of the rest of me. When the spring of living water is released in the desert of my heart, the greening of all of me happens too. When the small spark of desire for God is fuelled within me, my whole self is warmed and quickened. And in spite of my perennial short-sightedness and my ever-readiness to be seduced, like an image is clarified when the waters settle, like shapes sharpen when the mists lift, a saving grace has always risen in my deepest, darkest, most blessed places.

Time and again, when I begin to retaliate, to burn with vengeance, to judge wildly, to brood as only I can brood, an image of the sky or the ocean breaks into my churning heart. And then I quickly find freedom. Like a plane zooms under or over the angry confusion of clouds and squalls, or like Superman transcends the puny weapons of the mere mortals who envy his unusual powers, I escape into new space and bigness. I'm healed by a glimpse of what I can be like. I break through into another place in my soul where the air is pure and the light is lovely. In Christ, I too can be huge as the sky, fathomless as the ocean, invincible as Michael's army, once I allow my hidden self to be filled with the fullness of God.

With grace and practice we learn that we have a choice. It is always a revealing exercise to examine our fundamental reaction to the negativities of each day-ful of living. Gratitude, for instance, as a basic option, makes space for a decision, a conscious choice. Scarcely a day passes without the opportunity for putting the following demanding affirmation into practice: 'I can choose to be grateful even when my emotions and feelings are still steeped in hurt and resentment. It is amazing how many occasions present themselves in which I can choose gratitude instead of complaint. I can choose to be grateful when I am criticised, even when my heart still responds in bitterness. I can choose to speak about goodness and beauty, even when my inner eye still looks for someone to accuse or something to call ugly. I can choose to listen to the voices that forgive and look at the faces that smile, even while I still hear words of revenge and see grimaces of hatred.'

The freedom of this kind of centred response makes us truly ourselves – a gift to God, but not without considerable risk. The risk is in the openness to the Spirit of Life that will not be tamed. The spiritual writer Harry Williams puts it this way: 'Absolute love, God's love, makes us fully ourselves, instead of the half people we generally are. And to become fully yourself is a terrible risk. It would commit you to God knows what and lead you to God knows where.'

This, of course, is the final seduction. All the other seductions are but a shadow-part of the last union. Humanity is seduced by God. God by humanity. The Irish poet W. B. Yeats is sure that 'God possesses the heaven but he covets the earth ... oh! he covets the earth.' The mutual seduction is climaxed in the cosmic human-divine kiss we call Jesus.

'Wheelchair hearts'

I'm alone for a moment – at the bar on the ferry home, half-way between Calais and Dover. It is Sunday morning and the sun is shining on the green-blue sea. Our parish pilgrimage to Lourdes for holiday and healing, is almost over. Our hearts are full of stories of pain and joy, of some dark moments and many bright ones, of shared secrets and glimpses of the mystery of our human spirit.

Holidays and healing. They go together. They go together at many levels of experience. For instance, we were all in a new environment. Our winter bodies were plunged into a continental summer. The often-lonely routine of our predictable daily lives was suddenly and delightfully transformed into a community context of compassion. Unexpected experiences filled our nights and days. Everything was new and exciting. We found ourselves in a village of mystery and paradox where multi-coloured millions perennially gather. Like the apostles on the Mountain of Transfiguration, 'it was truly good for us to be there'.

At Lourdes they tell stories of how one day God's mother appeared to a country girl, and of how the lives of pilgrims, for a century and a half, have been changed forever. We loved being a part of that human journey. We would look at the few stray clouds meandering across the French sky and see them as the sacrament of the pilgrimage of humanity in search of holiday and healing. We took part in everything. And we all had our own reasons for doing so. Each morning and evening we found our place in the processions of light that wended their way around this holy place. We were part of the human quest to discover the love and meaning at the heart of our difficult lives.

Holiday and healing, mystery and paradox. Let me try to explain. At Lourdes – this metropolis of teeming emotion – everything is turned around. It is a place of divine contradiction. It is a humbling experience for those whose hearts are open. It is here that we are brought to our knees. We begin again to realise that God's ways are not ours and we surrender to a higher, loving Providence. As I sip my beer, I'm amazed at the way I have missed the hints and clues revealed to us by the God of

Surprises. This God is always different. Why are we so surprised that the God who once took the shape of a tiny, vulnerable, help-less baby at Bethlehem, to reveal the essence of divine healing, should once again confound our sceptical and doubtful logic by touching us, through our lovely Mary, at Lourdes? Without the miracle of Bethlehem, the miracle of Lourdes makes little sense to many of us.

This paradox was played out in many ways during the past week of holiday and healing. One example of paradox arose from the honest sharing that happened in the Dovecoat Chapel at L'Astazou ACROSS, half-way through our visit. Our leaders, in their handbook, encouraged us to 'come with minds open to the spirit, prepared to put our whole selves into the moment'. What came up for us at such times of sharing surprised us. We, the giving helpers, began to realise that truly we were the re-ceivers.

The roles were somehow reversed. Even though we were the ones who walked behind the wheelchairs of our physically un-able sisters and brothers, we were, in fact, the ones who were blessed with the privilege of being their servants. And so often too, it was us, the 'able-bodied', with our unable hearts in emo-tional wheelchairs, who so desperately needed holiday and healing through the love and acceptance of our 'guests'. Within our group there were many stories told of such 'small miracles'. Lourdes, we agreed, is not the place for wearing masks.

Now that the white cliffs of Dover are coming into view and our group is stocking up with duty-free gifts, I offer one last re-flection for those who had difficulty in 'buying into the legend of Lourdes' and its commercial and materialistic trappings. Such people are not alone. I, too, admit to a 'doubting Thomas' inside me. In fact I feel sure that many of us carry a small, sceptical voice about what goes on at Lourdes. For those of us who are aware of such hidden and disturbing thoughts, there is another way of entering into the spirit of the place.

I think it is possible to be part of the mystery of Lourdes at a very fundamental level of experience. From all time, and in all cultures and religions, there is a 'famine of the heart', a search-ing for the transcendent, a quest for God. Our human condition is always unfinished. Deep in our souls is a yearning for comple-tion. God has implanted in our hearts a longing for intimacy and belonging. St Augustine said, 'You have made us for yourself, O Lord, and we are forever restless until we rest in Thee'.

And that is why people are forever on pilgrimage, drawn by a desire for the mystery of God. From the very beginning, people carry lighted candles and other symbols of infinite hope, like we did at the Torchlight and Blessed Sacrament processions; they bathe in water with naked bodies like we did at the Baths or blessed ourselves from the green river of liquid, holy history; they touch the rocks of mother earth like we did at the cave; they take off their shoes when they are on holy ground like we did for those who anointed our tired feet; they kiss the icons and images of salvation like we did and like the Pope does when he kneels down to kiss and honour the dust of the earth from which we came and to which we will return; they sing and chant familiar refrains like we did to the rhythm of the rosary.

Perhaps Lourdes, then, can be experienced as an opportunity and an invitation to join our sisters and brothers of the world over, in the journey of their souls, in the rituals of death and life, of despair and hope, of pain and joy, especially when we gathered in our own particular 'wheelchairs' around the universal elements of bread and wine at the magnificent spectacle of the Basilica Mass, or in the more intimate setting of our own group's eucharist.

Lourdes is the world in microcosm, the church in miniature. All of life is here. It is open to all who are searching for meaning, for healing, for wholeness. It asks for no spiritual passport. If you are hungry, the table is set just for you. If your wounded heart is open, it will be healed. Beyond historical facts and proofs, beyond denominational distinctions and conditions, beyond the unartistic memorabilia of the shops, one can hear at Lourdes the voice of a passionate God saying, 'Because I love you so much, I only want to heal you.'

As I finish these lines, a little girl and her two small brothers are rushing to the window of our bustling ferry, waving and shouting, 'Hello England, Hello England.' Yes, while it was good to be there, it is good too to be home.

Beyond intimacy

Are you aware of 'spiritual milestones' in your life? Can you recall little personal breakthroughs for you, into the meaning of, for instance, the mysteries of creation and incarnation? Very often these have to do with a sharper focus in our awareness of the presence of God in creation, brought about in any number of ways, such as through reflecting on a poem, a conversation, a baby, or on the writings of the mystics. Or they may have to do with a fresh insight into the wonderful implications of the incarnation, through a good sermon, a good hug, a good laugh, for a deeper grasp of the divine value of all our experiences. Or such moments of growth may be about a richer understanding– arising from a house-group discussion, a son leaving home, a daughter getting married, the death of a parent – of the significance of the familiar and routine celebrations of sacraments, of traditional doctrines of the church, or of long forgotten prayers and holy practices.

While such windows may well spring open for us suddenly and unbidden, nevertheless, the locks and catches will have been gradually cleaned and oiled, but not always in a deliberate and conscious way. Some kind of quiet energy is usually at work in unrecognised places within us before the small revelations of delight happen. With reference to how children learn, the eminent educationalist Jerome Bruner reminds us that 'discovery, like surprise, favours the prepared mind'. Like the seed that is busy about its business in the womb of the earth during winter; with the coming of spring it rewards our waiting, to keep us wondering and exploring for more beauty tomorrow.

Anyway, just now, as I continue with the struggle to prise open the secret of the love and meaning at the the centre of all created things, another heart-thought rises up within me. It is about the intimacy of God in the deepest core of our being. Already the reader will be familiar with the belief, either through spiritual reading or meditation or from a natural instinct, that God is everywhere; that the Word became flesh to reveal to us the amazing mystery of God's desire to live among us and within us; that Jesus is the sacrament of the human-divine marriage; that the church is the sacrament of the spirit-filled community – 'the world where the world is truly itself'; that the seven sacraments are the 'house-warming' celebrations of the indwelling Blessed Trinity, at home in our truest selves; and that therefore, the whole point of Christianity is the delicate and difficult learning of the universal lesson to love each other and all things else, always and everywhere, with no exception, in the inescapable commitment to the basic thrust of our human and divine nature.

I want to take this understanding one step further. I want to explore the notion of God's intimacy with us, God's desire to be involved in our lives, God's delight in our acceptance of divine incarnation to a point of total identification. Is it possible that, close and loving as our grasp of God's place in our lives may be, it is still very incomplete and dualistic? Are we still operating from a notion of a God 'out there' who comes nearer to us at certain times; a God who responds to our invitation to occupy our inmost recesses; a God who, however much we are consumed by a longing for communion, is still someone clearly distinct from ourselves and who approaches us from outside? (There is nothing in this reflection that does not honour the church's teaching about divine transcendence or the *apophatic* tradition of the mystics – the doctrine of the unknowability of God.)

With humility and reverence, this then is the sacred secret I wish to touch. In the wilderness of a Kerry valley I recently met a contemporary mystic who spoke about his fear of entering into the holy places to be approached only on bended knees. He told me about the danger he felt when writing about the boundaries between God and humanity. He feared that his arm 'would be withered' if he dared to pursue his fatal attraction into the 'sanctum sanctorum – the terrible yet fascinating mystery' of God's mind. I mention this only to remind myself and you that there are no-go areas where angels rightly fear to tread. While our present reflection is taking place on safer ground, and does not presume to be as profound or threatening as my friend's explorations into God's mysteries are, nevertheless, it seems a sensible precaution to take off our shoes at this point!

A few images may help to clarify the 'spiritual milestone' I feel I have reached. When each day I pour some water into the chalice at Mass, and watch it become totally and irretrievably lost in the wine, I wonder about God's intimacy with our human nature. Is it possible that God and myself are so at one? Is God's heart, while separate from, indistinguishable from my own? Are all prayers that begin with 'Oh God...', still dualistic and misleadingly separate? Are we calling on a God that we still image as one step removed, One who is somehow 'over-against' humanity, still living somewhere else and coming to us from outside? Is it really possible that my very essence is the essence of God; that God is more me than I am myself?

What other examples and images have we? Take the intimacy of marriage. Intense and complete as this may be, as beautiful and holy as many have experienced, is there still a union that lies beyond – a communion that is holier than the oneness of marriage? During a moment of deep affection or gratitude a person might say to the beloved 'I could eat you'. And the climax of the eucharist is the reception into our body-spirit of the sacred species. 'Receive who you are,' the priest used to say when offering the consecrated bread and wine to communicants. This, too, is an ultimate kind of intimacy.

We become, truly and irrefutably, the very body and blood of God. Or maybe the holy communion is the confirmation and guarantee that this is what we already are! How much further can we press the incredible revelation without 'our arm being withered'? Can it really be true that in our deepest essence, and from the very beginning, we are inextricably bound up with God? That the beauty of our imagination, the breathing of our lungs, the energy of our bodies, the thoughts of our minds, the feelings of our senses, the beating of our hearts, the desires of our souls are already the very expression, in time and space, of the Creator-God, the Almighty Being, the Tremendous Lover? We say and hear so often that in God 'we live and move and have our being', but, as we well know, it takes a long time to recognise in our hearts what we know and believe with our minds.

The hermit and potter Nick O'Keeffe suggests that when we pray, asking God to be present to us; when we beg of God not to abandon us; when we cry out to God to pour divine love into us, we are misunderstanding the meaning of incarnation, because God is already essentially within us. 'The major task then is not trying to persuade God to "be with us" ... When we place the emphasis where it deserves, we stop concentrating on waiting for God to do what God has already done and continues to do. We turn the searchlight on the point of difficulty in our lives and in our world where that Presence is unable to move freely.' All we have to do is surrender to the love that is already within and surrounding us at every point of our truest selves.

In a letter to the world, *The Monastic Journey*, that had its origin in a request from Pope Paul VI, Thomas Merton wrote:

God seeks himself in us, and the aridity and sorrow of our heart is the sorrow of God who is not known to us, who cannot yet find himself in us because we do not dare to believe or trust the incredible truth that he could live in us, and live there out of choice, out of preference.

The message of hope the contemplative offers you, then ... is that whether you understand or not, God loves you, is present to you, lives in you, dwells in you, calls you, saves you, and offers you an understanding and light which are like nothing you ever found or heard in sermons.

The contemplative has nothing to tell you except to reassure you and say that if you dare to penetrate your own silence and dare to advance without fear into the solitude of your own heart and risk the sharing of that solitude with the lonely other who seeks God through you and with you, then you will truly recover the light and capacity to understand what is beyond words and beyond explanations because it is too close to be explained; it is the intimate union in the depths of your own heart, so that you and he are in all truth One Spirit.

Once the dammed up flow of God's energy within us is unblocked, once it is set free to inhabit its rightful homeland, a whole network of intimacy is set up. The recognition of the interconnectedness of all creatures is intensified in the surrender to the original source of human life which is God's love. We begin to notice both the barriers and the potential that exist in others – individuals, families, communities, ethnic groups, religious and social groups, nations and continents.

'It is only when those barriers have been wiped away, suffered away, struggled through, graced out of existence that we will be free,' writes O'Keeffe, 'free to be loved and to respond in kind, total surrender by "letting go to become who you have always been", whole, saved, redeemed, like Christ, ready for total bliss. Let us pray.'

The place within

While in all honesty I must admit that I don't see eye to eye with Pope John Paul II on a number of current issues, nevertheless, with millions of people I have always admired the man's integrity, authority and his relentless pursuit of truth. In *The Place Within** I have discovered one of the sources of his depth and attractiveness. These poems reveal his true soul – that part of him that is often hidden beneath the uncompromising line that he repeatedly offers to the world. The *via creativa* is well served by such healing creativity.

This is a most moving book. While suffering, I suspect, from the process of translation, as all second-language poetry inevitably does, where words are uncomfortably forced into an alien literary context disturbing the native flow of the original, the impact of the poems is still profound and lasting. They are carved from the quarry of the writer's personal agony and ecstacy. They reveal the soul of a man who loves to write, who became an actor, who worked in a stone-quarry and chemical plant, who was scarred by his hiding from the Gestapo during the German invasion of his homeland. The power of the poems, their imagery and forcefulness, their homespun philosophy and theology, were honed in 'the place within' of one who has lived long in the land of pain and beauty.

There are many intermingling themes throughout the collection. An almost Celtic spirituality of creation underpins some wonderful lines. Titles like *Shores of Silence, Song of the Brightness of Water, A Tale of a Wounded Tree, Space Necessary for the Drops of Spring Rain* indicate the writer's sense of divine immanence in all that God has made.

Oh – and a particle still remains
of that amazement which will become the essence
of eternity.

(Many decades later, in his recent Jubilee Letter, *Tertio Millenio Adviente*, Pope John Paul returns to this theme of creation-theology.)

The *via negativa* also winds its dark way between the pages of

the book. There are many lovely glimpses of the hiddenness and
ordinariness of God. For instance:

> You, Immeasurable, take but a little cell,
> you love places uninhabited and empty.

In a brief conversation between Father and Son, a forgotten and
desperately-needed model of revelation embraces our hearts.

> Son, you will be gone. Before time began
> I saw in your depth
> everything that was to be.
> Father, love must surge with glory.
>
> Son, look at the swelling ear of corn
> on the verge of your luminosity;
> one day they will take it from you
> when I give your light to the earth.
>
> Look, Father, my eyes
> are near to my love,
> gazing eternally
> at this day bursting with green.
>
> ... Son, when the day comes
> I will give your bright light
> to the corn on the swelling earth.
>
> ... Father, I leave your sun-flooded gaze.
> I choose human eyes
> and meet their gaze
> flooded with the light of wheat.

With another insight into the presence of God in all creation,
into a world created and sustained in the light of the Word, the
poet places these words in the mouth of the mother.

> I knew: like the light that lingered in ordinary things,
> like a spark sheltered under the skin of our days
> – the light was you;
> it did not come from me.
>
> And I had more of you in that luminous silence
> than I had of you as the fruit of my body, my blood.

Allured by a beauty that is captured in *Song of the Inexhaustible
Sun*, the Pope writes:

> Then, that evening with Nicodemus,

then again on the seashore
where I return each day,
bewitched by your beauty.
All this, Nicodemus,
that land, the fishermen's mooring,
the transparent depth,
and that Figure so close, so near

– all this stems from a White Point,
a point of the purest white,
encompassed in the human heart
by the red flow of blood.

Like the intermingling of the water and wine at the Offertory of
the Mass, there are images of intimacy between the divine and
the human in John Paul's reflection on *The Samaritan Woman*:

It joined us together, the well;
the well led me into you.
No one between us but light
deep in the well, the pupil of the eye
set in an orbit of stones.

Within your eyes, I,
drawn by the well,
am enclosed.

Over fifty years ago, consumed by his humble and heart-felt
longing for another consummation, the poet wrote:

Oh, do not spurn this wonder of mine, Lord,
which to you is nothing…
but for me now this is all,
a stream that tears at the shore
in muted motion,
before it can declare its yearning
to the measureless oceans.

… Then a miracle will be,
a transformation:
You will become me,
and I – eucharistic – You.

I find echoes of an incarnational theology of childhood in these
lines:

Yet day by day You multiply
my feeble ineffectual lot,

surrendering your infinity
to my fallible thought.

Can I ever repay my gratitude to the sea
whose quiet waves come out to seek me
as I am led astray, day after day?
– and to the sun
for not spurning me, its journey done,
and for keeping evening and dawn
not far apart?

… What can I give you for that familiarity
which you start in a child's eye
and complete in the glory, untouched
by shadows of sorrow?

Looking at his hands, 'hard and cracked from the even knocking of hammers', our Pope reflects on the power of pain:

Hands are the heart's landscape.
When they split, the pain of their sores
surges free as a stream.

Death is regarded as 'only the sun's rays too short on the sundial of hours'. It is later described as 'an experience of the limit', and hope as that which reaches beyond it.

No layer in my memory alone
confirms my hope,
no mirror of passage recreates my hope,
only your paschal Passage,
welded to the deepest record of my being.

The book ranges far and wide. Bishops, for instance, on their perennial round of duties, will identify with John Paul's vision of youthful energy. Maybe challenging images from his skiing encounters with the snow-lines of his beloved Alpine slopes have crept into his poem on *A Bishop's Thoughts on Giving the Sacrament of Confirmation in a Mountain Village*:

In their features I see a field, even and white,
upturned, their temples a slope,
their eyebrows a line below.
The touch of my open hand
senses the trust.
… In the map of their wrinkles
is there the will to fight?

Shadow moves over their faces.
An electric field vibrates.

The shape of the face says everything
… how telling the eyes of a child,
constantly crossing a strange equator
… Invisible pressures are trapped in the atmosphere.
yet there is light enough
to approach in this dark.

While we are often reminded of our longing for God, we rarely
reflect on God's longing for us. In a poem called *Magdalene,* the
Pope combines the pain of a mutual yearning:

At times love aches: there are weeks, months, years.
Like the roots of a dry tree my tongue is dry
and the roof of my mouth. My lips are unpainted.
It takes long: Truth sounding out error.

But it is He who feels
the drought of the whole world, not I.

In the final part of the book entitled *Redemption Seeking Your
Form to Enter Man's Anxiety,* the poet writes out of the *anima* of
his soul, with reference to Veronica as a symbol of redemption.
In the poem *Sister,* he meditates on what in the past was called
'the sacrament of the present moment', or today referred to as
'living in the now':

No ready footpaths for man.
We are born a thicket
which may burst into flames, into the bush of Moses,
or may wither away.

We are always having to clear the paths,
they will be overgrown again;
they have to be cleared until they are simple
with the mature simplicity of every moment:
for each moment opens the wholeness of time,
as if it stood whole above itself.
You find in it the seed of eternity.
When I call you sister
I think that each meeting
contains not only the communion of moments,
but the seed of the same eternity.

(*The Place Within – The Poetry of Pope John Paul II,* Hutchinson, London,
1995.)

Just before jumping

Here we are, Kathryn and myself, wheeling around the sky over East Yorkshire, searching below us for a safe place to land. But, before that, will our parachutes open? What am I feeling just before I jump out of this plane? I promised myself beforehand that I would try to remember my emotions at this precise moment. Familiar as I am with fear, I presumed that I would be sick with worry about a faulty parachute, a bungled landing, and how to face all those people around my hospital bed saying 'I told you so!' I also wondered whether my life (and especially my sins) would flash before me, as I tumbled into space. Would I regret, in the event of a very unpleasant ending to the whole venture, not having told the special people in my life how much I loved them, and others how much they had hurt me? And would I regret not having said and done, out of human respect, all the things that my most real and true self longed to reveal and accomplish?

As it turned out, it all happened quite quickly. There was one intense moment of wild trust, of total abandon, of a desperate kind of 'letting go', and then I jumped. While my thoughts were shouting 'Hold on, you fool', some small, clear instinct was saying 'Go for it'. I seemed to be jumping somewhere between my head and my heart. I will never forget the timeless seconds of total confusion, disorientation and awful panic, as Kathryn, young and brave, was swept out of the open Cessna plane door, swirling into a vortex of space, like a feather in a storm. And I was next. In spite of the painstaking efforts of Chris, our experienced instructor's expert coaching, I more or less made a hash of my jump. Unable to remember our carefully rehearsed routine for flight control, or find my ripcord, or my designated spot for landing, I drifted out of sight and landed somewhere between Hibaldstow and Brigg, just managing to avoid a farmer's carefully heaped up pile of horse and pig manure in a Lincolnshire field. However, in the process, as I floated down, I was intoxicated by the amazing view denied to most sensible human beings. Believe it or not, I had a little time to think on the deeper meaning of what I was doing, apart from the financial gains for our new church, a kind of spiritual reflection on this unusual experience – a theology of jump!

To put it bluntly, and to avoid getting too heavy about the whole happening, I was linking this jump in the first place with the risk of believing in God (or in anybody, for that matter), each day of our earthly lives, and then with taking the final risk of surrender called 'death' on the last day of those same lives. My scrambled thoughts, just before I jumped, were about the 'leap of faith' I take every day, when I try to place my life and work under God's providence; when I doggedly commit my living and loving into a deeper and stronger power than my own un-aided efforts; when I endeavour to hand over my control and my manipulation of the future to One whose ways are seldom the same as mine. Hanging in there, under my spiritual para-chute, between heaven and earth, I felt I was taking a kind of 'dive of passage' from the known to the unknown, from the cer-tain to the uncertain, from being stuck in security to surrender-ing in trust. Is it true to say that something like this happens every time we trust a friend with a secret, or make a stand for what we believe in, or risk being laughed at because we dare to be different?

Just before I jumped I asked myself was it too much 'up in the clouds', so to speak, to see this blind tumble downwards as a sort of dry-run for another more important one, a small prepara-tion for death, a shaky rehearsal for that dark and empty night where no stars shine. After all, there are many similarities. Death is the last and unavoidable tumble into the abyss, into total nothingness – the final leap or push that challenges intensely even the stoutest, faith-filled soul. Maybe this is a kind of prac-tice jump, a dry run, supported by my young friend Kathryn, and surrounded by car-loads of loving friends (and an ambu-lance) – for the real thing, the ultimate exit, waiting at the end.

I hope you are still with me. To sum up, I now see this whole experience as a 'small sacrament' of what pervades the totality of our Christian lives – the danger of believing in God, the courage to tell the truth, the risk of not conforming to the expect-ations of others, the free feeling of being true to oneself, the infi-nite space we find in letting go of possessive clinging and yet the fear of nothingness at the end. In no particular order, these thoughts were crowding my mind. I was so eager to break into places I had never been before, to travel through new land-scapes towards new horizons. I was convinced there were so many untapped powers of healing and creativity yet to be ex-plored within my being. There is something about reaching an ultimate boundary in jumping like this; about glimpsing another order of things, about touching the beyond and finding that failure can be good for you and that falling isn't really falling at all.

A final thought came to me as I ran with the wind, high over the furrowed fields below, in the direction, I think, of Scunthorpe. After many months of thinking about the jump and several hours of immediate training, the actual moment of truth – the seconds just before jumping – can never be completely prepared for. The frozen heart still misses a few beats. Like mine did when Kathryn smiled and leaped, and before I (without the smile) leaped. I thought about our Christian faith. We go to Mass, we read the holy books, we listen to talks, we pray every day and yet, in the end, there is no easy way to repeatedly place all our trust in the hands of God. Our finest theologian, Karl Rahner, describes such faith as 'a ghastly leap into the void of groundless space'.

And so too, at the end of life, where the dying person is privileged with the time to make the final act of surrender to the emptiness and fullness of God, only the same huge courage of the Spirit will transform the frightened traveller. There is no adequate preparation either, for this last, shocking, blind leap into eternity. I suppose what I'm trying to say is that for these three moments of trust – the parachute jump, the daily faith in God and in each other, and the last leap into the night of death– it is of the greatest importance to be adequately trained and prepared. But, at the end of the day, it is going to be a soul-sized encounter between two tough and mysterious powers of light and darkness, between raw courage and raw fear.

After all the theologising, spiritualising and agonising about the parachute-jump, maybe Kathryn, the 17-year-old captain of our small team, had got it right. Even though she planned the whole thing from the start, and for all the right reasons, such as providing funds for her community's new church, etc., 'I'm jumping,' she laughed, 'for the sheer hell of it!' Either way it is all about resurrection. After all, aren't we both alive to tell the tale.

P.S. Having written 'Just Before Jumping' I wonder now about God's thoughts just before dying to become a baby and Jesus' thoughts just before dying to become bread and wine.

Redeeming the dark

I turn around and there, below me, is 'Noddfa'. It is nestling in a small wood. 'Noddfa' means a safe haven for travellers. The Sisters of the Sacred Heart of Mary had given that Celtic name to the lovely place in which we are resting awhile from our journey through life. I am climbing a hill in Penmaenmawr, a lovely village on the north coast of Wales.

Like a river that forever meanders into perennial mistakes and cul-de-sacs on its inevitable way to its ultimate home, so too do I move in fits and starts on my personal journey Godwards. Sometimes like now, it is all uphill. Tomorrow I may simply go with the flow. But half-way up this hill I know that I see something more clearly. Let me explain.

A unique revelation of Christianity concerns the pain in our lives. How does the pain in our lives hold the key to our growing? As with all that pertains to the mystery of life we are at the heart of paradox here. How can what we instinctively recoil from be good for us? How can something negative have a positive outcome? So we find freedom at the heart of our fear – is this but wishful thinking? And does the light really begin to shine in the darkness?

I want to approach this ever-present mystery in two ways. The first way is at the level of simple devotion – a few theological and prayerful reflections about the implications of the death and resurrection of Jesus Christ for the daily crosses we are called to carry. *It is the way of trust.* The second way centres around a kind of mental strategy for dealing with the disturbing visitations and challenges that relentlessly come our way – a practical plan for structuring the basic faith-vision that flickers or flames within us but , please God, will never go out. *It is the way of letting go.*

I believe that even for Jesus Christ himself, to transcend the negativities of the human condition, a great deal of stress and confusion was necessary. It is very important to understand this. Because he was human there was no other way. The path to freedom is fraught with resistance. The gate to peace is guarded by dragons. Once Jesus was dignified by humanity he also became subject to its conditions. One of these is that if you dare to love be prepared to grieve. Jesus reached his Easter through his Good Friday, his crown through his cross, his glory through his agony.

And because he accomplished this transition successfully and gloriously, so can we all. This is another vital truth to make our own. Put theologically it means that by virtue of our solidarity in the human flesh with Jesus, and because we are truly adopted siblings with him in the family of God, then his breakthrough into divine splendour and his passover into the risen life is ours too – we are asked only to reach out and claim it. The victory is ours– *but so is the struggle*! The outcome is guarantee – *but so is the encounter*. 'If you dare to love, be prepared to grieve.' Jesus revealed the living potential in all death. Through the many little deaths of his journey from fear to trust, he dismantled the stranglehold of the negative forces that were destroying the precious energy within him – and that are still capable of holding us lifeless today. The doctrines here are clear. In the painful journey of Jesus through despair, loneliness, temptation the way is now open for all of us to be free – to travel confidently through our Good Fridays to our Easter Sundays.

God's amazing secret is now out. Forever our diminishment holds the promise of a brighter future. Every cross is a potential bridge; every failure a potential success. I think this is one of the most extraordinary revelations within our Christian tradition. It is a blessing of incredible proportions for the whole salvation of each human person. And it leads us immediately into worship.

I praise the Lord for this wonderful news – that my distress becomes my strengthening, my darkness gives birth to a bright morning, my fear leads to another freedom. Because Jesus revealed this to be so, I know it can be (and is) true for me too. If this is not salvation from hell then what is? And what a grace this is – to be able to redeem my darkness! It is redemption indeed to be convinced that, if the doctrine of the resurrection is true, then nothing whatsoever, no circumstance, no suffering, no cracking by chaos of sanity and dignity, no betrayal, no oppression, no collapse of sense, structure or relationship, no guilt over careless sins, can justify despair, can justify the fear that darkness has the last word.

St James writes: 'My brothers and sisters, you will always have your trials but, when they come, try to treat them as a happy privilege. Be sure that your endurance carries you all the way, without failing, so that you may be perfect and complete, lacking nothing.'

And I pray for this daily miracle in my own soul. I pray for the deep joy that follows my new awareness – that my face and body will reflect the glad surprise of this truth; that my words and walk will spread a new hope to faltering hearts; that my beauty will awaken the sleeping beauty in all I meet. My whole being is now a constant yearning, a fiercely hoping waiting for this abundant life, this promised transformation, this daily discovery of freedom. I seem to be committed to this pursuit of losing the will to control, the pull to power, the subtle manipulation, the avoidance of necessary loss. It is a living prayer that holds my heart these days, a prayer more open and more honest and more total than ever before. It is like a cry to be possessed.

In Peter Shaffer's *Amadeus*, Salieri despairingly whispers, 'To be owned – ordered – exhausted by an Absolute. This was denied me – and with it all meaning.' In a sense, Salieri becomes Everyman and voices our distraction, a tortured mediocrity – every bit as intense as a tortured genius. When half-gods go the gods arrive. I must dream the darkness into insight. I must work the vision.

But a final word to end this section. When I pray this prayer for wholeness and for freedom, for independence of all creatures and all created things, for dependence only on God; when I pray that my love for others will be passionate and compassionate but not possessive, manipulative or addictive; when I pray that my only desire will be a burning quest for God, then I know, as surely as I know that Jesus Christ suffered and was crucified, that I too will suffer and be crucified. Because there is no other way. If there were, Jesus would not have died on a cross. The emptying of oneself is torture. Our deepest being needs healing, and divine healing and pruning and fine-tuning happens in darkness. The perfection of loving comes through hard learning and many mistakes. And very often, the greater our need to love and be loved, the greater the hurting we cause in our confused efforts to reach for what attracts and allures us. And, therefore, the deeper must be the divine discipline over our wayward hearts. In *The Prophet*, Kahlil Gibran writes:

Much of your pain is self-chosen.

It is the bitter potion by which the physician within you heals your sick self.

Therefore trust the physician, and drink his remedy in silence and tranquillity.

For his hand, though heavy and hard,

is guided by the tender hand of the Unseen.
And the cup he brings, though it burn your lips, has been
fashioned of the clay which the Potter has moistened with
His own sacred tears.
(Alfred A. Knopf, 1977, p 52)

The other side of the vision of what my life can be points towards certain tactics to ensure my growing. Becoming free and
staying that way calls for watchfulness, readiness and a kind of
strategy for dealing with my wayward emotions. I'm thinking
now of the negative emotions that shut out the light from my
inner house. Let me try to put some order into my thoughts here.

I must first of all get really in touch with my feelings. This is a
well-known piece of advice but it stays in our head. It takes constant fine-tuning to be always aware of our emotions. And not
just the top layer of feeling but the hidden, stubborn forces that
so often control our reactions and block our growing. Mostly we
do not know how we really feel. Do I hate myself? Do I feel
guilty? Is there a meaninglessness in my daily life? Am I truly in
touch with the negative voices that so influence my decisions
and actions?

Gently, patiently, every moment, pay careful attention to
what is going on inside you. Be present to every moment at two
levels – the level of noticing what is happening around you in
the usual way, but also be aware of your inside reactions and re-
sponses to your environment. It is as if you were watching yourself having all these feelings with detachment and affection.

Remember that we are discussing the difficult emotions that
bring distress of one kind or another. Having become aware of
them, identified them to some extent and acknowledged their
presence within us, we then quietly welcome them. We welcome the distress! (We think of Jesus here – '...a death he freely
accepted...') Whatever the unwanted feeling may be, however
hurtful and disturbing its effect, we gently accept it into our
lives, without excessive fear, without panic. *Only accept.*
Deliberately and consciously we open ourselves to its presence.
We do what we normally avoid doing like the plague – we attempt to befriend the pain. We welcome and befriend the darkness that we fear.

At this point two very important realities are emerging. In
the first place we are not escaping from our feelings; we are not
avoiding them, suppressing them or denying them. To do this is
psychically unhealthy and ultimately self-destructive. Most of

our neuroses arise from our refusal to face our necessary pain. The second significant fact is that in discerning and welcoming such negative moods and feelings we are acknowledging that we are greater than our emotions, that they are but a part of us, that we are not identified with our guilt, our depression or our fear. The negative is not in control – it is kept at a distance. It is disempowered. The real me remains untouched because the true me is free. Every negative thought will pass when seen in this light.

This awareness is hugely important for a number of reasons, the main one being that it enables us to take the next step which lies in the skill of letting go. Of what must I let go? *Of my desire, of my attachment.* All our sorrow, according to Eastern wisdom, springs from our attachment to a whole range of desirable states, things, people. It is almost certain that whatever distressing emotion you are encountering in your moment of trial – the fear, anger, depression, anxiety – springs from excessive desire or conditioned expectations. And such deep-seated programming is met and challenged and disempowered by one or other of the following resolutions. So, holding my fear before me, I say to my deepest self:

a) I can let go of my desire for control and for power;
b) I can let go of my desire for affection and esteem;
c) I can let go of my desire for security and survival;
d) I can let go of my desire to change the situation.

Because negative thinking so stubbornly dominates our lives it often requires relentless repetition to dislodge our mental habits. It is helpful to repeat the above exercise many times a day in the context of prayer.

For the Christian, the new power that floods the soul will be the fruit of the Holy Spirit of the Risen Christ.

The reason for these suggestions is based on the knowledge that our negative feelings are not reality. *They are about the way we see reality.* The feeling is in us; it is not out there. The tapes that were recorded in my childhood heart keep repeating relentlessly the dire admonitions and warnings of our 'cautious elders'. But the inside tapes of yesterday are not the outside facts of today's reality. Either way, we are powerless to change the situation around us. Anthony de Mello writes: 'We spend all our time and energy trying to change external circumstances, trying to change our spouses, our bosses, our friends, our enemies and everybody and everything else. But the negative feelings are in *us*. We don't have to change anything out there to make ourselves free. We simply take our power into our own hands. No event, condition, situation or person has the power to disturb or hurt us.'

All this is a kind of habit of the heart. How to keep our peace in the face of failure, disappointment or loss? Is there a way of balance and centredness even though we are moved deeply by a passionate dream? In the *Bhagavad-Gita* we hear Lord Krishna advise Arjuna, 'Plunge into the heat of battle and keep your heart at the lotus-feet of the Lord.'

Homecoming

It's been a slow slog through a persistent winter. Easter has come and gone. My brother Míceál and myself are taking a few days off. We're heading for Chrysalis, a holistic centre for spiritual growth, shyly set into the flatlands of Co Wicklow. On our right, as we head north from Baltinglass, I can see the Bog of Allen, a seamy, stagnant, shapeless mass of water and soggy turf. It mocks how I feel. These days my thoughts, emotions and energies are all over the place. Everything within me, like those murky, muddy waters, seems to be draining away, formless. Anxiety fills me – about my work, my health, my future, my relationships, myself. Shadows of depression haunt my heart. I'm really at a very low ebb. And when the tide is out, every pressure leaves its mark.

The view is changing. In the distance I can see the bold Broadstairs mountain range and, to the west the river Slaney, like a liquid blessing, is flowing through fields now green again. How I long to be greened and fertile once more, like the valleys and hills that now come into view, protecting and thanking the winding river of life that flows though them! I noticed the comforting boundaries – those hedges and walls, those river banks and bridges – so secure, so appropriate and so natural. Unlike the mutilated Bog of Allen, everything here is in its perfect place. Without any intense effort, the unfolding of life is happening as it was meant to happen. A vague hope stirs somewhere inside me. Maybe I too can still repair my broken boundaries, and recapture my lost rhythm, my drained vitality, my unbalanced centre.

What follows are my reflections about that April weekend at Chrysalis when something like a silent metamorphosis took place in the cocoon of my soul. The theme of the days was the necessity of awareness, the way in which we are present, or absent, to ourselves. Without awareness there can be no centred growing, no deepening of the spirit. And how difficult it is to be truly and quietly aware! What a desperate struggle the mind's thoughts and ideas put up to avoid surrendering their mastery over our lives! Subtle and insidious, they infiltrate the necessary vacuum within, without which there is no space for the desired grace to emerge.

Even writing about it has its own seduction where words can impersonate the reality. Knowing something is so different from being and becoming it. There is a tyranny of knowledge. I am now coming to suspect all kinds of plans and methods of meditation, notes I take from talks, books I read about self-healing, and ideas to do with changing and improving my life. Of course there is a place for such helps and guidelines. They are necessary, but only up to a point. Most of my own ministry, for instance, is about such matters. But just now I see them as the finger pointing to the moon. But as we well know, only the fool looks at the finger. It is the moon we seek, not the finger. It is the goldmine we're after, not the map. The rich veins of the golden blessing we are promised lies deep within us and will only reveal themselves after unforced but relentless commitment to the inner work of silent, trustful waiting. Somewhere here is the point of disclosure, the leap of faith, the encounter with darkness.

This inner work calls for a combination of dedicated discipline and yet an easy flowing, for a will of steel and yet an open, receptive and trusting heart. This is paradox but not contradiction. To the purists of enlightenment my words may be inappropriate or even misleading, but today I know no others. They are the best I can offer when faced with the tangled and complicated, yet simple and all-revealing mystery of the inward journey of my soul this very evening. I'm trying to put together what has come to me during these hours at Chrysalis – some realisations about embarking on one way of finding my true and but temporarily lost soul.

It is very important to trust the quest for emptiness. This quest is at the heart of all traditional contemplation. It has to do with waiting patiently, endlessly letting go, and blind faith. Take time, we were told, to draw into yourself your wandering mind. There is an inward focus of attention. This is about watching your straying thoughts and gathering them from the past and future into the *now*. It entails the leaving of anxious forebodings and the coming into the present. The gentle challenge is to draw back from the day-dreaming and fantasising about yesterday and tomorrow and to come home to the centre of yourself at this very moment.

The exercise of developing body-awareness is one such recommendation. It is only when we stop rushing towards some desired goal that we somehow arrive there. This means a radical 'slowing down'. It means taking one thing at a time. It is a leav-

ing of the mind and a coming to the senses. There are those who
try to remain 'mindful' by continually persisting in the exercise
of talking themselves through what they are doing at any particular moment. For instance, 'Now I am washing the dishes, not to
get the dishes done, but simply to wash the dishes.' At the age of
sixteen, during my first week in the seminary, I remember pin-
ning the three words *'Age quod agis'* (Do what you are doing) beneath the one-shelved desk in my student room. (I also remember that my room-mate at the time, for some strange reason, tore
this non-threatening piece of paper from its place and committed it to the dust-bin!)

Anyway, most of you will be aware of the exercise I'm referring to. It is about being grounded and centred. It is about 'living
in the now'. Another 'way into' this contemplative consciousness is that of transcendental meditation. There are various
models of such awareness. At Chrysalis we persevered with the
familiar *Sadhana* exercises of de Mello. But there is no perfect
model. They are all means to an end. In simple terms they all
have to do with keeping our thoughts and our body in the same
place! This seems to be the basic aim of all *awareness* techniques.
Another popular model recommends the use of a 'mantra'. At
that time I read the following paragraph in the *The Heart of
Creation*, one of the many books explaining the wisdom and
methods of John Main. I quote it for its simplicity.

> Sit down. Sit still and upright. Close your eyes lightly. Sit re-
> laxed but alert. Silently, interiorly begin to say a single word.
> We recommend the prayer-phrase 'maranatha'. Recite it as
> four syllables of equal length. Listen to it as you say it – gen-
> tly but continuously. Do not think or imagine anything –
> spiritual or otherwise. If thoughts and images come, these
> are distractions at the time of meditation, so keep returning
> to simply saying the word. Meditate each morning and
> evening for between twenty and thirty minutes.
> (John Main, *The Heart of Creation*, Darton, Longman and
> Todd, 1988, Intro.)

As I persist with such meditation, forgotten pieces of spiritual
advice come back to me with fresh meaning. Good insight bears
repetition. It is the travelling that matters, not the arrival. It is
what is happening now that is important, not the end product.
The wisdom of this truth is very much with me at the moment. I
have always carried within me a great urgency toward completion. Whether it is the compulsion about a new project that is

struggling to get off the ground, about an agenda for physical exercise or stages of prayer, about the building of a new church (currently underway), about the formation of various ministries within the parish, or about the production of this very book, I find I lose my peace of soul, over and over again. I become impatient with the many steps that must be taken for the goal to be reached. I want to rush the details for the final plan to emerge.

How very foolish is this way of living! How stressful and damaging it is to the well-being of mind, body and soul! How self-important and untrustful! The meditations I refer to are helping me to begin a slow change in how I understand the meaning of God's time. The only graced place is in the moment of being or doing. The only interface between the Holy Spirit and myself is at the point of the present. The eventual outcome is something else. The ultimate end is beyond my concern. If each second of time, each small step of the way, each detail of the overall outline is not seen as the *whole*, then the eventual result will be built on sand. It is all about the energy of compassion that must underpin everything we do. This bit of wisdom is of great comfort to me. It takes such a load off my shoulders! It reminds me of something I read in a parish newsletter recently – a letter from heaven.

My Dear Beloved,
Do not feel totally, personally and irrevocably responsible for everything today.
That is my job.
With so much love.
God.
(*God*, Celestial Press, No date given)

The motivation behind what we do reveals the state of our heart. Apart from appropriate expediencies, the hurry, anxiety, urgency and impatience that we bring to our work betrays our true motives. Everytime I ask myself the question 'Why am I really doing this?' I am forced to do some soul-searching. I often remember another passage from Kahlil Gibran:

Work is love made visible.
And if you cannot work with love but only with distaste, it is better that you should leave your work and sit at the gate of the temple and take alms of those who work with joy.
For if you bake bread with indifference, you bake a bitter bread that feeds but half man's hunger.
And if you grudge the crushing of the grapes, your grudge

distils a poison in the wine.
And if you sing though as angels, and love not the singing, you muffle man's ears to the voices of the day and the voices of the night.
(Kahlil Gibran, *The Prophet* , Alfred A. Knopf, 1977 p 28)

Finally, it was with great delight that I came across the following passage by Daniel Berrigan about 'staying with it'.

It's hard, and yet not so hard, to realise you haven't made much difference and that things in the world are worse than when you started ... When you turn to the Bible for illumination on the question, it seems as though the more godly a work is, the less likely is its accomplishment in one's own lifetime. All the prophets died with things in shambles, like Jeremiah ...

So the value is in the work itself, rather than in the outcome. You stay with the work because of its own goodness, not on the basis of whether it succeeds. And that takes prayer.
(Daniel Berrigan, from an interview in *America*, 1996)

The probable Trapezist

'Don't follow the Tremerchion sign,' shouted Joe as I headed off from St Beuno's, 'It's pointing in the wrong direction.' Tremerchion is a village in North Wales not far from the Jesuit Centre for Spirituality where we were staying. This afternoon we would begin a three-month retreat so I wished to have a last run around the beautiful countryside before the wrestling with the dragon would begin! As I loped along Joe's advice set me thinking about wrong signals and false guides.

'Be probable trapezists.' I began linking this phrase that I had recently come across with the Tremerchion signpost. This second exhortation sounds like an invitation to take up a highly dangerous profession. But we are not in the world of circuses. William Yeomans explains that the trapeze in question was the money-changer's table on which he would bounce coins to test their genuineness by the ring they gave. (The word 'probable' here come from the Latin *probare* – to test.) The 'trapezist' needed a very true and trained ear to distinguish between the real and the counterfeit. This image came from ancient Eastern bazaar life and was used by Christian spiritual directors when they spoke about identifying the deceiving whispers of our often misleading hearts. So much of growing is about discerning. Is the signpost trustworthy? Is the sound-signal flawed? Is my heart telling me the truth?

It was well known in those times, as it is now, that once a person begins to move towards, or rather be drawn by, divine love, strange counter-forces come into play. Some kind of resistance is set up. Persuasive arguments against change are murmured deep inside – arguments of prudence, of safety, of 'common sense'. Almost all of these arguments were begun in childhood. The various disciplines have their own names for this fear of growing, of healing, of transformation. Whether this resistance be described in emotional, psychological or devotional terms, it is important to be ready for the phenomenon – to anticipate it and to identify it. Nobody escapes it. And because it is a master of disguise, this confusing inclination is not easily discerned. The reassuring sign, after all, is not trustworthy. After a second spin, the bouncing coin sounds out of true.

The subtlety of the resistance within us to following the light that beckons us forward arises from the fact that its voice is so plausible. One hears or sees no hissing serpent or screeching demon. The persuasion is impressive. In his *God of Surprises*, Gerard Hughes explains, 'It can enter politely, plausibly, respectably, even religiously, germinate quietly and peacefully for a while, then suddenly erupt in savagery and destruction.' (Darton, Longman and Todd, 1985, p 119) There are many names for such spirits of confusion and fear. One of them comes to mind – 'Father of Lies'. This is a chilling title – so obviously sinister that, given at least a reasonable state of spiritual health, we feel we could swiftly challenge and disarm such a threat. But a more accurate description of the pervasive nature of the infiltration of our souls might be found in the title 'Father of Half-Truths'. We are far more likely to grant entry into the sanctuary of our hearts to the partial truth than to the stark lie. The latter we identify at the door of our perception; the half-truth is already a friend at the family fireside, sometimes for a long, long time, before the disguise is penetrated.

When I succeed in observing the pattern of my own choices, the way I decide for or against a path of action, a decision, an option for change, it is as though there were two strands of energy or persuasion within me. The one may be challenging but always affirmative, supportive, encouraging; the other is usually negative, cautious, maybe even cynical. One counsels risk and hope, trust and courage; the other opts for certainty, repetition, the status quo. One is dynamic, explorative, open; the other conservative, sometimes parsimonious, closed. These intense 'counsellors' are often 'look-alikes' and only after close observation will they sometimes reluctantly reveal their true identity. This process of penetrating the impressive disguises is what spiritual guides refer to as discernment.

The discernment of spirits is a special grace. In a language borrowed from religious attitudes of past centuries, many 'directors of souls' employ a more militaristic idiom. The 'enemy' in the camp is named as such. The battle-lines are drawn. To win the war is the aim of the strategy. Satan is victorious when the soul is brought to a point where it is lost in a dull, grey confusion of mediocrity – and remains unaware of its wretched condition. The Lord is triumphant when each soul wakes up to its shining glory through intimacy and unity with the God of Love and Beauty.

But whatever the mode of expression, it is truly a blessing when we become aware of the force and counter-force, the graced movement and the persistent resistance, the call and the doubt that takes place in our deepest spirit. The awareness of what is going on in us is a hard-won gift. It is never easy to reflect on our experiences, to replay our reactions to such-and-such an encounter, to honestly review some stance we vehemently took during the day, to explore our deeper reasons for going OTT about what began as a rather trivial exchange with someone, to probe, maybe painfully, into carefully hidden motives and attachments – desires that we deny even to ourselves. Oh how skilled 'the probable trapezist' must be at times like these. 'Reflection is the prayerful searching of my heart, facing up to my emotions and testing their worth in terms of how far are they creative or destructive. What is really going on in the unseen depths of my soul? What I seek is that interior knowledge, the heart's way of knowing, the creative insight of the artist rather than the rational analysis of the philosopher.' I am convinced that the greatest need in the world just now is for people who are prepared to fearlessly examine the deeply flawed 'doctrines and principles' that seduce and prejudice us into negativity, insecurity and even violence.

This kind of work on oneself is not for the feeble or the timid. It takes more than a little courage to face the inner, subtle counsellor and unmask him for an imposter. There is a serious risk in eventually confronting the trusted travelling-companion of your soul's secrets and calling her bluff. Power, prestige and possessions are never far below the surface of our motivation. Pride and greed neither rest nor slumber. In fact all of these intruders roam unchecked around the temple of our inner selves, their deadly identities unrecognised in their casual familiarity.

Gerard Hughes reminds us that 'Riches and honours can become our idols, our Mammon, so that our lives revolve around our bank balance, whether its abundance or deficit, or around the esteem, or lack of it, in which we imagine we are held ... We fail to honour one another because we do not value and cherish each other for what we are in ourselves – images of God – but we value people for the wealth they possess, the power they have.' (p 122)

More often than not, discernment, as we have already pointed out, is extremely difficult. On the one hand we are dealing with assumptions and attitudes that have become part of the furniture of our soul – half-truths and well-meaning cautions that haunt and colour our efforts to change ourselves and transform our community. These ingrained brakes and blinkers have little to do with genuine prudence or carefulness – sown in our childhood memories, they come from an era of fearful parents and a fearful church. Written over the corridor arches of many of the seminaries in my day were words that Jesus never said, 'If you keep the Law, the Law will keep you.'

On the other hand, spotting the deep-seated deceit in our fundamental options about the meaning of life and Christianity is made so difficult because of 'what everybody else thinks and does'. When so many seem to be travelling in a certain direction, we feel fairly sure that they all cannot be wrong. When the most respectable members of our political party, when our business partners and peers, when our church groups all agree with us, then how can we be wrong? That is how powerful and insidious the spirit of deceit, the father of lies, 'the enemy of our human nature', the invisible 'Mammon' of confusion can be. This 're-spectable' attraction can be 'any idol in our lives, any created thing which becomes the focus of our praise, reverence and service. It can be patriotism, my country right or wrong, or it can be the way in which we practice religion, when our dedication becomes dedication to particular structures or formulations of the Christian message, and their preservation in the form familiar to us becomes more important than the love and service of God …' (p 120)

The whispering beguiler almost always plays on our pride or greed, especially our inner, emotional greed which often springs from our pervasive sense of insecurity. Painful as it is to discipline our avarice for money and things, much more acute is the pain of curbing the spirit. Spiritual poverty is about disentangling our clinging to everything that contributes to a false sense of self-importance, 'our popularity, status in society, our physical health, strength, beauty, our intelligence, qualifications, achievements, our ideas, including our ideas about God and spirituality … we feel crushed when overlooked or not appreciated because our deepest securities are being attacked and our whole self-preservation instinct rallies all our forces to repel this attack on what we suppose to be our inmost being. What we are defending is not, in fact, ourselves, but our false notion of our own worth and meaning … If I have poverty of spirit, I can listen carefully and with interest to personal criticism from others. Humility is freedom from every form of inner enslavement…' (p 123)

Moment of disclosure

There I was at the dentist's, down Wakefield Road in Garforth, waiting to be called. Like those around me in the waiting-room, I was pretending not to be afraid. I looked out the window across Joe Barrowman's big fields. I needed a distraction. I reached for the magazines. One of the ubiquitous *Magic Eye* books was waiting to be engaged. I picked it up and read the instructions on the cover. *For a new way of looking at the world, 'diverge' your eyes and do not focus on the image; instead, let the image come into focus.* So I sat back and began to stare at the picture on the front page.

As I focused, or rather unfocused, a kind of transformation took pace. Something started happening to the flat, two-dimensional drawing of your average assortment of swimming fishes. Suddenly I was part of an enchanting underwater world of 3-D excitement. The picture had taken on the depth and rich perspective of a mysterious, subaquatic, quasi-tropical reality. For a rare moment (for me!), I was out of time.

'Fr O'Leary, please.' Swiftly I surfaced as the magic in my hands shivered back to the ordinary. But once the screaming drilling and the messy mouth-washings were over, I began to use my *Magic Eye* experience as an image of a new awareness in my life.

The impact of the incarnation on the Christian consciousness can be described as the gift of insight into the meaning of things. At some point in our lives, if we refuse to resist, a kind of 3-D effect enriches our perception of reality. As a result of divine revelation, the flat becomes deep, the ordinary extraordinary. In the light of the mystery of God's becoming human, our frame of reference shifts, a refocusing takes place and our way of attending to what happens is drawn into a new setting.

On that morning at the dentist's, even my nerves forgot to play me up, as I gaped and gawked at the changing scenery before my nose. Once I got the hang of it I was hungry for more. I still remember the amused expression on the dental assistant's face as she tried to call me back out of my amazement. Something like this, I believe, is what happens, at the level of grace, when the Spirit of understanding develops within us the mind of Christ.

There are moments of conversion in our lives – significant and unexpected surprises when the wall cracks and we see heaven through the split; when the focus shifts and we are in another dimension; when the routine and familiar break open to reveal a dynamic beauty and rhythm. Such moments are often called sacramental. Something like it happens when we fall in love. We take a delight in looking at and being present to the one who transforms our life. We are profoundly shaken and even fragmented and now need new terms of reference. So we go back to the drawing-board of our heart's original design, to the laboratory of meaning, to that safe place where we can stand to look around us and make whatever readjustments or even radical and fundamental paradigm shifts in our consciousness and perception of reality.

Jesus looked for images to portray hints of mystery and depth. These were 'focusing' places and times and things such as mountains, rivers, seasons, birth and death, bread and wine, to reveal the universality of the divine presence in all creation. This is the essence of the sacramentality that the truest Catholic tradition of Christianity has struggled to preserve over the centuries, and recently lost.

It is about opening up the ordinary to find within it the deeper mystery. It is about discovering, when lost in the forest of crowded trees and the daily undergrowth of entanglements, the hidden, faery fort of joyful, flowing order. It is about stumbling on to the sudden oasis that gives meaning to the desert and so greens my dry sense of purpose. This is what sacraments do, each in its own most exciting way – those very sacraments that we so often relegate to the periphery of our religious agendas.

Why did my *Magic Eye* experience speak to me so clearly and move me to write down this reflection? Because first of all it reminded me that I had to be ready for the revelation. I was approaching the exercise with a measure of expectation, having read the cover-blurb. Such gifts rarely happen by accident. Discovery, like surprise, favours the prepared mind. Second, I felt *drawn into* the depth of the ocean scene, not left outside, watching in. The idea of sacrament, whether applied to Jesus Christ, to the church or to the seven celebrations, has a warm and welcoming dimension towards full participation. (I recall the catechetics of the seventies where we consumed much coffee over the differences between sign, symbol and celebration.) Sacrament is the doorway to the sacred; the small window on to the unfathomable.

Sight becomes insight. Knowledge becomes wisdom. Information becomes understanding. Acquaintance becomes allurement. And observation becomes involvement. The background to this holy process is called mystery. Mystery is the context of all our knowing, communicating and encountering. Mystery is the ocean saying 'I will support you, carry you and care for you. Filter me and drink me; harness me and use my fearsome energy; calm me and you can dive into me, and swim and sail across my waters. But meet me humbly, unlike the first Adam. Because you will never tame me, or drain me, or know me. You must remember that. Respect me or I will destroy you.'

This morning, I want to end my reflection with a summary (to be developed throughout the book) of three such moments of disclosure that relate to my life, now that I hear the footsteps of another spring coming up along the A1 from the south. The first concerns the freedom that surrounds me since I opened myself wider to the call of being a *servant* of God, in Christ, for others. No matter how profoundly we understand (or think we do) the many meanings of 'washing each other's feet', there is always a whole range of further layers of understanding waiting to be encountered. Accepting this invitation with fresh insight (or obeying this command) seemed to lift me above my petty moaning about being badly done to, above the dingy doling out of my time and energy, above the miserly measuring of my received rewards and appreciation for work done. My perception of duty and service had expanded into another dimension. Something had happened at the boundaries of my spirit.

Freedom, again, was my overwhelming reaction to another shift within me, regarding the cost of discipleship. This shift had to do with the *totality* of loving and being compassionate. As with servanthood, above, so too the horizons of compassion seem always to be further than where we stand. At every instant we must strive to raise the limits we set on loving. At every instant it must be complete, unconditional. I found the very enormity of the challenge to be exciting and liberating rather than depressing. Here was a God-size enterprise if ever there was one! This inner breakthrough most assuredly happened, also, at the soul-edge – another limit-situation. It had to do with the *letting go* of the enervating effort to get even in tiny ways; with con-

serving the energy of our spirit so often dissipated in unwar-
ranted feelings of hurt or offence at careless or ill-judged remarks; with overlooking, without too much bother, the many
events of each day which bring some measure of distress.

I have little doubt that our hearts carry a low-burning yearning to be like the light that, with the shift of a February cloud
over Wetherby, has lit up, for a bright minute, my little Carmel
room, tucked peacefully away within the folds of the furrowed
fields of West Yorkshire. The splintered shadows that criss-
crossed the floor and walls were caught up into the sunshine
that white-washed every corner with instant surprise. When
half-gods to the gods arrive. Giving in to grace is like *recognising*
something that was obvious and waiting to be found. It is like
being delighted at finding yourself in a suddenly familiar place
called home.

Third, and most unmistakably, freedom again is what lifts
my spirits when I surrender my controlling impulse, to a more
demanding level of *trust*. The graced invitation to escape into
trusting usually comes in the nick of time. Or rather I allow myself to hear it just before I panic. When we fear that we alone are
rowing our boat so small, in the sea so big, at dark midnight,
surrounded by dense fear, we suddenly hear, with intense reassurance and joy, the splash of oars, far beyond us, out in the unknown distance.

So strong is our desire to have things our own way, so en-
trenched is the need to dominate and control, so fearful are we
of risking the presence of a providence that in fact provides our
ultimate security, that we need daily meditation to keep this secret before our minds and hearts; to learn how to be gentle and
sensitive; to learn how to wait and be still; to notice things and
begin to believe not just that it is safe to trust, but that our *only
hope* is in letting go the reins and allowing our Tremendous
Lover do the driving. Some of us are willing but we are also wil-
ful. There is a blind, primitive hardness that quickly surfaces
when our patch is threatened. The heart of stone needs to be
fleshed. The soil needs moistening.

I often wonder whether one can practice letting go; whether
it becomes easier with the habit. Or can one ever make a habit of
it? Because it is always so hard to do. And the moment I have
achieved some measure of success at it, I discover a whole new
mountain of the ego to be encountered. I find myself digging
down deeper into the multi-layered mass of hidden attachments

and into the subtle but tough entanglements of pride. To loosen up these solid, compressed conditioners of the quality of my life needs large showers of spring grace.

Mine, O thou Lord of Life,
Send my roots rain.
(G.M. Hopkins)

PART IV

The Moment of Compassion and Transformation

Living Pentecost

If people were asked, after reading through the gospels, to find one word for the kind of person Jesus was, many would choose 'compassionate'. His compassionate heart seemed to inform his life. 'And Jesus, seeing the crowds, was moved with compassion.' (Mt 9:36) This profound adjective has depths of meaning, combining the finest elements of caring, of selfless service, of sensitive attention, and of true openness, humility and self-discipline. It is about the grace of love, stripped to its radical essential. It is about self-giving purified of self-interest. Compassion springs from an awareness of the connectedness of every aspect of creation and life. It has to do with a sense of identity with all forms of existence. It has deep roots in the heart of the Creator.

When God becomes visible, tangible and available on this earth the result is incarnate compassion. We look to Jesus to see the face of God. The Word, a self-portrait by the Creator, is drawn with the lines of compassion. Throughout the gospels, even when the word itself is not used, we can feel the movement of this instinctive gut-reaction. In Greek the movement of compassion means a deep-seated impulse that comes from the very bowels of the human being. Matthew quotes Jesus as saying 'Don't be afraid', 'Don't be worried', 'Don't cry', and Mark points out that he was more moved by the last penny of the poor widow freely given into the temple treasury than by the grandeur of the Temple itself; and that while everyone else was so excited about the raising of Jairus' daughter, Jesus was more concerned that she should be given something to eat.

The prophet shares not only in God's knowledge but is filled to the brim with God's own feelings and emotions. For Jesus, it was God's essential compassion that possessed and drove him; he was its actual embodiment.

All his convictions, his faith and hope were expressions of this fundamental experience. If God is compassionate, then goodness will triumph over evil, the impossible will happen and there is hope for mankind ... Compassion is the basis of truth. The experience of compassion is the experience of suffering or feeling with someone. To suffer or feel with humanity, nature and God is to be in tune with rhythms and impulses of life. This is also the experience of solidarity with each person, with each part of creation and with God. It excludes every form of alienation and discrimination. It makes a person at one with reality and therefore true and authentic within the self ... This made Jesus a uniquely liberated man, uniquely courageous, fearless, independent, hopeful and truthful.[1]

But compassion is no soft option. It is, in fact, an intensely-felt way of dying. It destroys suffering only by *suffering with and on behalf of* those who suffer. A Buddhist prayer is to use suffering so as to end suffering. A sympathy with the poor that is unwilling to share their sufferings would be a useless emotion. One cannot share the blessings of the victims of our inhumanity (the *anawim*) unless one is willing to enter into their painful plight. And that is what Christians are called to do. Jesus wasn't just compassion incarnate, he also said to his followers: 'Be compassionate as your Father is compassionate.' This calls for the most sublime graces of trusting in, and letting go into, the ever-present, all-pervasive loving providence of our tremendous lover.

In his *Commentary on the Psalms*, Thomas Aquinas writes, 'We find these two things, compassion and justice, in all the works of God. Through compassion human beings imitate God ... since God is compassion itself.' He reminds us that we know from the life of the Incarnate Word, how 'divine compassion has no measurement ... it is the greatest of the mysteries of God'. Notice that the Angelic Doctor links compassion with justice. This fourth *Moment* of the book is about the transformation of people's attitudes especially in matters of equality and justice, peace and freedom. Lived compassion is built on these pragmatic dimensions of active ministry or else it dissolves into empty sentimentality. And justice without compassion can be too severe, peace without justice can be utterly false, freedom without responsibility can become wanton licence.

Compassion, as we have seen, springs from the intimate inter-relationship of all things. God's compassion becomes a little more understandable, then, when we realise that all creation, and every aspect of it, is the fruit of God's womb. God sees the divine Self in everyone and everything. Only when we too see and know and feel the oneness of our universal sisterhood and brotherhood, can we 'suffer with' in an authentic and saving way. Only when we feel an intimacy with the elements of nature, with the turning of the seasons, with the pulse of the earth, can we passionately desire what Aquinas calls 'the common good'.

Compassion moves outwards. It will not be trapped into individual soul-saving. It grows only when given away and it can only happen in community. It is a 'reaching out' kind of virtue that is forever purified in the sharing. And it enriches the giver, because there is a sense in which our redeeming compassion is directed towards ourselves. We are a part of everything and everything is a part of us. This is another glimpse of the amazing revelation of incarnation. 'Blessed are the compassionate for they themselves shall attain compassion,' writes Matthew, and, in his *Commentary on St Matthew's Gospel*, Aquinas comments, 'To be compassionate is to have a heart that suffers from the misfortune of others because we think of it as our own.'

The common good
The reason that we are dwelling so much here on this aspect of the Christian life, is to emphasise the ultimate goal and focus of the previous three *Moments* of our story. Personal transformation leads to social transformation. 'It is much better and more divine,' Aquinas reminds us, 'that (compassionate endeavour) be done for a whole people and for states (than for a single person only) ... The common good of many is more Godlike than the good of an individual.' (*Commentary on Aristotle's Ethics* 1, L 2 p 15)

At the end of the day, in the evening of our lives, there will be but one question. 'Were we compassionate throughout the decades of our time on earth?' (Mt 25) Everything else is secondary. The whole point of our religion is tragically missed if we follow another agenda. What is shockingly revealed in the mystery of incarnation is God's own need and demand, in the powerlessness and vulnerability of each other. The sovereign deity has no need of our praise and thanksgiving (Weekday Preface IV); the Incarnate God, however, pleads for our understanding of God's own vulnerability in each other. The almighty and transcendent Creator may well have infinite ranks of angels for an eternity of support; but the Incarnate God longs for our scraps of time and words of comfort for our neighbour. The infinite and changeless Being is beyond the range of our deadly inhumanity; yet the Incarnate God silently waits for the healing touch we offer each other.

As we saw in the first *Moment* of our theological glimpses, so deep is our dualistic thinking about heaven and earth, about soul and body, so conditioned are we to follow a two-tier type of Christian thinking, that we still divide the sacred from the secular, the holy from the earthly, the God of Jesus from the human heart. The birth, death and new life of Jesus, his every word and action, spell out for us in absolute clarity the startlingly urgent realisation about our responsibility for saving each other in particular, and the whole world in general. We persist in missing the point. We resist taking Jesus at his word, even at the point of his death. We forget that in his own body he reconciled all divisions, between God and us, between ourselves and each other. 'Christ has put an end to all barriers, and since no division remained, the Jews and Gentiles became one people.' This is what St Paul says: 'I affirm that Christ has made both into one by the method of breaking down the middle barrier.' (*Commentary on the Letter to the Ephesians 2:14*, p 462)

There is a sense in which we too are called to reconcile in our own lives the seemingly irreconcilable divisions within humanity and between human beings and the natural world. Thomas Aquinas quotes the words of St Ambrose, '... feed him that is dying of hunger; if you have not fed him, you have slain him ... the bread that you withhold belongs to the hungry; the clothing that you store away belongs to the naked; and the money that you bury in the earth is the redemption and security of the penniless.' (*Summa Theologiae* 11-11, q66, a7) We have already reflected on the revealing words of Jesus Christ to St Teresa of Avila:

> I have no hands now but yours
> to embrace my wounded people;
> I have no eyes now but yours
> to look with compassion on my suffering ones;
> I have no tongue now but yours
> to speak redeeming words to my hopeless children;
> I have no feet now but yours
> to bring the good news of freedom to my oppressed family;
> I have no ears now but yours
> to listen with love to my voiceless victims of injustice.
> (Author's translation)

Transforming Eucharist

Against the background of a theology of creation and of a truly incarnational understanding of revelation, christology and sacramental theology take on a radical shift in meaning. Whether we reflect on the sacramentality of Jesus Christ, of the church, or of the particular sacraments, a new perspective on the role of being a Christian today unfolds before the eyes of our souls. For instance, Fr Edward Schillebeeckx has written: 'The church reveals, proclaims, and celebrates in thankfulness the deepest dimension of that which is being fulfilled in the world ... The church is, in fact, the world where the world has come fully to itself, where the world confesses and acknowledges the deepest mystery of its own life, the mystery of salvation ...'[2] And Karl Rahner refers to the individual sacraments as the revelation and celebration of what already lies within creation.

An immense revision of sacramental theology is waiting to be written in a popular form. This balancing revision will invigorate the church. It will reveal the person of Jesus, the Church of God's People, and the individual sacraments as confirming and celebrating the holiness of every aspect of creation, of nature and of human experiences. It will restore the blessing of the unity and intimacy between God and ourselves that was once-for-all achieved in the incarnation. It will affirm and guarantee the silent but irrepressible intimations of the human heart that 'nothing human is alien'. The challenge to those involved in Christian formation, in adult education, and in effective catechesis for a new millennium, is to pursue the rediscovery of this basic tradition which will usher in 'the new springtime' that Pope John Paul longs for.

For example, it seems such a pity that so many rich veins of meaning at the centre of the eucharistic celebration have remained unexplored for so long by so many of us. (A following reflection will take up some life-giving and traditional revelations to do with this sacrament in more detail.) Just now, in the spirit of this fourth *Moment*, let us look briefly at the eucharist as the sacrament of compassion and transformation. So much has been written and preached about the Sacred Mystery in terms of individual piety, of personal salvation and of a time-bound concept of transubstantiation. Also, many of us are quite familiar with a eucharistic catechesis and celebration based on the re-enactment and re-presentation of the historical Last Supper, when Jesus made himself, and thus eternal salvation, available to all for all time. Holy Communion is food for the soul, and saves us from our sins. There is no end to the flow of good literature and defensible practices of private eucharistic devotions generated, for example, through the decades of this century.

But there are times when we feel deep and satisfying fulfilment in meditating on some long-neglected aspects of the eucharist such as its consecration of human compassion and its universally transforming symbolism. Just as we perennially make our God too small, so too we often make our eucharist too small. To be sure, in Roman Catholic terms at least, a persistently loyal devotion to the Mass during generations of persecution has kept the faith of our fathers and mothers vibrantly alive and well all over the world. What causes anxiety are certain common and misleading strains of eucharistic understanding where a static kind of dualism prevails; where the breaking of the bread and the crushing of the grapes are not seen in a truly sacramental way; where the living memory of the dying and rising of Christ are not seen as symbolic of the breaking of our lives in eucharistic living; where the holy signs of bread and wine are not seen as the sacrament of a world, suffering injustice and war, waiting and groaning for salvation.

Touching the mystery
The faithful reader of this book will by now be aware of the main strands of incarnational theology that interweave repeatedly throughout its pages. Our consideration of the eucharist, for instance, springs from the traditional Christian vision of a world already filled and permeated with God's loving presence, a world that tends towards the celebration in sacrament and symbol of its own amazing story, its beauty and its hopes, its struggles and its successes, a world evolving inexorably into the final *Omega* of Jesus Christ when, one day, God will be all in all.

Here in the eucharist, the mystery unfolds; the real presence of our ultimate being 'in Christ' comes to us through the shared 'fruit of the earth and the work of human hands'. In this light, the eucharist intensely symbolises a holy and whole creation: nature and history, the produce of the earth and the productions of human creativity, the self-expression of the human and the self-communication of God are subsumed into one sacramental intensity. In a world threatened with ecological disintegration and cultural uprootedness from nature, the eucharist nourishes faith into gracious, ultimate wholeness ... In the 'holy communion' offered in the eucharist, not only does God communicate himself in the body and blood of Christ, but also, in a profound sense, gives us back to ourselves. Our humanity is nourished into an ultimate awareness of its embodiment in a material cosmos. The most intense moment of communion with the divine is, at the same time, the most intense moment of our communion with the earth ... The Lord invites us to reconnect with the cosmos as he has done, to claim it as our own, as our larger selves, in a world of divine incarnation.[3]

These insights are not easy to understand. They challenge us to explore the mystery more deeply than we have wanted to do, or dared to do. They invite us to enter into unfamiliar but highly rewarding horizons of mind-expanding dimensions. They call us into ways of thinking about the incarnation and the eucharist that we are quite unprepared for. Rahner reminds us that when the church gathers to celebrate the eucharist, our humanity is united with the glorified humanity of Christ, and we too take part in the fulfilment and transformation of the material universe, which began in the resurrection. Such revelations arouse the passion for the possible within us. We sense something soul-sized in contemplating the vision of a universal transubstantiation, a eucharistic universe, a cosmic communion. Teilhard de Chardin, for instance, stirs our souls with his vision of a consecration of the world:

When the priest says the words 'Hoc est corpus meum', his words fall directly on the bread and directly to transform it into the individual reality of Christ. But the great sacramental operation does not cease at that local and momentary event ... All the communions of a lifetime are now one communion. All the communion of human beings now living are one communion. All the communions of all people, past, present and future are one communion ... In a secondary and generalised sense, but in a true sense, the sacramental species are formed by the totality of the world, and the duration of the creation is the time needed for its consecration. 'In Christo vivimus, movemur et sumus' – in Christ we live and move and have our being.[4]

At the end of this final *Moment*, we further develop our exploration of the transforming and compassionate connections between the incarnation and the cosmic implications of the first creation.

Cosmic connections: The new story
Even though references to the cosmos have been made re-
spectable once again by Pope John Paul II in so many of his letters and encyclicals, many people for some strange reason are
still wary of such terms. However, arising from the unprecedented studies of scientists and physicists in recent years, the old
debate between theology and cosmology can only intensify in a
new millennium. It is an 'old' tradition even though there is little
evidence of a serious consideration of it in the doctrines we grew
up with. But there is an abundant source for reflection in our
tradition, in the Hebrew and Christian scriptures, in writings
from the early church, and in the theological and spiritual treatises
of many saints, scholars and other mystics throughout the centuries. The significant developments during the last decade or so
about the implications of the incarnation for a deeper understanding of the cosmic story, arise from a number of reasons.

> These developments include the emergence of creation-cen-
> tred theologies, the promotion of a new dialogue between
> science and religion, the rediscovery of the importance of cos-
> mology, and the recognition of an ecological crisis ... The
> credibility of christology in the future will depend to a large
> degree on its ability to enter into a meaningful conversation
> with the emerging post-modern cosmologies ... [especially
> since Christianity] is a religion whose centre of gravity is the
> Word of God becoming flesh and entering into a new com-
> munion with human nature and the world in which that
> human nature exists.[5]

The good news is that there is now an emerging body of work
devoted to these issues. It is good news because scarcely a day
passes without some revelation about what is happening and
what is being discovered 'out there' in space. This very evening,
for instance, the BBC *Horizon* programme examines NASA's
'stunning findings' of life in Mars 3.5 billion years ago! It has
been my good fortune, in the course of my sabbatical wander-
ings, to sit at the feet of modern prophets such as the theolo-
gian/scientist Fr Thomas Berry and the physicist Brian
Swimme.

The 'new story' they tell is of cosmic proportions. The revelations they unfold in their talks and published research is barely
digestible by our hungry minds and hearts. We need to remember that the vast universe as we know it through astronomy and
astrophysics came into being some fifteen thousand million

years ago, give or take three or four billion years in the interests of accuracy! The 'new story', according to Berry, holds within it a strong emphasis on the fundamental unity between the galaxies, the earth, life forms and the emergence of human existence. Human existence is perceived as the earth in a particular mode of self-consciousness.

The scientists, catching up with the theologians, now assure us that everything comes from a common origin. The universe, in fact, has poured into us the creative powers necessary for its further development. So often, in our unreflective mode, we see ourselves as almost totally distinct from our world and all the things of matter. But, in fact, we are the self-awareness that provides the space for the universe to feel its own breathtaking beauty. As the heart is to the body, so are we to the universe, and to God. In the words of Julian Huxley, quoted by Teilhard de Chardin, 'humanity discovers that it is nothing else than evolution become conscious of itself.' Brian Swimme compares the earth without a human to a child without a parent.[6]

Recognising and nurturing our origins
There is a sense in which we can set the beginnings of creation into the context of our own long-term infancy. These days, we are perennially searching for our ancestral roots. We have a need to seek out and recognise our origins. It has to do with a desire to belong, to be at home within our extended family, within our planet earth, within our universe and ultimately, within God. Albert Einstein is often quoted as identifying the most important question for each human being – is the universe we inhabit a friendly place or not? The response will significantly determine the shape of our lives and the degree of satisfaction and joy that we experience. Were we destined from all time to be created from our primeval parents or did we happen by accident, or through a later intervention by God? Freeman Dyson, a contemporary physicist, suggests an answer. 'It almost seems,' he writes, 'as if the universe must in some sense have known that we were coming.' The theologian's reasons for putting this sentiment in much more confident terms are easy to find today.

Faith affirms that we have been addressed by a Word of promise that uncovers the meaning not only of our individual lives and of our whole history, but also of the entire universe. Even though the Word breaks out into the daylight of consciousness with the birth of persons and human history, faith allows us to discern a great promise even in the earliest moments of the cosmic adventure. When we are convinced by faith and science of the bonding between our own lives, humanity as a whole, and the known and unknown realms of space, only then are we filled with a new compassion. This compassion is inevitable once we recognise the intimacy of long infancy over billions of years with God's grand design for the future of creation. And this original vision of God, this divinely implanted seed of compassion, then gives rise to a maternal and relentless impulse to protect and transform all of life because, in the end, it is ourselves we are taking care of.

For a long time, a question about two disconnected aspects of the mystery of our faith has occupied my mind. I suppose you could see this pre-occupation in terms of what is traditionally described as faith seeking understanding – *fides quarens intellectum*. So I often wondered at the strange space between our picture of the God of the churches and that of the God of creation. The one seemed to me so full of a sense of loss, of guilt and of homelessness. As exiles we do not really belong here. We are strangers in a foreign land, pining for our true home in heaven. The other picture is a vibrant one of God's delight in this world, of creativity, diversity, excitement and wild, divine extravagance. The world is God's beloved body and we ourselves are the very temples and home of God. How could I reconcile these seemingly opposite pictures of creation and incarnation as handed down to me by the same Christian tradition?

The 'Four Moments' of this book weave in and out of this dilemma, trying to hold on to what is essential in both, trying to lose nothing of our fundamental, inherited wisdom. On the one hand we study and pray the stories and devotions of the churches that focus on the dark death of our Saviour, at the hands of our originally sinful condition, arising out of a well-documented Fall. On the other hand we rejoice and wonder over the stories of a love-struck God who unconditionally blesses us with incomprehensible giftedness; who created an extraordinarily beautiful universe full of quarks and dark holes, that is unfolding with ever-increasing magnificence before the awe-filled eyes of our minds and hearts and bodies. So how do we reconcile the naturally graced and environmental imperative to love and cherish the earth as our home and God's home, with the other religious imperative to live as though we were guilty outcasts and homeless? It was only during the last few years of trying to focus my scattered glimpses of these two seemingly irreconcilable pictures and imperatives, that one possible and tentative shape began to emerge.

A sense of sacrament

The following paragraphs are about building a bridge between these two given realities. How can God's self-emptying into a fallen world, God's dying on a cross in Jesus, and creation's self-transcendence, the flowering of an evolving, naturally stumbling process, be held together? I remember one day in summer listening to Fr Barnabas Aherne, a most highly respected scripture scholar, as he pondered about 'realised eschatology' and the time when God will be 'all in all'. He spoke about the possibility of our universe gradually, inevitably evolving into what we vaguely call 'heaven'. This observation shocked those of us who had been nourished on a dualistic diet of the fallenness of material things and the urgent need for all of us to transfer our exilic presence here as swiftly and as uncontaminatedly as possible to another shore. But his throw-away line has stayed with me all these years.

Karl Rahner, in his theological and spiritual writings, was the first visionary to put the pieces together for me. He set out to recover a traditional and forgotten understanding of sacramentality. We have touched on this liberating insight in the three previous *Moments*. He clarified the notion of Jesus as sacrament. Jesus is the sacrament, not just of the chosen people, not just of all humanity, but also of the whole world and of all creation. The 'line of promise' running through the stories and prophecies of the Hebrew scriptures have resonances of universal implications.

In the *hypostatic union* in the one person of Jesus, we find the unique and irrevocable meeting between creation's graced openness to divine fulfilment and God's creative and loving desire to achieve this intimacy. In Christ was completed and perfected the first longing of creation for God and God's own desire to fulfil that longing by becoming eternally united with humanity and creation. In Christ, the listening ear of a groaning and straining creation heard the divine music it was coded to hear from the beginning – the unceasingly uttered Word of a self-surrendering God. Christ revealed, once-for-all, and in his own human self, the 'hidden agenda' of God's initial creation, by being at once 'the way forward' for the final and unrepeatable break-

through of that creation into God and, at the same time, by being
'the way in' for the ever-approaching, self-disposing divine
emptying of God into the world that God had first conceived out
of love.

In his evolutionary christology, Rahner tells us that Jesus
Christ is God's gift to the universe, bestowed definitively and ir-
reversibly. The substance of the promise to Israel and the church
is, in the final analysis, nothing other than the very being of God.
The same divine self-gift that planted hope in the hearts of our
ancestors in faith had earlier aroused the cosmos into being, and
continually stirred it toward further evolution. Revelation is the
self-gift of the promising and beckoning God, not just to history
but to the entire world of nature which includes us. Cosmic
evolution itself becomes a sacramental revelation of God's personality. From the moment of its creation, nature too, even apart
from human existence, has felt the promise of God. This
promise, charted in the Hebrew scriptures as relentlessly surfac-
ing in the stormy oceans of evolution and human history, may
be read both cosmologically and historically, as finding a resolu-
tion in the Messiah. He is the focal-point of the 'breaking in' of
God's promise to the entire emergent universe, and the 'breaking through' of the waiting readiness of the universe and humanity for that blessed moment of disclosure and fulfilment,
and therefore of healing and redemption. In the second *Moment*
of our book, we referred to Jesus as 'the scandal of particularity'
– how could the almighty being of a transcendent God be encompassed in one particular moment of time, in one particular
human being, in one particular spot on the earth? But maybe
there is no 'scandal' here. Once we develop a 'sense of sacrament' along the lines we are pursuing, through prayer and reading, we find that, in the divine economy of creation and salvation in space and time, there can be no other way. God will, and
must, be true to the finite nature of God's new way of being in
creation, of becoming incarnate as Emmanuel (God with us) in a
human being, and of continuing that essential and sacramental
presence in ordinary things like bread and wine.

God's self-emptying: Creation's self-transcendence
Recently I read a most revealing book, *Mystery and Promise: a
Theology of Revelation*, by John Haught. It has helped me enormously in finding a coherence for this section. In the following
paragraphs I am deeply indebted to his wonderful insights. In

the latter part of his book he addresses himself to some questions about the process of evolution in the light of incarnation. If God is all-powerful, why was not the universe created in its final, fixed state once for all? Why fifteen billion years or so of struggle, randomness, and waste before our own species eventually materialised? And why so long before God's secret was revealed in the man Jesus?

I am anxious at this point to reassure the reader that these are not idle speculations for idle minds. I truly believe that they have a direct relevance for the way we live out our lives each day as Christian people, for our understanding of the sacraments we regularly celebrate, and for the way we pray whenever we can. I believe, too, that they have immense implications for the way we watch or listen to the Ten o'clock News, for the way we look at the moon on a cloudy night and for the way we hold our breath while a small child takes its first step.

What follows is not for speed-reading. It is to be slowly digested like rich food. Forgive me for giving advice, but it is to be lingered over, and reflected upon, as one would interiorise a letter of love. And so to the questions. This is how Haught endeavours to open a window with a beautiful view. With his permission, I quote him at length.

The cosmos in its finitude is unable to receive the boundlessness of God's self-gift in any single instant. A finite reality, even if it has the dimensions of our seemingly unfathomable universe, is never sufficiently expansive to contain an infinite love. Hence in its response to the overflowing self-bestowal of a promising God, the cosmos would be subject to an incremental intensification of its own being in order to partake ever more fully of the divine life given over to it. In other words, it would be invited to evolve. The finite world would move and grow (undergo a kind of self-transcendence) as a result of continual impregnation by the self-giving mystery of God. Evolution, when interpreted by the revelatory images of God's love, is both the expression of God's gift of self to the world and at the same time the world's response to the non-coercive, defenceless divine self-bestowal. Karl Rahner interprets the Christ-event cosmically as the definitive and irreversible moment of God's self-communication to the evolving world and at the same time the climactic reception by the world of God's revelatory promise.[7]

On reading this for the first time, two rather inept, inaccurate and very ordinary images come to mind. They may, nevertheless, partially clarify one aspect of this kind of 'doing theology'. One is the image of a cassette tape, where one tape gradually spins itself out as it releases its music on to another that grows and is enriched in the process. Another picture is that of the egg-timer or hour-glass. Gradually, one part of it empties itself out into the other which, in turn, finds a new fullness. These examples are misleading because they are mechanistic and without personality. Anyway, our author continues:

> The universe cannot contain the infinite in any single moment. Hence it is allowed, but not forced, to inch gradually forward by way of what science knows as evolution. Only after a period of time would it move toward a fuller participation in the promise that comes to light historically in the faith associated with Abraham. Christians, however, may understand the decisiveness of Christ as the moment in evolution when God's promise and self-gift, which have been continually and creatively present to the cosmos from its birth, are embraced by a human being without reservation. In Christ, the vision of God for the universe is accepted fully, and the significance of cosmic process eternally guaranteed.[8]

From the perspective of science alone, evolution is a happening without an intrinsic pattern of promise. It could be seen as a random series of events that could lead anywhere. But from the perspective of divine revelation, universal evolution is the love-story of a self-humbling God in the process of entering ever more intimately into our world and drawing it towards a graced fulfilment through its own transcendence. 'If we do not see things in the light of compassion,' writes Kathleen Raine, 'we do not see them at all.'

In the second *Moment* of this book, the *via negativa*, we touched on a theology of the cross. We reflected on the unfamiliar notion of a God who suffers in the Word-made-flesh.

> It is especially in the crucified man, Jesus of Nazareth, that Christians have discerned the disclosure of God's humility. The conviction of a divine *kenosis* could scarcely have entered our consciousness apart from this event. And out of this faith, theological reflection is gradually learning to regard the divine self-emptying as an eternal characteristic of God. Such humble condescension, manifest historically in the cross, is of the everlasting essence of God, and not just an ad

hoc historical occurrence only externally connected to God's inner life ... Creation may be understood, not so much as the consequence of God's self-expansion as of God's self-limitation. God's allowing the world to exist is made possible by a restraining of divine omnipotence. Divine power humbly 'contracts' itself, surrendering any urge to manipulate events or persons ... Creation is less the consequence of divine 'force' than of God's self withdrawal. It is especially in the image of the crucified that Christian faith is given the key to this interpretation of creation.[9]

All of this may seem too demanding, too 'way-out', too speculative for many readers. This, at first, was my impression too. But gradually it all began to make sense. It was as though, once I had worked through my intellectual resistance, I had known this revelation all along, by heart. The emerging synthesis did not entail any playing-down of the theological doctrines I had gathered from the 'penny catechism' or learned in the seminary. But it did mean that I had to do a great deal of sifting around for the origins and emphases of much of what I had been told. When I began to understand the historical context of the teachings I had received, and when I had read more widely into the vast theological riches of the Catholic tradition, I found that my head and heart were coming together. It wasn't that what we were told was wrong; it was simply that we had not been told the whole story.

Compassion for the earth
The previous *Moments* of this book prepare us for a passionate concern for all humanity and for the earth that sustains us. This issue is of particular and urgent immediacy at a time when our globe is now threatened by an environmental crisis of unprecedented proportions.

It has often been argued that an excessive anthropocentrism (over-emphasis on the human dimension of our world) is the main source of our current environmental crises. An exaggerated focus on human significance places value so heavily upon our own species that it thereby drains value away from the non-human aspects of nature. And this robbery leaves nature open to our own abuse. For this reason, our locating of revelation as a cosmic and not just an historical reality already has salutary environmental implications, for it counters the excessive anthropocentrism that has deformed so much of Christian theology. God's gift of self is offered to the whole of the universe and not just to humans ...[10]

It is only in the light of incarnation that the Christian can make all these observations with confidence. As the reader will be well aware of, there is much more to the 'new story' than has been touched upon here. The exciting dialogue will continue for many a day, as the secrets of the universe are revealed before our eyes. In this final part of the book, what needs to be understood is the oneness and intimacy of everything. For Paul, Jesus is the Wisdom referred to in the Hebrew scriptures. Wisdom is the artist who played with God in crafting the first creation. The same creative Word of God that is active in the beginning is now the same creative Word that was made flesh in Jesus. And it is that Word that still urges humanity into the new evolution of human and cosmic compassion.

When we struggle to hold creation, incarnation and the continuing activity of the Holy Spirit in human hearts and in everything together, we find glimpses of meaning in the words of Brian Swimme. 'The human face,' he suggests, 'is there in the structure of the first fireball.' This suggestion brings to mind the remarks of Tertullian, during the infancy of Christianity. He is quoted in Vatican Councils I and II as holding that when God was creating Adam and Eve from the mud of the earth, his blueprint, so to speak, was God's own shape in the figure of Jesus Christ. This observation must surely give us much food for thought. What is needed in theology today is a rediscovery of this revelation about the indwelling of God in the grand scheme of things, a relocation of redemption in the context of creation, and a new understanding of ourselves in relation to each other and to the cosmos.

This would mean, in effect, that the Logos of God was and is personally present in the earth and in the universe. In the light of the incarnation, therefore, the earth and the universe today assume special divine significance, analogous to the divine dignity of the person, deserving similar respect and reverence. There is something sacred, indeed sacramental, about the earth and the universe and their mutual processes in virtue of the incarnation. Through the incarnation, God has taken 'matter' into God's self ... It is hardly surprising that it was a cosmologist, A. N. Whitehead, who with his keen sense of the presence of God pervading the cosmic processes, could write, 'The world lives by its incarnation of

God in itself'… The final word, however, must be reserved for T. S. Eliot who captures and encapsulates the spirit of our reflections:

These are only hints and guesses.
Hints followed by guesses; and the rest
Is prayer, observance, discipline, thought and action.
The hint half guessed, the gift half understood
is Incarnation.[11]

In this fourth section of *Passion for the Possible*, we are trying to make connections – connections between creation and incarnation, between incarnation and continuing incarnation in today's world. We are trying to understand that when these connections are even partially made, we are filled with compassion. This compassion springs from seeing all people as the children of one Parent, and therefore as sisters and brothers sharing one home. This home is the world we live in, our gracious mother, who in turn is dependent on her extended family of the whole universe and the wider cosmos. This revealed awareness is the source of the compassion that compels us to reach out and transform each other, and to take a new interest in, and even passion for, the health and well-being of our beloved planet earth.

It is only when we see ourselves as one with others, with the world and with the universe, that the grace of compassion fills our lives. When Jesus wept over Jerusalem and spoke so lovingly about the elements of nature, he was deeply aware of the unity of all things. He saw himself, the people of the world, and all creation as part and parcel of God's own self.

He is the image of the invisible God, the first born of all creation; for in him all things were created, in heaven and on earth, visible and invisible … all things were created through him and for him. He is before all things, and in him all things hold together. (Col 1:15-18)

Included throughout the *Moments* of this book are suggestions about the nature of sin arising from each of the 'theological glimpses'. In terms of this last section, the notion of human sinfulness would take on some of the following faces. It has something to do with our blindness to revealed truth. Jonathan Schell remarked that 'in extinction a darkness falls over the world, not because the lights have gone out but because the eyes that behold the light have been closed.' If our metaphor of the world as God's body is accepted, then sin is the refusal to be part of that body, the special and unique part we are called to be for God to be 'all in all'. To sin is to refuse to take responsibility for nurturing, loving and befriending this body and all its parts. Sin is the refusal to realise one's radical interdependence with all that lives; it is the desire to set oneself apart from all others as not needing them or being needed by them. Sin is the refusal to be the eyes, the consciousness of the cosmos. 'Unblinkered,' the Buddhists remind us, 'the eye sees rightly: unblocked, the ear hears accurately.' Sally McFague outlines the implications of seeing the world as the body of God:

> It is the basis for a revived sacramentalism, that is, a perception of the divine as visible, as present – palpably present in our world. But it is a kind of sacramentalism that is painfully conscious of the world's vulnerability, its preciousness, its uniqueness. The beauty of the world and its ability to sustain the vast multitude of species it supports is not there for the taking. The world is a body that must be carefully tended, that must be nurtured, protected, guided, loved, and befriended both as valuable in itself – for like us, it is an expression of God – and as necessary for the continuation of life. In the metaphor of the world as the body of God, the resurrection becomes a worldly, present, inclusive reality, for this body is offered to all: This is my Body.[12]

We are asked today to redress an imbalance in our inherited theology and spirituality that is leading to dire consequences for the future of our world and even of creation itself. By refusing the balance of radical interdependence, we, the only conscious ones among the beloved, disrupt the ontological order and threaten life itself. McFague reminds us that this destruction is only too evident in our oppression of others owing to gender, race, or class, and in the genocide of other peoples, the deterioration of the ecosphere, and the threat of nuclear disaster. What results from the human selfishness that is addicted to the exploitation of all that is not 'self' is estrangement and alienation, the wounding of the body of God, the fragmenting of relationships at all levels, the refusal of living interdependently. Hierarchies, dualisms and outcasts become the norm: the inclusive vision of universal fulfilment is perverted beyond all imagination.

If ever the traditionally accepted scriptural definition of sin as 'missing the mark', as a misreading of the compass of life, as an unawareness of 'right relationships', needed a context, it is to be found in such attitudes. Sin is here understood as a costly blindness, an original and deep-seated flaw from which none of us is free. There can be no *via transformativa* in a dualistic doctrine of creation and incarnation. A monarchical, dualistic model of the mystery of God's becoming human encourages attitudes of militarism, consumerism, racism and sexism. It condones control through violence and oppression leading to elitism and individualism. It sees non-human life as a source of manipulation for the well-being of the dominant species. But an inclusive, non-hierarchical model of the world as God's body encourages holistic attitudes of responsibility and care for the vulnerable and oppressed. It acts through persuasion and attraction. It has a great deal of wisdom to share about the body and nature. It is fuelled by compassion and it loves to celebrate.

Passion for the possible

Sometimes the title of a book can only be finalised when it has been written. But this title was in my heart and head long before the first sentence was put down. I still think that it is an apt summary of what the book is about – the fierce desire to explore the potential for self-esteem arising from our own divine beauty, for a sense of our capacity for finding the healing light in our dark moments, for a new appreciation of our God-implanted creativity, and finally for our calling to redeem humanity and the world before it is too late.

This profound awareness, this passionate desire, this inexorable thrust towards completion, is already the work of God in us, whether consciously known as such or not. It is the unfolding of the promise entrusted to the world from the beginning of time. It is the growing, relentless and infinite seed implanted in the good earth of all life – the seed that will never die no matter what storms blow in winter nights. In spite of the nightmares of our experiences, it is still the blessed awakening of God's dream enclosed in every human heart.

Like all true visions, the 'passion for the possible' outlined in these pages is more about glimpses and hints than about logically structured arguments and doctrinal examination. Although I have taken pains to indicate the orthodoxy of the theology from which these reflections spring, the connecting and linking throughout the book may seem vague and haphazard. All I can say is that if you trust your heart as well as your head, something will resonate within you. It is written for searching souls, for those who may feel alienated from the main-stream churches but whose mystical, contemplative and prophetic gifts are as good as new. These are the enduring elements of our blessed heritage by virtue of our birth and of our baptism.

> We bear a divine seed within us, the seed that wants to thrust through all the encrustations of the material world, to grow and reveal itself. Humans are in a continual process of liberation from the constraints of the ego. Our feverish search for meaning is simply that evolutionary power of the divine ... The more we open ourselves to our divine core, the better and more quickly we shall solve our social and political problems. The men and women of the future, to paraphrase a line by Karl Rahner, will be mystics, or they won't be at all.[13]

These are soul-sized enterprises. And they take time to mature within us. Like the seed that grows while the farmer sleeps, the vision once glimpsed works its way within us and can never be forgotten. 'Do not forget the things your eyes have seen, nor let them slip from your heart. Rather tell them to your children and your childrens' children.' (Deut 4:1) There will, of course, be conflicts of orthodoxies arising from our childhood religious education, a shaking of the foundations of our inherited doctrinal formation, there will be personal and painful turmoil, there will be the immense fear of change and of letting go into new ways of thinking. Even for those who are open to the Spirit, there may be a long wait. But once the flame is lit, the fire will burn. The outcome is secure.

No hickorynut spirit

High over Snowdonia this evening, as though pursued for their very lives, a desperate flock of ragged clouds suddenly came up from the east and raced off towards the ocean in a spectacular display of sun-filtered formation. I recalled, as I admired this spectacular pageant of the skies, a remark made by Herman Hesse at a similar moment. He saw the moving clouds as a sacrament of humanity's eternal pilgrimage home to God. A quarter-moon was already lifting herself high into place with a quiet elegance. I was on my way back across the Clwyd valley to St Beuno's Retreat Centre where my companions were waiting. The small lambs had finally stopped annoying their mothers with their insatiable nudging and muzzling for milk. The sea was a distant murmur. Suddenly, on this becalmed evening, and for no reason that I can remember, I found myself thinking about heaven and hell.

For some strange reason, I have never been particularly worried about what happens to me when I die. To be sure, I do not feel deserving in any way of a heavenly reward, but from an early age I decided to leave that whole issue to God. Fellow-students, in my seminary years, were always unhappy about this rather cavalier approach to the grim threat of a Last Judgement. 'Do you worry,' I used to ask them, 'about the welcome that your Mom and Dad will have for you when you arrive home for Christmas? Will they remember your name? Will there be a bed for you, some food, a place to be comfortable? Will they tell you all the news about what's been going on in the lives of those you love?' Suspiciously they would give the obvious answer. Gradually they would see the point that I was making. Along these lines I have often presented reasons for my seemingly presumptuous and irresponsible attitude to my final destination.

More than once, the expression of this simplistic hope has landed me in hot water. I have often elaborated on such sentiments by adding that I have great difficulty in believing that God ever punishes people for the sins of their lives. Amid shouts of 'What about Hitler? What about Judas?' I would then explain the orthodox Catholic position on hell and on those who might be in it. Traditional teaching obliges us to assent to the reality of some kind of hell, but does not insist that it is inhabited! I am still surprised at how upset people become when I play down the punitive side of God's parenthood. Even when I try to point out that our sin always carries within it its own destructive elements, diminishing our true humanity invariably and relentlessly in the here and now, there is still a popular demand on the part of the 'righteous' for another more fearsome and eternal burning for those wretched sinners.

Anyway, as I trudged home this evening, I wondered about these 'last things', and whether I could find an acceptable way of looking at them. Maybe its true, I reflected, that the only part of us that lives on after we die is the love we have in us when we die. If there is no love, there is no after-life. The whole promise of life for the loveless person has come, literally, to nothing. For such a person, if any such soul exists, which I doubt, the hell is the loss of heaven, not a prolonged and repeatedly inflicted torture that defies the worst horrors of any concentration camp. We are born to create and incarnate love in the world and in each other, as God did in creation, as creation did in Mary, as Mary did in Jesus, and as Jesus did in his death and resurrection.

If, in the course of our lives, we have managed only to diminish and destroy the precious graces of love and trust; if, by our selfishness and closedness, we have added only to the lovelessness and fear of the world; and if heaven is made up of the intimate transcendence of compassion within the fallenness of our flawed nature, then maybe there is nothing left in us to live on in our empty souls. And even then we must ask if there is such a thing as the completely empty soul. Maybe, at the very end, each person has a final choice – to opt for or to refuse the freely-offered invitation to join the company of the blessed. But for those in whom all light is extinguished, and in whom all love has long been absent, maybe there is no possibility of choice. Choosing heaven implies at least a desire for shared joy.

Let me start again. The purpose of incarnation is to establish forever that love is all that matters. For the Christian, this revelation is a 'given'. Jesus was love personified. A long time before him, creation itself was an act of divine love. The whole story of a universe evolving into the fleshing of God is a stunning lovestory. The whole point of the 'Word becoming human' is that each one of us would continue, like Mary did, to incarnate heavenly compassion into our earthly condition. Through mutual forgiveness and openness, through our daily living out of the eucharistic sacrament, we co-create with the Holy Spirit that final consummation when God will be 'all in all'. Where God is, love is. Where there's no love, God is absent.

If then, at the end of my days, I have no love in me; if I have not opened myself to giving it, receiving it, or drawing it out of others; if I have persistently refused it, denied it or disbelieved in it, then what of the eternal do I carry? If it is in the finite only, and not in the infinite that I live and move and have my being, then surely the death of my body is the death of all of me. Everything dies when I die. 'We only take with us when we die,' said the colonel in *Babette's Feast*, 'what we have given away while we lived.' There is no remainder; nothing is left over. Dear God, what is the point of demanding a further attrition beyond the loss of everlasting ecstacy? Why do some 'righteous' Christians still cry out for the atrocity of an eternity of mad devils pitch-forking escaping and grief-stricken souls back into a cauldron of never-ending despair?

But even as I reflect on these huge issues, I wonder if anyone ever fulfills the conditions for eternal non-existence. How can someone who is the fruit and child of a totally loving Mother-God, whose very existence is created only from a passionate de-sire for its everlasting joy, persistently and wilfully deny its own birthright, freely and persistently spurn the ever-present and gracious offer of a healing salvation and a fulfilment of every pursuit of happiness, no matter how mistaken, misguided or terribly misjudged the evil object of this pursuit may be. The Rhineland mystics of the middle ages were often accused of bor-dering on the 'brink of universalism' in their understanding of God's will for the salvation of all creation. Our own Julian of Norwich, for instance, has been accused of this 'heresy' when she maintains that the indestructable seeds of our Tremendous Lover's life, infused into every living thing, can never be negated.

One last thought on the phenomenon of purgatory. This 'doctrine' is disregarded by many because of its traditional de-scription as a 'mini-hell'. But in all main religions, both the pro-found thinkers and the heart-people, understand the human need for a *space* to grow, a *time* for our eyes to get accustomed to the light, an ante-room of adjustment before the revelation of a great presence. Every time we opt for loving rather than fearing, we must die a little. The laws of nature and of life, in our earthly condition, allow only for a *gradual* kind of growing, through pu-rification and simplification, towards further graced ways of

being and becoming. We may fall in love through a sudden conversion, but staying in love takes longer! Nor can we stand
much reality, if it comes all at once; or much truth. All I'm saying
is that, given the fallenness and flawedness of our ambiguous
but lovely nature, it makes some kind of sense to believe in the
necessity of a *process* of healing, of redeeming, of completing,
even in the next life, before our originally blessed souls can live
with ease and joy in the bright presence of the full light of God's
selfless love.

> Tell all the Truth but tell it slant
> Success in circuit lies
> Too bright for our infirm delight
> The Truth's superb surprise
> As lightning to the children eased
> With explanation kind
> The Truth must dazzle gradually
> Or ever man be blind.

By now the racing clouds have escaped their celestial pursuer,
the moon is beautiful and I am back in my silent room. My last
thought for the reader is not to take too much notice of my wandering mind. I'm only thinking 'out loud'. The Buddhist teacher
always reminds the listener to ignore all that has been said. Let
your heart discern what is worth remembering. Throw the rest
away. But before I finish I want to tell you how delighted I was
to discover, just now, the reflections of an old Cherokee woman
who had 'figgered things out' along the lines of my own reflections:

> Granma said everybody has two minds. One of the minds
> has to do with the necessaries for body-living. You had to use
> it to figure how to get shelter and eating and such like for the
> body. She said you had to use it to mate and have young 'uns
> and such. She said we had to have that mind so as we could
> carry on. But she said we had another mind that had nothing
> at all to do with such. She said it was the spirit-mind.

> Granma said if you used the body-living mind to think
> greedy or mean; if you was always cuttin' at folks with it and
> figuring how to gain more profit off'n them ... then you
> would shrink up your spirit-mind to no bigger'n a hickor'-
> nut.

> Granma said that when your body died, the body-living
> mind died with it, and if that's the way you had thought all

your life there you was, stuck with a hickor'nut spirit, as the spirit-mind was all that lived when everything else died. Then, Granma said, when you was born back – as you was bound to be – then, there you was, born with a hickor'nut spirit-mind that had practical no understanding of anything. Then it might shrink up to the size of a pea and could disappear, if the body-living mind took over total. In such case, you lost your spirit complete.

That's how you become dead people. Granma said you could easy spot dead people. She said dead people when they looked at a woman saw nothing but dirty; when they looked at other people, they saw nothing but bad; when they looked at a tree they saw nothing but lumber and profit; never beauty. Granma said they was dead people walking around.

Granma said that the spirit-mind was like any other muscle. If you used it, it got bigger and stronger. She said the only way it could get that way was using it to understand, but you couldn't open the door to it until you quit being greedy and such with your body-mind. Then understanding commenced to take up, and the more you tried to understand, the bigger it got.

Natural, she said, understanding and love was the same thing; except folks went at it back'ards too many times, trying to pretend they loved things when they didn't understand them. Which can't be done.

I see right out that I was going to commence trying to understand practical everybody, for I sure didn't want to come up with no hickor'nut spirit.
(*The Education of Little Tree*, Forrest Carter, University of New Mexico Press, pp 59, 60)

Awakening to the possible

The greatest poem ever known
Is one most poets have outgrown
The poetry, innate, untold
Of being only four years old

Tom, aged four, very early one morning rushed into the bed-
room exclaiming in great excitement,
   'Marg, I can breathe! I can breathe! Watch me! Watch me!'
Deep noisy breaths in and out, then,
'Can *you* breathe?'
'Yes.'
'Show me, show me!'

Why would I want to start reflections on the transforming heart
with that very personal memory, which for me is still so vivid
and poignant? I think because in reflecting back on my own personal journey these last few years, and in observing what is happening to others around me, that incident seems to catch the
essence and mystery of beginning to live with a child-like freshness towards life, with a heart that can appreciate and celebrate.
What is usually seen as a very routine and rather mechanical exercise, breathing, is all at once an occasion of illumination and
reverence. Unless we become ill in some way and begin to find
breathing difficult, we hardly give the intricate workings of our
respiratory system a second thought, just taking breathing for
granted. But Tom that morning experienced real feelings of awe
and delight in discovering something about himself, something
so exciting, so surprising, so new, that he had to share the great
news.
   What he managed to communicate to me that morning was
far more than he ever could have imagined. He had entered into
a level of awareness that transcends the mundane, that was in its
truest sense exploring the realm of the mystic, and it burst forth
from him in a spirit of genuine reverence. His pleasure and excitement were infectious, but the beauty of his spontaneous out-
burst, paradoxically, lies in the recognition that it is the ordi-

nary, everyday workings of our lives that have the capacity to become moments of insight and transformation. In such moments we have a glimpse of what it means to be living with an almost tangible sense of the mystery and power of our human nature, already graced and blessed, and part of a universe created to manifest in an untold variety of ways, God's loving and sustaining presence. Our everyday reality wants everything to be healed and whole and new. How far this is from what we sense much of the time, and what we witness so often in the world around us! Yet my own experience over the last few years of being in the company of others who are trying to follow the prompting of the Spirit stirring within their hearts, has led me to rejoice in the many signs of healing and transformation that are springing up here in Garforth, offering fresh hope and meaning to wounded and broken lives.

The observation of a trusted friend who has regularly visited this parish of St Benedict's during the last twenty-five years is similar to comments of many others, and to feelings of my own: 'This place feels really alive! It is good to be here!' How is it that you can feel when a place is really alive? What is it that gives you that intuitive 'knowing' that something amazing, something life-giving and hope-filled, is going on? What is it that attracts others to want to become part of it all? I could have begun these reflections by describing in detail the practical developments in our small part of the planet these last few years, but somehow it felt more important to try to convey a sense of the 'heart' of our community, to convey the feeling of being involved in a process, an uncharted journey which we are trying to navigate together, and of discovering and connecting with many other people and places where this seems to be happening too, not knowing where it will all end, but trusting that God is at the helm.

That is why I started with Tom's story. It is because so many of our hearts are coming alive more and more to who we are, to the presence of God in each situation; because we are growing more courageous about trusting in the love in which we are held, even (and perhaps most especially) in the darkest times; because we are beginning to trust each other enough to reveal our own weakness and vulnerability – and because of all of this, small miracles begin to happen, and we find we are approaching life in a different way. Like Tom's, ours is a journey of discovery, about ourselves, about new possibilities and challenges, and,

like him, we want to share the good news. The fire within us becomes contagious – others begin to light up around us. There is a
natural outpouring of energy which reaches out to touch and
heal other hearts, and begins to open people to their own unique
worth and potential. The more we experience beauty, grace, and
healing in our own lives, the more we are able to notice and delight in those qualities in others. This is especially true when we
are in touch with our own woundedness. Then we can reach out
in compassion to those around us who are hurting too. Perhaps
that is the only real test of our journey together as a community,
and of my own personal struggle to grow. Are we becoming
more compassionate? Are we moving any closer to developing
and experiencing patterns of forgiveness, generosity, and joy in
our lives? Are we reaching out and searching for ways of healing and nurturing, of repenting and celebrating, of sacrificing
and sharing lavishly, of honouring the sacred air, water, soil and
resources of our mother earth? In short, to use our parish logo,
'St Benedict's, A Place To Grow,' ... are we growing as individuals, and are we creating the opportunity and time to honour and
nurture each person's efforts to do the same? The only starting
place for me can be my own story, in the hope that it might illustrate something of the way a 'Spirituality of the Heart', or
'Creation-centred Spirituality' has enabled this process of transformation. This process is often evident in the tiny miracles of
compassion and outreach amongst people here who are struggling to be more fully human these years.

My introduction to the four paths of creation spirituality had
an immediate and dramatic effect. It was as if some part of me
that had been dormant for decades suddenly came to life. What I
heard and read, what I experienced resonated so deeply within
me that it was as if at last there was a way of articulating and exploring the deepest parts of myself. An emphasis on an incarnational approach to theology allowed me to see how distorted my
image of God had become. No longer did I feel that I had to
prove myself worthy of love, but began to realise that I am always held in love, even in my sinfulness, and for all eternity. It
has become possible to appreciate what St Paul was telling the
people of Rome.

Nothing therefore can come between us and the love of
Christ ... For I am certain of this: neither death nor life, no
angel, no prince, nothing that exists, nothing still to come,
not any power, or height or depth, nor any created thing can

ever come between us and the love of God made visible in Jesus Christ our Lord. (Rom 6:35, 38-39)

That love is expressed in and through the created world, and what a delight it has been to be graced with so many epiphanies of the beauty, diversity and sheer extravagance of the Creator in designing such a universe. I would have to own that the re-reading of the creation story, and the growing awareness of my interconnectedness and role in the ongoing creativity of the universe, has been a wonderfully energising realisation, but at the same time rather like a disclosure of something that deepest intuition had always known to be true. Like so much else in the inner journey during these last few years, it has been as if scales have fallen from my eyes, and there is a radically different way of 'seeing' from then on.

This brings with it a truer sense of self, and a desire to become all that one is created to be. Beginning to reflect more deeply that we are 'made in the image and likeness of God,' which I learned 'by heart' in childhood, has indeed been a heart-journey, a love-story. That my imagination, intuition, and creativity are an extension of the activity of the divine Creator is an overwhelmingly beautiful revelation, and a source of immense energy and possibility. A vital dimension to this soul-journey has been that another person trusts, respects and honours the movements of my heart. To have such a companion, a 'soul friend,' to listen, to delight in, to encourage and inspire is perhaps the greatest empowerment. Because another trusts and believes, it becomes more possible to believe in one's own giftedness and creativity. Because another accepts without judging, it becomes possible to take risks, to move forward, knowing one is held and supported, and knowing too that it is all right to fail.

It is also God's wisdom that in the mystery and paradox of growing, much dying has to happen before the new life can begin. Seeds only grow well when planted in the dark, and the husk has to break open before the new shoot can emerge. There has to be much letting-go, much unblocking of all that blinds us. Beginning to understand this is perhaps the true basis of any desire to live the full life Jesus longs for us to enjoy. As Fr Richard Rohr puts it, 'It's finding what you don't need to be you.'

The greatest gift my soul friend has offered is some insight into that dynamic of letting-go and trusting, that in the waiting times, the empty times, when there is real pain, or you feel abandoned or betrayed, in those times are the opportunities for real growing. God is at work honing and pruning, suffering with me, and assuring me that weak and sinful as I can be, doubting and troubled, with all the shadow, resentment, jealousy and fear, all the wounded parts of me, all that is me, I am loved and cherished and held in the palm of God's hand.

The loving acceptance, the timely challenges, the shared joys and sorrows, the words of comfort and encouragement, the guiding lights are deeply felt experiences of the incarnation, of how through human loving, we experience the touch of Christ. To have the experience of a 'pilgrim guide', willing to share mutually the pain and joy of growing, is a rare and beautiful grace. So it is that at a time in my life when I might have been gently winding down in my career as a teacher, with more than enough in a very busy family life to occupy me, there has been a new energy and confidence to become involved in all sorts of ministries that before would have seemed beyond me.

None of this has been without the difficulties and resistance that accompany any form of change, especially within relationships, where familiar patterns are expected. In befriending, rather than avoiding, the birth pangs of new beginnings, from within the very struggle itself there comes a shift in perception, a quiet but dynamic trusting in the unknown way ahead. To journey, to be open to change, to grow, become characteristics of the life-style that feels most authentic. This sense of being ever open to be shaped and changed was captured beautifully by David Whyte in his poem, 'The Faces of Braga.' On visiting a Buddhist temple high in the Himalayas, whose entrance was guarded by wonderfully hand-carved figures with smiling faces, he compares their creator to God, fashioning, honing and shaping features, especially through weakness, pain and struggles. If only we could submit ourselves, in complete trust, to the blows of the carver's hands, then we would be transformed,

> our faces would fall away,
> until we, growing younger and younger toward death every day,
> would gather all our flaws in celebration, to merge with them perfectly,
> impossibly, wedded to our essence,
> full of silence from the carver's hands.

I knew what he was trying to say, for I'd begun to trust the more intuitive and imaginative part of myself, in realising that every new day brings fresh opportunities to choose life, to be present to each moment and allow God's ways to emerge, in other words, trusting the 'mystic' within. It is difficult to convey adequately in words the tingle of excitement and sense of harmony, of unity with a greater whole, but at the same time an awareness of that deepest longing for completion that can only happen with God.

Trying to discern and integrate the sinful and fragile parts of oneself enables one to walk humbly beside others who feel weak and vulnerable too, and it becomes an opportunity for mutual healing and growing. So it is that here in Garforth there is an expanding team of people who are treading a similar path together. These women and men continue to explore the dynamic between making the 'inner' journey of self-awareness, whilst at the same time seeking to become ever more compassionate in reaching out to those in need. Deepening our trust in each other, we have been able to plan and facilitate courses in a 'Spirituality of the Heart', as we attempt to offer opportunities to others, fired as we are by the movements within our own hearts.

In offering a different kind of spiritual renewal through the four paths of creation-spirituality, we are keenly aware of the need to offer talks and reflections that are based on sound theology and tradition. At the same time we offer ways of finding meaning in our life-experiences through all our senses, of becoming more in tune with feelings. For many of us this has meant developing new skills such as creating prayerful rituals, preparing talks and facilitating 'art-as-meditation' workshops. This type of workshop experience involves developing a sensitive and prayerful approach to using a variety of creative media, such as movement, painting, claywork, writing, aromatherapy and massage, as a way of inviting people to explore the depths of their own creativity, imagination and capacity for healing. It is because the members of the team have found art-as-meditation so powerful that people have been willing to risk new ventures, develop new skills, attend courses in an attempt to honour and bless the course participants. The capacity to encourage the gifts in others and enable people to feel confident using them, has only been possible because members of the team struggle with their own inner work, and because of the spirit of acceptance and trust which has grown, again not without difficulties and much letting-go. The awareness that we all need the creativity of each other to build community and care for our universe gathers its own momentum, so that there are now more than forty people enabling each person to discover the divine image within, the one in whom God delights. We call it a 'spirituality of self-esteem'.

Perhaps it seems a little unusual to include such a personal story in the fourth section of this book, the section concerned with transformation. Since first encountering a 'Spirituality of the Heart' the realisation is unfolding more and more that the extent to which one can reach out in true compassion to others is directly related to the extent one is deepening one's own inner life. Once this process of awakening to the holiness of each human heart begins, there is a profound change within oneself, within all our relationships with each other, and with our mother earth, too. A different attitude of mind begins to take hold and real delight comes in enabling each person to recognise the gift he or she is, to encourage true potential to blossom, to bless and affirm every tiny, courageous effort when people take new, and often faltering, steps. There is a surge of compassion for the weak and the vulnerable because of being aware of one's own weakness and vulnerability. But more, there is a deep realisation of how much it is ourselves who are healed and blessed every time we reach out in love. A heightened sense of our shared and graced humanity brings with it a desire to build community, to restore and heal all the broken and wounded parts of our common body, and to enable others to do the same. Indeed, as we are creating a new church building here in Garforth, there is an increasing number of people whose deeper concern is that we become a community of welcome and reconciliation; a place where we each know we are valued and needed, and where, together, we seek to discover ever new ways of living out our service of each other, expressed so powerfully in the symbolic 'washing of the feet' on Maundy Thursday.

For those of us who have embarked on the journey we call a 'Spirituality of the Heart', there are signs of immense changes in our lives. It has been remarkable to witness the growing confidence in people's capacity to develop, and use in the service of others, gifts they never suspected they had. What began as a yearning to discover deeper meaning in life, to grow spiritually, has turned outwards. There is a definite pattern here, a phenomenon which is both exciting and challenging. And the mystery is that the one sustains and energises the other. Without discovering, accepting and loving who I am, and all that I am, how could I ever truly love another? Without immersing myself fully into life, without recognising the destructive patterns and forces operating within myself and within the world, I am disconnected, adrift. Authentic spirituality makes the connections. Recognising the longing for wholeness within myself becomes a passion to restore wholeness, to seek reconciliation and justice in all spheres of life. Nurturing the divine wisdom within allows the prophet to emerge, the one who can speak truth, challenge and have the courage to act, because a light has been lit that will never be extinguished.

This journey has to begin somewhere, but where it will lead us is for the 'God of Surprises' to disclose. For me, and for many others like me, the process of deep change continues. The experience of the Spirit's transforming power means life will never be quite the same again. We recognise that for any growing there will be profound change, a kind of dying to be born anew filled with resurrection energy. And where has this process started? Most certainly it has begun with the heart!

Postscript
Since first writing this almost a year ago, there has been perhaps the greatest challenge to discover meaning at the heart of life, the loving hand of God in the midst of immense sorrow, because of the untimely and fairly sudden death of my husband. The journey of the last eight months has demanded all kinds of 'letting-go', of plans, hopes and dreams and ultimately for Keith, of life itself. It has been a privilege to have been able to accompany him each step along the way, and more, to experience the immense compassion of this community for all our family. These days, as I write, there is no clear vision of the way forward, and plans made a year ago seem unreal. The November days themselves, in all their damp greyness, seem to echo the weariness of my heart. For at times there has been such a hollow and empty feeling of having nothing left to offer, a fear too that the surge of creativity is gone forever, and a profound sense of aloneness. I have discovered a remarkable paradox, that it is perhaps only from within the heart of a loving community that one can truly allow oneself to encounter these feelings rather than trying to avoid the pain. From within the feeling of being held and supported, it becomes possible for the dark winter-time to be endured, to be experienced as a waiting time, a fecund generative period. Continuing to trust, in the darkest days, that the lightness of spring is there is made possible by the mantle of compassion that has been wrapped round me. And there have been soul

friends who have never doubted me, who have given me confidence again because their belief in me never wavered, who have known what I've needed when I was beyond knowing myself. I offer deep gratitude and blessings for all those whose love keeps the flame in me burning.

The mirror and the window

Rounding a bend in the road, yet another sweeping vista blessed my eyes. Most of my vacation days at home in Kerry involve a lengthy walk. Whichever direction I take, the Two Paps of Danu – a symmetrical pair of mountains of natural beauty – overshadow every step of my way. With the changing light and shifting shadows and sudden mists there is always a new element of surprise to heal the walker. This morning was no exception. Heavy with rain the wind almost glistened. It was, to be sure, like magic, but the usual ache of incompleteness was gnawing away inside me. I was somehow not connecting with the beauty around me. As though I could not enter into what I saw; as though an invisible filter blurred its impact on my soul; as though it was all 'out there', objective and remote. This distress was nothing new. It is like a faithful shadow to the substance of what I see.

And then two lovely ideas arose in my mind. They came like angels to the rescue. They emerged as disarmingly simple images from my tangled thoughts about creation and incarnation. One – the mirror image – sprang from a belief I hold about the part that each one of us plays in the continuing story of our growing world. In short, as I surveyed the fields and trees and wandering streams that reflect the perennial low clouds of the Irish southwest, I suddenly felt myself to be a mirror reflecting back to mother nature what she looked like through the eyes of her own child, me. I saw myself as begotten by the world, flesh of her flesh and now needed by her, to bring home to her the unique beauty of her everchanging face.

A few examples of this personal revelation came to mind. There was a first time, when on the threshold of humanity, one of our primitive, evolving ancestors leaned over a river and beheld her face in some still waters, millions of years ago – a once-for-all momentous breakthrough for human beings. Or there is the time when someone in solitary confinement since birth, for instance, is given a mirror to see the face he had only felt with his fingertips for so many decades. Or again, when the first photograph of a life-long 'pen-pal' is enclosed after a long wait. Without this moment something is forever substantially incomplete. In a vaguely similar way I felt that our human eyes feed back to mother earth what she looks like in every part of the world and in every turning of the light. Without this moment the song would be forever unfinished, the story ever unended, the dance never applauded, the loving unconsummated.

So this morning I thought 'I am the eyes of Gaia.' (Thus named by the Greeks who saw the earth as a living, breathing, feeling, growing mother.) Without me she would never know her allurement, never delight in the beauty that captivated the souls of her followers. Sprung from her womb, constituted in my body by the very same elements and materials as her own body, I am an unbroken extension of her evolution. Full of zinc, iron, potassium, sodium, just as she is, I have grown from my mother and become detached, like every baby does, and can now walk and think and be self-reflective. But I have sprung from her loins. To forget this is to die. Today a lost intimacy was restored when I felt myself to be my mother's eyes; a weakened bond was strengthened when I rejoiced in this special gift I could lay before her.

It followed, of course, that this whole new realisation about the meaning of my presence to the surrounding countryside enriched and enlivened my joy in looking and seeing. My blinkered heart was free again. A missing vividness was back in focus. From this *Sliabh Luachra bothairín*, this ribbony little road, I was revealing to creation the outcome of her 15 billion years of growing. In the grand scale of things I had my precious, unique and necessary role to report back, so to speak, that a crucial point had been reached in our journey through time. As I said, I saw myself as a key note in the canticle of the cosmos, a vital word in the story of life.

Daniel Dancing Fish once wrote: 'As the eyes are to the body, so are we to the cosmos ... and to God.' This brings me to my second image – the window. I strongly subscribe to a theory of incarnation which holds that God created the world so that in due course God could become human and therefore enjoy all human experiences. (This theological model of revelation is completely orthodox, largely overlooked and is making a spectacular comeback in recent years.) God so loved the world that God assumed human nature in order to enjoy it. 'Sheer joy is God's,' wrote Thomas Aquinas, 'and sheer joy demands companionship.'

The incarnation proves that this is so. There is a sense in

which even God can be lonely. Through creation and incarnation God is forever committed to the sometimes tragic, sometimes hilarious vicissitudes of human life. The Word-made-flesh
in Jesus reveals the Word-made-flesh in all creation. God plays
in every creature and celebrates the divine artistry of humanity.
If everything, according to St Paul and St Thomas, is God's work
of art, then incarnational theology holds that God rejoices in beholding such beauty.

Hence the window image. It began to dawn on me that God
somehow needed my eyes as a window to enjoy and wonder at
the holiness of the rocks and hills surrounding the twin-peaked
mountains of Danu. The quality of my beholding and of my
presence to my native soil became so powerfully enriched when
I realised that I could offer back to my God this lovely gift that
God *needed* to receive. When I began to realise the excitement of
God at the unspoiled playground of the semi-wilderness spread
out below the sky, I too felt some of the 'sheer joy' that allured
God into creating the universe in the first place and, at a later
date, in Jesus Christ, making that creation his way of being personally present to, and in, all of us. As God looked out with
great compassion at the world of his time through the eyes of
Jesus, I made space in my heart this morning for God's delight –
even astonishment – at the way the small birds swerved and
swooped and climbed in fine formation, the way the smoke rose
and riffled from a few distant chimneys, the way the bellowing
of the cows sounded lonely over the windless woods.

This whole experience sharpened my way of noticing everything. We – the indwelling Blessed Trinity and I – became aware
of colours in their unobtrusive profusion and of shapes in their
infinite variety of free lines and careless curves. We observed
shadow and light all over the place. We listened anew to the satisfying crunch of gravel underfoot, to the faint, sharp, tinkle of
tiny waterfalls over small stones, to a croaky frog behind a few
loopy ferns and to the troubled rumble of distant thunder.

I came home with a sense of thankfulness and moved to
praise. I knew that my walk had been a pilgrimage of profound
worship. I had felt a deep intimacy with creation and its creator,
with the earth as my mother and with God as my lover. My infancy, I realised, did not begin 55 years ago but first in the heart
of God before time began, and then, when time did begin, in the
first scattering of potent particles in the womb of primordial
darkness.

The story of the mirror and the window will be a perennial one for me. Like life itself, it will be new every day. Like life itself, it will be forever mysterious. And like life itself too, there will be times when the mirror and window images will fail – because when the darkness is around there is nothing to reflect or to see.

The angels will then love the sun into another rising.

Sabbath time

After a long term, a long flu, and a long Holy Week, everything was pointing to the need for a break. So here we are, my brother and I, heading down the M5 to catch a promised early week-end heatwave on the south coast of England. My worn-out body is aching for the sun, my stressed-out mind for relief and my clogged-up heart for a little space. I tell my brother the following story:

> There was a white man, with many possessions, trying to get out of Africa. He was in a big hurry. Loaded down with trunks of booty and bars of gold, his native helpers were struggling to reach the coast in time. The last ship would soon be leaving port, before the storms came. Day and night they travelled, urged and goaded on by their anxious, greedy boss. They were exhausted and disoriented. One morning, within sight of the ocean, and after a brief pause during the night, the workers refused to move. Threats of lashings had no effect, neither did promises or bribes. Nothing would budge the silent tribesmen. They had moved to another place inside them. After a whole day of acrimony, confusion and desperation, the truth emerged. The unfamiliar pressures and deadlines had wrought havoc in the spirits of the natives. They had refused to move because they were waiting for their souls to catch up.

I think we both felt a little like those slaves! We had allowed our bosses to become structures, our employers to become stressers, our agendas to become deadlines. Such distress sprang partly from outside, almost inescapable, social expectations, from a grim brand of Protestant and Catholic work-ethic; and partly from a kind of internalised oppression arising from these life-situations. As a result, on this fine day, there was a sense of guilt that we were both trying to fight off! 'Just being' wasn't coming easy to either of us.

I began to think about what the Benedictine Sister, Joan Chittister, called 'the lost Sabbath', the holy time (*kairos*) that makes sense of ordinary time (*chronos*), the withdrawal from the action so as to understand it better, the stepping out of the parade

251

in order to see more clearly its direction, the moment of desert-solitude so as to stay grounded in the distractions of the streets.

The sabbath is meant to enrich life, to measure life, to bring reflection to life, to engender life with soul. The sabbath is for resting in the God of life and bringing more to life ourselves as a result. The sabbath stays us in mid-course and gives us the opportunity to begin again and again... (*Tablet*, March 22 1997)

In her article, 'The Lost Sabbath', Chittister regrets the rejection by western society of the Christian commandment to keep the sabbath holy. She distinguishes between 'play,' which is now marketed into big business, 'leisure,' which has become a cultural pursuit, and 'sabbath,' which exists to sanctify rest, giving our souls a chance to catch up with us again.

The 'sabbath mind' reflects on the worthwhileness of what we put our energy into during the rest of our lives, the appropriateness of what we, unknowingly, worship by our unthinking choices and decisions. We worship consumerism, freedom from the family and from religion, for instance, when we turn Sunday into the biggest shopping day and working day of the week. Sabbath time is about giving space to the contemplative within us, about paying attention to the silent needs of the mystical child that we all carry. It is about finding balance and perspective in the journey of our souls, about noticing, before it is too late, the wrong directions we are following, the cul-de-sacs we are entering, the U-turns we must quickly take. Are we, for instance, over-active workaholics concentrating on external issues and quantifiable pursuits, to the exclusion of the inner spiritual life; are we hopelessly self-centred, wallowing in our half-remembered, half-imagined grudges to the exclusion of a sensitive awareness to the needs of those around us?

There is a profound wisdom about the Christian insistence on observing the holiness of Sunday. Many of us remember well how meticulously we kept the letter of the law! It was even a sin to break any of the many Sunday 'obligations'. (Maybe this heavy-handedness was counterproductive, in serving only to deepen what is now called 'the Catholic neurosis' by further frightening those who failed to conform with the threat of punishment.) However, with hindsight, the reasons for such insistence make a lot of sense at a time when Saturdays and Sundays are used to mop up what spills over from the working week. The gradual erosion of what was once an almost universal and non-negotiable oasis in each week, and the subsequent and relentless

deprivation of any kind of reflection time for desperately-strug-
gling souls, is leading to an increasing thirst for things spiritual
and beautiful. People need time for good thinking, for discernment about the deeper values of our often-shallow existence and
experiences.

> Thinking has become the last thing we want to do on the sab-
> bath. We have substituted play and leisure for soul-searching
> and beauty, for intimacy and awareness. Our culture turns
> the sabbath into a race for escape, a passion for things, a col-
> lection of distractions. We don't stop to think much about
> anything. We don't stop at all, in fact. We work every day of
> the week and pack even more into the weekend. We take the
> children to play in the park while we sit in the car to finish
> writing a monthly report. The sabbath has become catch-up
> time instead of reflection time. We have lost a sense of atten-
> tion, of what the monastics call 'mindfulness'. No wonder we
> can come to the brink of human cloning and hardly notice;
> that we can watch the oppression of half the human race and
> take it for granted. (ibid. p 374)

I'm writing this at a time of debate within the Catholic hierarchy
concerning the future of the Holy Days of Obligation. (These are
special days set aside each year to commemorate sacred truths,
moments and people, and to be celebrated with the same reverence as the Sunday.) Should they be retained or abolished? As
well as the grieving of the loss of the Sunday 'space', the sabbath
'moment', many Catholics are equally distressed by the impend-
ing loss of these special days. Eamonn Duffy rails against the
powerful lobby that seeks their abolition. He sees this move as
another capitulation to secularism, another loss of nerve in the
face of popular pressure, another hostage to fortune for fear of
becoming unpopular with the masses.

> Holy Days of Obligation are awkward, burdensome; they
> cause problems for the conscientious, they are ignored by the
> lax. There is nothing new about this. What is new is the pro-
> posal to deal with the difficulties by abandoning the struggle
> ... One of the few witnesses against the relentless dominance
> of the economic in our lives is the ancient rhythm of the
> Christian liturgical year, breaking through, interrupting, and
> thereby giving meaning to the daily business of living ... The
> awkward demands of Holy Days of Obligation – in forcing
> us to rearrange our days and interrupt our routines at some
> cost to conscience or pleasure – are not, in fact, outmoded

restraints on our liberty, but exactly the opposite: important
reminders of our human dignity and freedom, signs of another
and greater timetable, a nobler scale of values, not dictated
by Act of Parliament or market forces or supermarket opening hours ... [Their abolition] is yet another step towards the
flattening out of the liturgy, the elimination of anything in
Catholic symbolic behaviour which might disrupt the secular
pattern of our lives, or mark us out as odd or non-conformist
members of our society; it is another dilution of the symbolic
force of liturgy, one more feeble retreat up the beach in the
face of the incoming secular tide. ('Days which are Different',
The Tablet , Jan 1997, p 37)

Since God sanctified rest in the most impressive manner by resting on the seventh day, I thought it appropriate to include this
reflection towards the end of the book. How we waste the opportunities for grace in each day, by not noticing its miracles.
How we miss 'the Colour Purple' in our grey lives. While all
kinds of things and people plead with us,'Look at me, look at
me,' we hurry on, trapped on the tread-wheel, blind to beauty. A
half-remembered prayer comes into my mind.

Slow me down, Lord, in stillness.
Ease my pounding heart,
Quiet my racing mind,
Soothe my frayed nerves,
Relax my tired muscles.
Bring me peace and joy.

Please break down the barriers
within my heart; and heal the
wounds of division within myself
and between myself and others.
Slow me down, Lord, and help me to let go of anger,
of anxiety and of fear by truly trusting in your love and
joy, unconditional and forever.

Lead me to a new and happier way of living and of loving
others this year, both at home and in places far away.
Slow me down, Lord, so that at each moment I can enjoy the
wonder and the mystery of your love.

Eucharist and transformation

It was a warm December in Gibraltar. The (in)famous 'levanter,' (the local cloudy mist) was halfway down the Rock and the barbary apes were halfway up as I looked out over the Straits. I was preparing a talk on the eucharist, and endeavouring to propose an alternative image about its meaning. My intention was to share with others a vision of the Mass that does not threaten orthodox doctrine but rather deepens and enriches the believer's participation at the Lord's table each week. I place this vision, or rather 'glimpse', in this final section – *The Moment of Transformation*. It springs from the theological notes that underpin the whole book.

To begin, for the purposes of this reflection, it seems to me that 'sacrament', in Christian terms, is not meant to be a notion or practice imposed from without, but rather regarded in the light of a world already filled and permeated with Love's essence – a world that tends toward the celebration in symbol and word of its own amazing story, beauty and hopes. The symbolic power of the sacramental action is to remember, affirm, celebrate and intensify the love and meaning at the heart of all creation; to remind ourselves, through the incarnation, that dualism is not from God, and that in truth, in historical reality, Love has always been incarnate.

Everyone is graced with the capacity for this vision. For each one, as for Francis of Assisi, the sun and moon, fire and water, the four directions and all the elements, animals and humans – all creatures – are windows on God or, more accurately, faces of God. Even the smallest particle of creation is a theophany, a sacrament, a revelation of God.

Apprehend God in all things, urges Meister Eckhart, for God is in all things. Every single creature is full of God and is a book about God. Every creature is a word of God. If I spent enough time with the tiniest creature – even a caterpillar – I would never have to prepare a sermon. So full of God is every creature.[14]

We therefore need new eyes to read the wind, sand and stars, people's hands, hearts and faces, beneath the first level of appearance. It is the vision of the heart we search for here. 'It is only with the heart that one sees clearly,' explains the Little

Prince, 'what is essential is invisible to the eye.' There are surprises and special gifts to help us all make this transition – moments which stand out from all the others, gracious moments
when the paradigm shifts and a single leaf becomes every tree,
each holy stream is the underground river of Love, a rock speaks
prophecies and a smile transforms a winter heart. We say that
such small epiphanies are sacramental because in them we
glimpse through windows of wonder something of the joy of
God incarnate in everything.

The eucharist is of a piece with the rest of reality and life; it is
the institutionalised expression in symbol of a story of love as
felt in human hearts. These hearts are, in turn, the self expression in human consciousness of the evolving love story of the
universe. And before that again, the whole cosmos, of which the
universe is a part, is the self-expression, in time and space, of the
first divine love in the heart of God. The bread and the wine,
therefore, around which we love to gather, have a long history.
The seeds, in fact, were planted a long time ago, in bright darkness, before time began. In the sacramental mode, with bread
and wine, the world is acknowledging its very being as flowing
from the womb of God at the beginning of time and in each
passing moment.

There is, of course, more to the eucharist than the long-awaited
celebration of exulting joy, praise and thanksgiving as the patient
soul of the earth finally evolved into a richer mode of life in its
humanity. What I mean is that humanity itself, in its breakthrough into intelligence and human love has, especially in its
famous visionaries, prophets and messiahs, been able to reflect
back to its cosmic ancestry, very sketchy but unbelievably exciting revelations about its origins, history, evolution and maybe
even its destiny. The eucharist brings to self-consciousness,
identifies and names for the universe some of the deepest dimensions of its miraculous growth. It achieves this because,
once upon a time, a human being, Jesus, at the forefront of the
evolutionary journey, enlightened by Love herself, recapitulated
in his life, death and resurrection what is already going on in the
birth from nothingness of the cosmos, and in the dying and living that is the constant in its growth. There is, therefore, a central
and stunning truth revealed and celebrated in the eucharistic
drama. Because of the history of this man, millions of people believe that the ubiquitous death built into the innermost heart of
the cosmos and of every creature of life is essential to the love

that powers the universe relentlessly onward to the glorious realisation of our full dignity and majesty.

The play and struggle between the dying and rising in the loving heart of the living cosmos, together with the eventual outcome of delight of that sometimes bloody conflict, is revealed, clarified, named, owned, and celebrated by the universe at every true eucharist-gathering, 'with a directness and an intensity like that of the incarnation itself'.[15] Thus in a ritual in time and space, involving bread and wine and words, in one privileged and symbolic moment, the eternal significance of the mighty cosmos is encapsulated.

In the dynamic presence of the bread and wine on the table we have symbolised just about everything that can be predicated of humanity, the earth and everything on and in it, the universe and the cosmos itself – the past, present and future of all creation. These rich and simple elements gather up the intense agony and ecstasy of the world, its darkness and light, its failures and mistakes, its strivings and hopes, its indomitable creativity.

Today a new light has dawned upon the world.
Love has become one with humanity
and humanity has become one again with Love.
The eternal Word has taken upon himself
our earthly condition
giving our human nature divine value.
So enchanting is this communion between Love
and humanity
that in Christ the world bestows to itself
the gift of
Love's own life.
– Christmas Preface III, *The Roman Missal* (my translation).

In eucharistic celebration it is we who are changed and realigned with our true nature. Taking part in Communion 'does nothing other than transform us into that which we consume'.[16] Jean Luis Segundo suggests that we should not just be 'gospel consumers' but 'gospel creators'. Perhaps Christians should make continual efforts to authenticate their sacramental life by being not only 'eucharist consumers ' but of necessity 'eucharist creators' too, committed to establishing a new world order in which the universe itself is seen as the Body of God in which the basic needs of all humanity are provided for and the resources

of the world justly shared. The fact that the eucharist is today
celebrated in a world where over one thousand million people
are regularly hungry asks a profound question of all eucharist
consumers. Sean McDonagh devotes his book to this issue.

> Hunger, malnutrition, lack of opportunities to grow and har-
> vest food, the erosion of the genetic base of our staple foods,
> the control of seeds by a few giant companies and the contin-
> ual degradations of fertile croplands are all interrelated. One
> cannot celebrate the eucharist today without being chal-
> lenged to do something about this appalling reality.[17]

When we eat the bread and drink the wine we are identifying in
the most complete way with the cosmos and with the love that
created and continues to create it. We symbolically transform
the cosmos into our very lives just as the cosmos will one day
transform us into its body. Full participation in the eucharist celebration should not be entered into lightly. We may not be able
to afford the cost of discipleship. Our desire for justice and peace
among the family of humanity and in the non-human kingdom
may not be, as yet, passionate enough. The original sin of humanity lies in the lack of hunger for community. 'The only real fall
of humanity is its non-eucharistic life in a non-eucharist world.'

In light of new cosmological insights from the likes of
Stephen Hawkins and many others, I am here involved in revis-
ioning theological language and concepts. If I am on the right
track, a startling fresh and simple image of truth emerges.

Let me review this image again. The creative Love of the universe that has relentlessly inspired the evolutionary journey of
its own Body, guiding it through the crucial breakthroughs in its
quest for human love, negotiating the deadly temptations towards extremes – either those of random and aimless selection
or premature closure – urging it along the cosmic milestones of
destiny, this Tremendous Lover is really and truly present in the
fruit of her/his Body, this bread and wine. That this mysterious
and lovely story is true we know because that same Love has
now revealed it to be so. It is revealed in a favourite Child, graced
through his human consciousness in an extraordinary manner
with the very vision of Love itself. Quite recent in the evolutionary calendar, this cosmic moment of divine disclosure in Jesus
Christ exploded with the same split-second and perfect timing
that marked all previous breakthroughs of universal import.

The experience of sharing and consuming Love's Body, the
Blessed Sacrament of the Universe, the Cosmic Bread of

Incarnate Divinity, the Sacred Wine of a Growing Humanity, the Holy Communion of all forms of Life, brings, as well as deep joy, forebodings, where the future appears as a yawning chasm into which a mutilated and drained earth must fall. Let us look briefly at some reasons for such deep concern.

Thomas Berry writes about the failing of our present energy sources as pollution darkens the skies and poisons the seas, as tensions between nations and within nations intensify, as military methods grow more destructive, as the multitudes of humankind double in numbers and people swarm toward the urban centres of crime and violence. The labour saving and leisure filling dimensions of the technological and industrial breakthroughs were creative, appropriate and very welcome. But in a turbulent age of change where political power and social sin are liable to run wild, the earth is exploited in irrevocable ways. Savage assaults were made upon the environment and people became destructive beyond imagination. The discoveries that initially brought enrichment and satisfaction to human hearts later 'went to the heads' of power-orientated men and emerged as manipulation and exploitation of all life-levels. The experience of sacred communion with the earth went underground, so to speak, waiting, in the darkness, to be rediscovered and nurtured into vibrant life. Human power over life and death has become frighteningly efficient.

> For the first time they (humans) can intervene directly in the genetic process. For the first time they can destroy the ozone layer that encircles the earth and let the cosmic radiation bring about distortions in the life process. For the first time they can destroy the complex patterns of life in the seas and make our rivers uninhabitable by any form of life. Some areas of river pollution are so bad now that not even bacteria can live in them.[18]

In its wantonness human power reaches destructively everywhere over the very topography of the planet from the emptying of the earth of its precious top soil to the filling of space with flying junk.

Berry numbers this change in the relation of human activity to the earth process among the major shifts of evolution such as the transition from non-life or from life to consciousness. I have no doubt that when the hoped-for awakening consciousness and the redeeming vision of humanity assume the fullness of spiritual power, the resultant transformation of the universe will rank with the morning of creation itself. What is at stake is a matter of

> ... the interior richness within our own personalities, of shared understanding and sympathy in our homes and in our families. Beyond this is our extended security and inter-communion with others in an embrace of mind and heart that reaches out to the local community, to the nation, to the larger world of humanity, to an affectionate concern for all living and non-living beings of earth, and on out to the most distant stars in the heavens...[19]

As we take, break, share, eat and drink the cosmic bread and wine and turn to embrace the stranger at the 'kiss of peace', how aware are we of the kind of dying we may be called upon to make?

> Let us plant dates, even though those who plant them will never eat them ... We must live by the love of what we will never see. This is the secret discipline. It is a refusal to let the creative act be dissolved away in immediate sense experi-ence, and a stubborn commitment to the future of our grand-children. Such disciplined love is what has given prophets, revolutionaries and saints the courage to die for the future they envisaged. They make their own bodies the seed of their highest hopes.[20]

In one sense we are at the beginning now. There is a mission of cosmic proportions to be accomplished – a world to win and a universe to save and a Body to be healed. To live the Ritual. To be the Myth. To see the world as God sees it; to live it into health as God does. 'The eye with which I see God is the same eye with which God sees me.' (Meister Eckhart)

A massive re-education of the heart is called for. Luckily we have the teachers. There is also, it seems to me, a readiness for change, a potential for transformation. There is a growing sensi-tivity to new strategies of concern, a kind of genetic awareness of the need for imminent action. There are pockets of conspirators all over the world; and when these small streams of conscious-nesses seem to make but little headway into the dry mainland, we must believe that at another invisible level, the waves of transformation are already sweeping through:

> For while the tired waves vainly breaking,
> Seem here no painful inch to gain;

Far back, through creeks and inlets making,
Comes silent, flooding in, the main.

The two tables: eucharist and world

What is so delightful and profound about the Mass, the summit and source of our Christian lives, is its unfathomable mystery. It can be explored in terms of its sacrificial-meal dimensions, its aspects of praise and thanksgiving, its themes of covenant and conversion. Today I wish only to reflect on its significance as the sacrament of our daily lives: the sacrament which gives meaning and therefore healing to every single thought, feeling and action from dawn to dusk and from dusk to dawn: the sacrament of our astounding universe whose long-held secrets are only now being revealed through the miracles of scientific technology.

When conversation touches hearts, the mystery is engaged and aspects of eucharistic living emerge. Every shared sandwich or brilliant banquet is a moment of grace when people stop playing games and sensitively encounter each other in the search for truth. Sometimes the exchanges will be heavy and serious, sometimes playful and humourous. Either way they are the raw material of eucharistic celebration. Let me try to explain what I mean.

Think of the levels of emotion within the experiences of people as they care for their happy and sick babies, as they try to cope with success and failure bringing shared joy or depression, as they are overwhelmed by the agony and ecstacy of their relationships in conflict and reconciliation, as they commit themselves to a project or long-held desire for equality or justice, for a new age of peace. Such passion and commitment are of the essence of our lives as parents, family, friends, lovers, colleagues, neighbours, responsible citizens and, I'm afraid, as perennial sinners. Finally, multiply such moments *ad infinitum* all over the universe both now and during its long history.

Now think of the God who lives in the profoundest depths of all of us. And think, because of God's incarnation in each human spirit from the first creation – an intimacy only fully revealed later on at the first Christmas – of the possibility that maybe every human emotion and its expression in word or glance or touch, is at the heart of God's emergence within the human community: that this is the divine intimacy of continuing incarnation, the evolving warp and woof of the fabric of God's design for our contemporary society. Is it possible to believe that all of this is celebrated as often as we go to Mass?

The table of the eucharist stretches wider still. Our Catholic tradition protects a deep Christian cosmology enshrined in the elemental symbols of bread and wine. Current literature is beginning to resurrect a most moving and beautiful sacramental theology where the eucharistic liturgy assumes cosmic significance. This is the aspect of our weekend worship that Dermot Lane hopes will be more imaginatively celebrated especially today, 'in view of the presence of so much ecological degradation and destruction of God's creation'. (*The Furrow*, September 1996)

Every time we celebrate the saving mystery we remember and reactivate God's initial creative work and God's subsequent and continuing redemptive action in the past and present. We affirm, celebrate and intensify the constant presence of grace in our midst from the fiery beginning of our cosmic story, through the fifteen billion years of evolution, into the current thrusting, straining and groaning of the world, forever painfully giving birth to new beauty. In his Prologue, John reminds us that Love has always been incarnate. That is the mighty love story that we celebrate around the table of the Lord of the Universe. The celebration is about the liberating force of this sacred memory, with its assurance about the wholeness and holiness of all the dimensions of creation. It is prophetic in signalling a most powerful counter-sign to the almost unbelievable, dualistic and divisive greed that is decimating the resources of mother earth.

Getting our minds, or rather our imaginations, around all of this is not easy. That is why we are gifted with the eucharist. The eucharist is the sacrament of the holiness of these loving and community-building aspirations that are forever birthed in the human heart. It is the weekly reminder and guarantee that this is so, that nothing is wasted, that all in the end is harvest.

A deep-seated tradition of dualism, whereby the sacred is set up as over against the secular, makes it very difficult for many Christians to feel secure in such a neglected but thoroughly orthodox tradition. While their hearts rejoice in the recognition of this beautiful vision of the love and meaning at the centre of life, their minds are conditioned by a grimmer and more barren story of a basically wicked world.

The amazing insight we grapple with today is about the humanity of God, the focus of the real presence of Jesus in our world, the intimate movement of the indwelling Spirit within our most secret and often ambiguous desires. A creation spirituality struggles to identify the authentic presence of God in the emerging experiences of everyone. Whether trivial or important, whether about disappointments or achievements, whether about fear, hope or pain – in these places we find what Hugh Lavery called 'the really real'.

When are we most ourselves, most honest, most free from masks and pretence, most off our perennial guard and out of hiding? Is it when we are at home, at work, at play? Is it when we're ill, at prayer, in bed? When, and to whom do we reveal our most real concerns? Could it not happen, for instance, in a most sublime manner, at those fleeting or ordinary or once-off moments like the casual sharing with a trusted friend – or maybe even with a friendly stranger?

What I'm trying to clarify and identify here, is the locus or address of the truest reality of the human spirit. Having explored that, I'm then trying to emphasise that here, too, is the holiest and most authentic experience of the divine. A fully-fleshed and full-blooded theology of incarnation, unique among all other religious traditions of revelation, contains the almost incredible truth that here, and here only, and for us humans, is the only way of experiencing God. (It is important, at this point, to protect the authenticity of many other officially accepted 'channels' of mystical revelations, but all in the end are conditional on our experienced humanity.) It is becoming more obvious from recent theological writings about the original Christian vision of incarnation, together with a trust in the teachings about 'developing doctrine', that a whole forgotten model of sacramental theology is waiting to be explored.

Let me offer two tiny examples of such writing, one old, one new. Working, as I do, in a parish called 'St Benedict's, the spirituality of this patron saint of Europe is never far from our minds. Archbishop Weakland reminds us that in the saint's advice to the cellarer of the monastery (ch 32 of his *Rule*), he states that the person chosen by the abbot should 'regard all the utensils and goods of the monastery as sacred vessels of the altar'. In a very real and simple way, Benedict ties together spirituality and life, the sacred and the secular. Monastic tradition was much influenced by this closing of the dichotomy between liturgy and life, the dualism of sacred and profane that has often plagued Christianity since early times.

The second example is taken from the thoughts of Karl Rahner. He reminds us again and again that there is no event in which we cannot experience God. There is nothing in life so secular or sinful that we cannot find God in it. It means that we live in a fallen world, which is, in fact, permeated by grace. The eucharist is not a refuge from a trivial or common-place world. We should never treat it as an escape from the emptiness and meaninglessness of our lives. God is in 'the bits and pieces' of each day, as the Irish poet puts it, even the ones that seem furthest from heaven. To believe this is an immense challenge. Why would God want to be present to such 'ordinary' moments? But if we have the courage and patience to look, we may be surprised to find a God we could never hope for or imagine.

According to Rahner, each moment of our lives is like a grain of sand lying just alongside the ocean of mystery. Every event, no matter how profane or mundane it might seem, is a potential experience of God. In fact, the experience of God does not normally take place in religious ways and at sacred times, but in the material of the failures, difficulties, responsibility, fidelity, forgiveness of the human condition. 'The explicitly religious moments of our lives, experiences of the church's liturgy, for example, are necessary and important symbolic manifestations of the presence of God in all our moments. But they are just that; they are not the only times that God is present. We will be only able to recognise the presence of the absolute mystery in the liturgy if we first recognise its abiding presence throughout our whole lives and in all the world.' (Michael Skelley, *The Liturgy of the World: Karl Rahner's Theology of Worship*, Pueblo Books, 1991, p 83)

After the resurrection, in the powerful experience of fellowship and community, the disciples indeed realised that Jesus, surrounded by sinners and outcasts, had given to the breaking of bread a new and universal meaning – not just in terms of passover meal, but in relation to all meals and encounters between people, from the innocent child's shared mid-day apple to the executive's more ambiguous banquet, wherever in fact reconciliation and trust and hope for the future are happening. Since the Paschal mystery is really present in every attempt to relate and reconcile what is broken, to recover and discover the energy of love, to create and to grow in trust, then the human predicament itself is the central dynamism for the specifically ecclesial celebration of eucharist.

Conscious of what has been achieved and revealed in

Christ's death and resurrection, the church carries the table of the world to the table of the eucharist for its interpretation, purification, transformation and completion, for the humanisation of creation, for a civilisation of love. It can do no less, 'for the partaking of the Body and Blood of Christ does nothing other than transform us into that which we consume'. (Vat II, *Lumen Gentium*, para 26) The pattern of a true and loving humanity revealed in Jesus, is the only paradigm for our actions and attitudes. Because Jesus lived a human life, thought with a human mind, loved with a human heart and was tempted in his human condition, then nothing, apart from deliberate, persistent and unrepentant destruction of love, is other than the raw material of the eucharist. (cf Vat II, *Gaudium et Spes*, para 22.)

> Leave this singing and chanting and telling of beads.
> Whom do you worship in this lonely dark corner of the temple with all the doors shut?
> Open your eyes and see that God is not in front of you.
> He is there where the farmer is tilling the hard ground and where the labourer is breaking stones.
> He is with them in the sun and the rain and his garment is covered with dust.
> Put off your holy cloak and, like him, come down on to the dusty soil.
> Our master himself has joyfully taken on the bonds of creation; he is bound with us forever.
> Come out of your private devotions and leave aside the incense.
> What harm is there if your clothes become tattered and stained?
> Meet him and stand by him in the toil and in the sweat of your brow.
> (Rabindranath Tagore, *The Hidden God*, quoted by Tissa Balasuriya, *The Eucharist and Human Liberation*, Orbis Books, 1979, p 165)

In his Jubilee letter, *Tertio Millennio Adveniente*, the Pope, calling for 'a new springtime of Christianity', has intimations of the cosmic nuances of preparing for the third millennium. He is well aware of the significance of creation theology in this regard. 'The fact that in the fullness of time the Eternal Word took on the condition of a creature, gives a unique cosmic value to the event which took place in Bethlehem two thousand years ago. Thanks to the Word, the world of creatures appears as a cosmos, an ordered universe. And it is the same Word who, by taking flesh, renews the cosmic order of creation.'

Let me try to focus my thoughts. Creation had waited for billions of years to achieve self-consciousness. Once this breakthrough was accomplished, the cosmos then needed to celebrate its incredible life-story with its mysterious beginning, its hazardous evolution, its split-second timing and its relentless success. For with the advent of humanity – its new and unique heart and mind – this became possible. After the Incarnation, the eucharist is one of its richest celebratory expressions. And this expression has to be symbolic – encapsulated in time and space. 'The earth, like an apple, is placed on the table.' Around the table bearing the fruits of the earth and the work of human hands, through the human voices, gestures and sacramental ceremonial of its offspring, the very cosmos itself is in worship before its God, offering itself to its incomprehensible lover-God in the ecstacy of its joys and the bitterness of its sorrows.

Just as we filtered the passion and glory of human living and loving through the lens of the Passover of Jesus as celebrated in the eucharist, thus revealing the presence of the living God incarnate, so too with the glories of the galaxies. The play and struggle between the dying and rising in the loving heart of the living cosmos, together with the eventual outcome of delight of a sometimes bloody conflict, is revealed, clarified, named, owned and celebrated by the universe at every true eucharistic gathering, 'with a directness and an intensity like that of the incarnation itself', as John McQuarrie puts it. (*Principles of Christian Theology*, SCM Press, 1966) Thus in a ritual in time and space, involving bread and wine and words, in one privileged and symbolic moment, the eternal significance of the mighty cosmos is carefully embraced and forever celebrated. In his prose-poem *Mass on the World*, Teilhard de Chardin moves our hearts:

> I will place on my paten, O God, the harvest to be won, this morning, by the renewal of daily labour. Into my chalice I shall pour all the sap which is to be pressed out this day from the fruits of the earth ... All the things of the world to which this day will bring increase; all those that will diminish; all those that will die ... This is the material of my sacrifice ... The offering you really want, the offering you mysteriously need every day to appease your hunger, to slake your thirst, is nothing less than the growth of the world borne ever on-

wards in the stream of universal becoming.
(Teilhard de Chardin, *Hymn of the Universe*, Harper and Row,
1961, pp. 19-20.)

In the dynamic presence of the bread and wine on the table, we
have symbolised just about everything that can be predicated of
humanity, of the earth and everything in it and on it – its flora
and fauna, of the universe and the cosmos itself – the past, the
present and the future of all creation. All labour is therefore
holy. All true work, as the Prophet tells us, is love made visible.
These rich and simple elements gather up the intense flow and
counter-flow of the world, its darkness and light, its failures and
mistakes, its strivings and hopes, its indomitable creativity. 'By
previewing the future, the eucharist gives a focus, a sense of direction, to a world that is in danger of losing sight of gifted origins
and graced endings.' (Dermot Lane, *The Furrow*, September 1996)

And then the eternal words of divine disclosure and universal revelation are spoken: *This is my Body*. They sound around
the earth like the angels' Christmas song and they echo off the
stars with the energy of transfiguration. They were first whispered by our Creator-Parent as the terrible beauty of the fiery
atoms shattered the infinite darkness of nothingness with
unimaginable flame, heat and light. And they are whispered
again, a thousand times a day, in the midst of God's holy people
around a table with a piece of bread and a cup of wine. *This is my
Body*. It is God-become-atom, become-galaxies, become-univers-
es, become-Earth, become-flesh, become-everything. It is a kind
of *Angelus* of hope – a remembering, a reminding, a recapitula-
tion and a confirming that the divine and the human, the sacred
and the secular, the holy and the profane, are all God's one body
by virtue of creation, first in time but revealed to us later, and
once for all, in the ultimate gift of meaning, the incarnation.

If all of this is true, what an adventure lies in store for us!
What a song to sing for a distracted world! What a story to tell
our children! The eternal child of a courageous faith, of a playful
imagination, sleeping in each one of us, must surely be stirred
with excitement and delight. This plunge into uncharted seas is
not for the faint-hearted.

But we have bread galore and wine aplenty
and multicoloured hearts quite crazy
with a madness straight from God.
Oh, we will wander long through lands so strange
and many seasons. There will be dragons fierce and blue birds

too and great wise fish in magic, stormy waters.
...and every now and then another dancing dive which
like first Eden-love
goes on forever.
(D. J. O'Leary, *Windows of Wonder*, Paulist Press, 1991)

The stature of compassion

The aim of this reflection is to recover the word 'compassion' from the shadows and bring it centre stage once again. It is such a word with profound meaning – a word that gathers in so much of what the *via transformativa* is about. I tend to think of compassion as a feminine virtue, one that is natural to the heart of a woman, one that is uniquely begotten by God our mother. Compassion has a ring of solidarity to it. Because all of us are aspects and images of the one divine source, the appropriate human response to other creatures is one of loving sensitivity. When we forget this elemental fact of our existence, the bond of harmony and peace is broken.

This was explained to us with deep feeling one afternoon in May 1988, on a hillside in Oakland, California, by the grandson of Mahatma Gandhi. He was tracing our hunger for peace back to our common origins in God. This concern is cosmic – it is more than the quest for personal healing. Both as individuals and as a planet we are genetically coded for compassion, for 'karuna'. 'Why do men fight?' he asked. Because compassion is dead. 'All wars take root,' he added, 'in the "I am here and you are there" attitude.'

On the day he died, Thomas Merton said, 'The whole idea of compassion is based on a keen awareness of the interdependence of all these living beings, which are all part of one another and all involved in one another.'

That is why compassion is to be distinguished from the kind of pity that makes distinctions – as much pity does – and the kind of love that is sentimental, where one person has a false kind of empathy. The 'karunka' – the compassionate person – feels about everybody and everything as she does about her very self. In fact she daily becomes more aware of all creation as herself. When she says 'I love you' she is no longer talking about giving or receiving; she means something like 'Your are that part of me without which I would be less than complete.' To be present to life in this way calls for hard-won self-forgetfulness and endless letting-go. This spirituality is not for all. Most of us are only beginning the long journey toward this understanding and vision. St John of the Cross preached about becoming nothing so that the 'all' might be achieved. This kind of talk frightens most of us. It is really scary to step out into the darkness alone, defenceless. Anthony de Mello was aware of this real panic in his listeners' hearts: 'When people hear me speak about these things they say, "Tony, listening to you, one is left with nothing to hang on to…" I then complete their sentence: "… as the bird said when it began to fly".'

An awareness of shared weakness is the beginning of compassion. This is its strength. And this is the source of the call. The call is to action, arising from the breaking down of the boundaries between the self and everything else. In the weakness, therefore, is the strength. At a certain time in our lives, our wounds will empower us with vision and with unfamiliar strategies for transformation. We are sensitised to others at the point of our own pain. The tree of our energy grows in the open wound. This healing energy is holistic – it works from the centre. And because we know ourselves to be one with the universe, we experience our own healing in the healing of the world. Mother earth heals us. To be compassionate is to be a wounded healer. We redeem and are redeemed even as we breathe. In owning their own suffering, our hearts participate in the cosmic pain of created being. We shine more brightly even as we lose ourselves in the wider wounds of a fallen world.

It is not only in the context of suffering that compassion is appropriate. It is about 'feeling with' across the range of emotions, and 'reaching into' across the barriers. The graces of compassion, for instance, arise from the awareness of our intimacy with the basic rhythms of the first creation. No other word catches this cosmic content, no other word reaches into the common ground of our origins and destiny, no other word expresses the emotional attitude that follows on our recognition of our lineage and extended family. Unlike most other positive emotions to which some element of limit might be placed, compassion, by nature and definition, has no boundaries.

> …compassion is about energy we give and take from all creatures, not just from human beings. After all, Martin Buber explained that I-Thou is not only an experience between people but among people and trees, people and animals, people and music and painting and other arts, and people and God. The selling of psychological personalism has often ignored compassion and reduced it to ego-feeling alone, just as it often tends to ignore the mystery and riches of silence and solitude where so much compassion is learned and developed.[21]

A shallow grasp of the infinite depths of the human spirit and its roots in divine love can be quite detrimental to the acquisition of true self-esteem or healthy psychological liberation. I have yet, for instance, to find the word 'compassion' mentioned at tutorials or in course descriptions. At this point in our reflections at the windows of wonder, we have moved away from forced and limited interpretations of 'self' and 'self-esteem'. We are moving, in fact, toward a gradual reinterpretation of self, leading to a loss of the dominant self, so that we can become more effective co-creators with God, participating ever more intensely in his life. Our compassion, in fact, may be extended toward God's own self. Because God is compassionate, God suffers with the *anawim*, the poor.

> Human compassion then becomes the relief of the pain of God as well as the relief of human pain. This theme of God in pain is an ancient one, well developed in Judaism and in certain thinkers ... Rabbi Heschel, in an interview given a few days before his death, declared, 'There is an old idea in Judaism that God suffers when people suffer. There's a very famous test saying that even when a criminal is hanged on the gallows, God cries. God identifies with the misery of people. I can help God by reducing human suffering, human anguish and human misery.'[22]

Compassion is about a passion for justice, freedom and peace. This passion is held with the urgency of a mother's commitment to her child. Compassion is powered by the memory of a grounding in a common life-source, by the awareness of the one sacred womb where all life was birthed, by a sensitivity to the unity and connectedness of all creation as though the whole cosmos were one vibrant body. How can I be unconcerned when part of me is oppressed, exploited, manipulated? How can I be unmoved when part of me is ecstatic? These are the questions of the compassionate person, the one who has transcended the self. The self that dies is the self that separates. 'I live now, no not I: Christ lives in me,' wrote St Paul. To St Catherine of Siena the Lord said, 'I am he who is; you are she who is not.' Anthony de Mello points out that this spirituality named compassion is in tune with the best tradition of Christian mysticism, Muslim Sufism, Hindu Advaita, Zen's atomism and Tao's emptiness.[23] Compassion is pure when it makes no distinction between the 'objects' of its loving concern. There is no question of loving others more than myself or of loving God more than others, because there is only being.

> For the entire insight upon which compassion is based is that the other is not other; and that I am not I. In other words, in loving others I am loving myself and indeed involved in my own best and biggest fullest self-interest. It is my pleasure to be involved in the relief of the pain of others, a pain which is also my pain and is also God's pain.[24]

Before bringing this reflection to an end it is important to consider the necessity of celebration in the flow of compassion. Both compassion and celebration bear witness to the transcendence of self toward 'the other', toward cosmos, toward God. Both are set in a social, universal and divine context, neither of them can happen alone.

They are appropriate partners also in their common underpinning of joy. Because the focus of compassion is the fundamental unity of all creation, it touches too on the humour and joy at the heart of all being. One can only celebrate this discovery, the discovery that certain people are reaching the underground river where all the streams unite and the sound they make is the sound of laughter. Because of the wonder of this, and of the sentiments of praise that rise, unbidden, from the heart – dimensions of the *via positiva* of creation spirituality – we reach for the simple and rich symbols of the earth to both interiorise and externalise these glimpses of mystery.

Since worship without sacrifice, according to Gandhi, is one of the deadly sins, the celebration that follows on compassion will carry the clear prints of the *via negativa* in the letting go and detachment that the compassionate person is engaged in. All clinging, distracting attachments, doubting, competing and whatever tends toward dualism must be let go if the spirituality named compassion is to grow. There is a sense in which we must lose the desire to control and manipulate life in general and our own in particular if our compassion is to stay sensitive and healthy, and if we wish to truly celebrate and not just go through the motions. Matthew Fox is convinced of the intrinsic bond between compassion and celebration. To be compassionate one must forget many things. And this is where celebration is so appropriate.

> For all celebration is an act of forgetting in order to remember. Thus celebration requires acts of forgetting and it is in the very energy expressed in celebrating (for example in folk dancing)

that such forgetting and remembering is effected. In celebration we forget the superficial in order to remember the deep. But the deep is simple and good; it invites us to celebrate.[25]

There is a *via creativa* identifiable in the 'work of compassion' and in the celebration of that work. One must be free to follow the path of creativity. Only then is one ready to celebrate compassion. The *via negativa* is about liberation. To let go of competitiveness, to transcend self-consciousness, to forget about crippling control, to forgive ourselves radically – these are the ways we become free to be creatively compassionate and to celebrate deeply. In *Circles of Love*, Henri Nouwen writes,

> I am constantly struck by the fact that those who are most detached from life, those who have learned through living that there is nothing and nobody in this life to cling to, are the really creative people. They are free to move constantly away from the familiar, safe places and can keep moving forward to new, unexplored areas of life.[26]

Finally, in creation spirituality the *via transformativa* is about the new creation of a global civilisation where justice and peace pervade the community. It is along this path that compassion runs, because the social change envisioned by the mystics and prophets demands, first and foremost, the liberation of the great variety of oppressed creatures, human and non-human, that we daily encounter. To be compassionate is the radical human condition for recognising, healing and freeing the *anawim*, a term that includes all victims of blind carelessness and unbridled greed, among whom mother earth is becoming daily more noticeable. Readers may remember the lists of spiritual and corporal works of mercy that we learned by heart from the catechisms of yesterday. These lists were a central dimension of compassion-in-action, which is about *creating* community, *making* peace and *doing* justice.

There is a place here for some kind of ritual in this spiritual evolution to hold the network of energies together, a liturgy to gather our past story into the present moment with hope for the future, symbols to express and deepen our compassion and creativity as we grow. One day soon the world will celebrate.

The imperative to oneness

Whenever I introduce people from different ends of the planet to each other, I am often struck by the fact that within minutes they have focused in on at least one person they know in common. A little reflection has clarified the situation. *Bottom Line* researchers have established that the vast majority of people in the world are linked by no more than two intermediaries. They have also concluded that two of the most isolated people in the world – say a monk in Tibet and a hermit in Appalachia – are linked by no more than eight intermediaries.[27] Philosopher and scientist Guy Murchie turns poet to communicate his sense of the interrelatedness of everybody.

What relation is a white man
To a black man?
A yellow man to a red or brown?
Closer maybe than you'd think.
For all family trees meet and merge
Within fifty generations, more or less –
In round numbers a thousand years:
Which makes all people cousins,
Siblings in spirit if you will.
Or, to be genetically precise,
Within the range of fiftieth cousin.[28]

Creation spirituality would bid us pursue the phenomenon of oneness still further. The fundamental interconnectedness and perennial allurement of all things for each other belongs to the exciting realms of deep mystery and emerging mysticism. Mysticism is all about interconnectivity. Fritjof Capra is a creation-centred physicist. 'The universe,' he writes, 'is seen as a dynamic web of interrelated events.' And the mystic Eckhart points out that 'Everything that is in the heavens, on the earth, and under the earth, is penetrated with connectedness, penetrated with relatedness.' Having indicated the manner in which humanity's family includes the animal kingdom, the whole of nature including trees and rocks, and the galaxies uncountable, Guy Murchie continues,

There is no line, you see, between these cousin kingdoms,
No real boundary between you and the universe –

For all things are related,
Through identical elements in world and world,
Even out to the farthest reaches
Of space.[29]

The emergence of a living cosmology is revealing ever-new depths to the mystery of unity. As the physicists explore relentlessly into the dark secrets of space, they confess to continual astonishment at the recurring patterns and harmonic flow that stem from and tend toward a ubiquitous oneness, the reawakening of a vibrant mysticism from a long sleep, also bringing home to us the interdependence of all living things which are all part of one another and involved in one another. In the creation tradition all people are mystics. The Jewish scholar Abraham Heschel wrote:

> The mystics, knowing that man is involved in a hidden history of the cosmos, endeavour to awake from the drowsiness and apathy and to regain the state of wakefulness for their enchanted souls.

Gandhi saw all life as one in a cosmic family in which each member helped to elevate the whole from a selfish, destructive level to a spiritual and productive one. And not only among the 'major world religions' do we find insights into the mysterious oneness at the heart of everything but also among the more ancient and more earth-centred traditions of native peoples all over the world. 'The earth and myself are of one mind,' wrote Chief Joseph of the Nez Puruse Indian tribe over one hundred years ago, 'the measure of the land and the measure of our bodies are the same.'[30] Such creation-centred reflections on 'oneness' are sometimes cosmological, sometimes mystical. These disciplines are intrinsically connected. The mystical experience is like the mirror image of science, a direct perception of cosmic oneness, an inside window into the mystery that science grapples with from the outside.

It is easy to maintain the sense of excitement and movement in this vision of intimacy at the heart of all created and uncreated being. The nature of the primordial ones is described and imaged in a variety of ways that portray a trusting dynamism – a flowing, an awakening, a dancing, an allurement, a loving, a creating, a returning.

'The world is a spinning die,' according to an old Hasidic passage, 'and all things turn and spin and change, for at the root all is one, and salvation inheres in the change and return of things.'[31]

But the symphony is rarely complete. There are usually instruments missing or out of tune. Or the acoustics are inadequate. There is often hard wax in the ears, or people's hearts are distracted. The magic is missed. The whole symphony is less perfect when the tiniest note is untrue. There is a Pigmy legend about the forest filled with the beautiful music.

A little boy finds the bird with the enchanting song and brings it home. He asks his father to bring food for the bird. The father refuses to feed a mere bird, so he kills it. And the legend says that with the killing of the bird he kills the song, and with the song, himself. He dropped dead and was dead forever.[32]

Every hurt we cause nature leaves a scar on ourselves. Every time we honour the smallest creature we honour ourselves. Once a Zen master stood up before his students and was about to deliver a sermon. And just as he was about to open his mouth a bird sang. 'The sermon,' he said, 'has been delivered.'

I wish to devote the remainder of this consideration of oneness and intimacy to a brief reflection on the unity and ecstasy of sexuality. I will also endeavour to explore the cosmic and mystical dimension of this unique and precious gift of God. I submit that human sexuality may be regarded as the sacrament of all-loving oneness and healing wholeness. It is the thrust toward unity, the energy within the human being calling for a breakthrough and a breakout from the physical and psychic loneliness that is never far from the human heart. True sexuality-in-action has a multiple unitive power. The persistently reopening wounds at the split between ourselves and the universe are in sore need of healing. In our sexuality we perceive the allurement of union at many levels. In its ecstasy we are in touch with the ecstasy of God. We discover that we are indeed a part of everything and one with the mystery of life. Our sexuality perceived as a gift brings home to us our createdness: when perceived as power we are moved by our creativity. 'To talk about God in relation to our sexuality,' writes Dorothee Soelle, 'means to be aware of love moving in us because in God we live and move and have our being.' In *To Work and To Love* she writes passionately about the vulnerability involved in true union and about the play of ecstasy and trust in achieving it.

> In long-term relationship, we move between the poles of ec-
> stasy and trust, sometimes closer to one, sometimes closer to
> the other ... These essential dimensions of our lovemaking
> are also expressions of our love of God, our relatedness to the
> source of life. We relate to God in ecstasy and trust ...[33]

Creation spirituality reminds us that our creation in God's
image means that we are created to become lovers like God, to
be allured eternally toward the perfect oneness that God is.

> Sexuality is a sign, a symbol, and a means of our call to com-
> munication and communion ... The mystery of our sexuality
> is the mystery of our need to reach out to embrace others
> both physically and spiritually. Sexuality thus expresses
> God's intention that we find our authentic humanness in re-
> lationship.[34]

If oneness is the perennial allurement in our lives, fragmentation
is always a diminishment. Separation and loss, both cosmic and
psychic, in childhood and in maturity, leave heavy shadows on
the soul. But we remember the unity from which we came and to
which we yearn to return. Sexuality is the guardian of our origins and the guarantee of our fulfilment.

> Relatedness to all that lives is the original experience which
> we lose in the process of differentiating and creating our-
> selves as individuals. Lovemaking is an attempt to find our
> way back to the old unity ... Sexuality reignites in us the
> oceanic feeling of an indissoluble oneness with the surround-
> ing world ... we undo the loss, assuage the grief, and recover
> a kind of passionate, primitive joy in our existence ... the
> time of separation and coldness ends; we enter another time.
> God is with us; we shall not want.[35]

It will take long time to restore the mystery of sexuality to where
it truly belongs – among the most beautiful windows of wonder
onto the love that is God. A fog of suspicion still surrounds this
rich and amazing gift of the human expression of love. Rarely
within contemporary Christianity is it understood as one of the
foremost incarnations of the infinite love that creates, sustains
and quickens all life. In fact, along with sin, it is one of the dimensions of human life where we are not encouraged to search
for the experience of the grace of the abundant life. All my memories of past studies of human sexuality have to do with temptations, anxieties and degrees of moral culpability. To recover an
understanding of sexuality that gives rise to gratitude and

praise for such freely offered ecstasy, there is a need to revision our theology and spirituality. Sexuality can only be truly celebrated when it is returned to its original roots in cosmology and mysticism. Personally I have relied on the insights which have given rise to these reflections to open up to me a clear new window on to whole expanses of this forgotten garden of divine delights.

The *Song of Songs* in the Hebrew scriptures is one of the finest biblical examples of a cosmic and mystical sexuality. It is cosmic in that the lovers return their love to the universe that gave it birth.

Love is always about cosmology. Lovers exist in a universe, not just in a personal relationship. Thus, for example, when the woman responds to her lover's comment on the secret fountain (in the *Song of Songs*), she includes an incantation to the winds of the universe:

> The fountain in my garden is a spring of running water
> flowing down from Lebanon.
> Arise, north wind!
> O south wind, come!
> Blow upon my garden, let its alluring perfumes pour forth.
> Then will my lover come to his garden
> and enjoy its choice fruits. (4:15-16)

> ... In this poem we are told the lovers emerged 'out of the wild, up from the desert, leaning and holding'. To make love is to enter the cosmological wilderness, to go beyond the human artefacts of city and civilisation, to return to the depths of darkness where spirit embraces matter and the Cosmic Christ is recognised as earthy and untamed.[36]

In *Year of the Heart* I have explored these themes more fully.[37] Human sexuality is healthy and full only when the cosmic connection is made. It is a participation in a wider and deeper ecological and universal bonding that began with the primordial act of creation and has evolved into a uniquely beautiful self-conscious exchange of creative love. Cut off from its cosmic roots and power our love-making will be less holy, our physical praise less true. 'With my body I thee worship,' countless couples have solemnly promised at the Christian sacrament of marriage. Why, I wonder, was this phase dropped from the new ritual?

Creation spirituality places human sexuality high on the short-list of original blessings. It calls for a mystical sexual awakening. The mystical dimension lies in the ecstasy of unity, in the playfulness of passion, in the vulnerability of trusting in the sacredness of creativity. A comment from C. J. Jung is appropriate here:

> Normal sex life, as a shared experience with apparently similar aims, further strengthens the feeling of unity and identity. The state is described as one of complete harmony, and is extolled as a great happiness ('one heart and one soul') – not without good reason, since the return to that original condition of unconscious oneness is like a return to childhood … It is, in truth, a genuine and incontestable experience of the Divine, who transcendent force obliterates and consumes everything individual, a real communion with life and the power of fate.[38]

Human sexuality, it seems to me, even with all its ambiguity and manipulation, its negative and distinctive powers, its history of, and potential for terrible pain and exploitation from the beginning of time, is still at the heart of the divine, creative power of the universe.

Manifesto for joy

To maintain a 'passion for the possible' we need to be constantly and personally nourished by reminders of some of the wonderful revelations contained within the mystery of the incarnation. At a time of media hype about low morale among the clergy, low church attendance among the laity and financial crises among the dioceses, here is a joyful charter of purpose and intention, as we prepare for a new millennium. In the midst of warnings and self-doubt, struggling Christians today deserve a clear reminder and affirmation of their profound holiness, their worth and beauty, and their limitless power to change the world. Beyond a temporary repairing and maintaining of the churches, we look for a dynamic new vision of the transforming power of the Risen Christ to usher in a new age of joy – a hymn of hope at a time of doubt.

1. The church is a community of human beings united in a common aim to create, with God, a new age of the good, the truthful and the beautiful. As individuals we are all called to the new adventure of discovering again the divine image within us. And as loving families we are called to be the rich and special soil in which this discovery grows and then spreads outwards.

2. We contribute to, and experience this new era of God's grace by letting go, as Jesus Christ did, of all the negative emotions that hold us back. Only then will we be empowered by our Tremendous Lover to renew the face of the earth. Anxiety and guilt have no place in the Christian life. Futile bitterness refuses the gift of inner freedom won for us at Easter.

3. The human spirit is the place where God is revealed. This we know through the mystery of the Word taking on humanity in Jesus Christ. Until we are convinced of our own holy beauty, we will never be amazed and delighted at the mystery of life. The vision of how special we are to God is the Good News we bring to each other.

4. Every member of the human race is an image of God, the Creator, and there will be no peace on earth until we live in the light of that revelation. We are called to reverence the holy

presence of God in each other's heart, mind and body. But especially in children. As Jesus pointed out, they teach us the playfulness, the trust, the freedom and the wonder of heaven.

5. It is myself that suffers when I blame, criticise, judge, condemn and refuse to forgive. Until I let compassion into my heart I can never be free. Christians forget that they are already forgiven, redeemed by the one great sacrifice of Jesus Christ. What remains is for us to grace each other and ourselves with that salvation. Heaven is on earth when a person forgives.

6. The mystery of the incarnation reveals the humanity of God and the divinity of the human being. We are already sons and daughters of God; soon we will be one with God. We resemble God in a most special way through our creativity and compassion.

7. Without the celebration of our creativity, our lives of faith become mechanical and our imagination dies. It is time for us to rejoice at, and to use, the infinite powers we have been graced with, to transform, to create and to heal. This change in us will nearly always arouse resistance, resentment or ridicule in many people around us. We must try to understand this.

8. Christians must move away from a merely individualistic notion of personal salvation. We are also called to transform humanity into God's family through the power of the Holy Spirit. This is a work of justice-making, of peace-making and of the liberation of all peoples. We are saved, not as individuals, but as a people. Christians are committed to the risk of deep sharing and surrendering to each other in trusting love.

9. Even though original sin is deeply lodged in all human hearts it is not the only reason for the incarnation. From all eternity God desired to create us as divine 'works of art', to be God's pride and joy. It was God's deepest wish, too, from the beginning, to become human in one beloved person, Jesus. Because of that, Christian belief in the dignity and wonder of every human being leaves no room for self-hatred, self-rejection, or low self-esteem.

10. Individually, and as a people, we all carry a mysterious darkness within us, a sinister tendency towards evil. The death

and resurrection of Jesus Christ, celebrated continuously at every moment of our revolving planet, proclaims the victory over all sin. There is no room for fear anymore in the heart of the trusting Christian.

11. The Christian is ready to change. To grow is to be challenged. To be holy is to be bold. The call is to build relationships across previously conditioned boundaries of age, gender, class, race, religion and nationality. The divine energy within us, both as individuals and as communities, is urging us to announce forth a new age of God's favour. We are a people of hope and vision.

12. The Christian must regain a sense of the mystery of life. We have lost the consciousness of our interdependence with all of creation. Each one of us carries within us the fifteen billion year history of the cosmos. Young people are often aware of this mystery. They are aware, too, that this sacred mystery is seriously threatened by ecological disaster, planetary death and human disintegration. Their faith is not dead; it may be buried from disillusionment – but it is not dead.

13. Every Christian, by baptism, is a leader. True leadership is love in action. When you lead by loving, your every gesture, word and decision will help to create a new world. You are called today to be a leader in your community. In 'collaborative ministry', where parish responsibility is equally shared between priest and people, an exciting vitality is about to renew the faith of God's people.

14. A spirituality of the heart – one based on the goodness of creation – announces a way of life in which healing blessings are passed to one another in the midst of suffering and experiences of darkness. We must see ourselves as wounded before we can be healed, as sinners before we can be saints. To be vulnerable is to be human and open to grace. 'When I am weak, then am I strong.'

15. Christians will stay true to the voice within their own hearts. They remember the original vision of their baptism. They trust the Spirit within them. Only then can they be true to the 'indwelling Trinity' and be fearless prophets in a dark decade. For this to happen, they will need, like Jesus needed, the support of a soul-friend, of loving colleagues, and of many angels.

16. This is the decade for the church to stop retreating, defending and protecting. Now is the acceptable time for believing again, for trusting and risking. When we look at our role-models in history – the holy men and women of immense spirit who lived life at full tilt – we can only wonder at what has happened to our hearts! Jesus and the prophets had a passion for the possible. They were on fire with a dream. We need a deep conviction and faith in the extravagant, empowering gifts of the Spirit if we are to turn that dream into a reality in this place, at this time …

17. The marginalised of our society stand in the centre of the Good News. The way of Jesus Christ is not the way of elitism and privilege. God's voice and God's own power, the gospel insists, must be discerned in the lives of the poor, the oppressed, the voiceless and the powerless.

18. The Holy Spirit will not be locked into any one form of religion, any one church. Until we believe that divine revelation is happening everywhere we can never be truly ecumenical. Christianity 'rejects nothing which is true and holy in all religions'. Let us in future do together everything that is possible and appropriate.

19. During this decade of evangelisation, the Spirit is pleading with us to believe in ourselves, to believe in the unlimited divine power at our disposal, to come forth with courage to do something beautiful for God before it is all too late. There is a world to save. And now is the acceptable time to begin. May your hearts burn within you as you continue 'to act justly, to love tenderly and to walk humbly with your God'.

End thoughts

Dear faithful reader, in our journey through the pages and *Moments* of this book we have ranged over many areas of human, non-human and cosmic developments at theological, spiritual and holistic levels. What follows is a kind of summary of aims and goals to be gently pursued as our desires and our very lives develop under the guidance of the Holy Spirit.

* *To be unblocked*. After decades of exploration into some of the central aspects of processes such as spirituality, enlightenment and healing, I find the term 'unblocking' most helpful. Unblocked, our souls will find their way home. According to the wisdom of Zen, our eyes, unblinkered, will unerringly see true beauty and our ears, once unwaxed, will hear the perfect truth. Christian mysticism holds that our hearts, unencumbered by the baggage of false teaching, will grow into God.

To grow spiritually it is not about adding something to the essence of our being: it is more about taking away what is inappropriate and misleading. As in touch therapy and holistic healing, we safely flow in the right direction when the log-jam of debris is disentangled from our clogged-up centres of energy, from the silted arteries of our spiritual bodies. The clouds rain, the sun shines, the farmer sleeps and, with nobody pushing it, the hidden seed is splendidly, effortlessly and mysteriously transformed into its perfect truth.

* *To be free*. Awareness is about freedom – the blessed freedom that is intoxicating. To be free from fear – from the fear of being hurt, of not being liked. There is immense joy in no longer trying to impress anyone, no longer having to explain yourself to the suspicious or justify your position or your actions to your critics. I'm not beautiful or unattractive because others say so. I myself am in complete control of the harmony or disharmony of my soul. This is so because of the free gift of grace that ultimately never fails me.

* *To be wise*. To be wise enough to see the gift in the hands of the

visitor with the bad news. 'Pleasant experiences make life delightful. Painful experiences lead to growth. What leads to
growth is painful experiences. Suffering points up an area in
you where you have not yet grown – where you need to grow
and be transformed and change. Every negative feeling is useful
for awareness and understanding. You get the opportunity to
feel it and watch it from the outside ... Gradually or suddenly,
you then get the state of wakefulness.' There are beautiful places
within us that never come into view until pain alerts us to their
presence. In more prosaic language, we have the choice of allowing our negative experiences to become stumbling blocks to
keep us down or stepping stones bringing home to us the heady
energy of our true potential.

* *To wake up* to the source of all our distress. The deadly virus
that poisons our happiness can nearly always be traced to one of
the following. There is usually either an illusion that has to be
dropped, an attachment that has to be detected, an expectation
that has to be exposed, a craving that has to be admitted or a
conditioning that has to be dismantled. Awareness is about
bringing these hidden persuaders to the surface. Self-knowledge
of a high calibre is often required to achieve this. Our distorted
view of reality may have begun many decades ago in the
wounds of childhood.

* *To hand over* the flow of our lives to God. To trust in the unconditional love of God. This beautiful strategy for our emotional
and spiritual health is sabotaged by a number of maverick viruses
of destruction. Our need to control our environment, to 'fix' our
circumstances, to label the mysterious, keeps us from ever growing. As long as we do not try to *understand* what's going on
rather than change it, we stay lost. We continue to interfere, to
manipulate, to expect. This is a deadly way of life. Because our
expectations cloud the acute delight of our experiences and trap
us into anxiety.

* *To be human* is to realise that the freedom we desire will never
be a plateau stretching securely into the future. Each day will see
us climbing, slipping, falling and rising. To be human is to be
somewhere between balance and off-balance, living, as has often
been said, on the edge of a knife. The dragon must be encountered. In fact the only way you know you're on the right road is
when you see the dragon approaching. No daimon guards the
downhill path. Another way of putting this is to realise that as

long as we intend living on the frontiers of our hearts, as long as we continue to explore the potential of our souls, there will always be fear. To be human is to know and feel this.

* *To accept* without resisting. Are you aware of how strongly and persistently you resist all calls to growth and freedom? This is a strange phenomenon. From dark places within us arises a denial of the light. It is very foolish not to examine carefully this powerful and negative force. Do not fight the allurement towards being free. Believe in the care that life has for you. Go with its flow. Trust in its compassion for you. And you must trust completely. It is total surrender or nothing. Once we resist we are back on our own futile resources again. A blindness enters our soul together with negative thoughts and feelings. It's like driving with the brakes on!

It is worth noticing that as we persist in our quest for wholeness and freedom, the resistance movement within us gets even more stirred up. This stirring up brings many unpleasant things to the surface. As we move more deeply into the inner being, irritability, conflict and confusion may occur. The energy channels are throwing out the mental garbage. The experience of surrender and emptiness is the most dangerous on the path because it is then that the shadow dances most seductively. At this point just observe its movement and transcend it through awareness and understanding.

The more hopeless you feel as the negativities pour up and out, the closer you are to the source.

* *To be here and now.* The awareness of which we speak is only possible *now*. God's secret, I often think, is about the sacrament of the present moment. So many are trapped in the past, held captive by the future and therefore unaware of the here and now. To be attentive; to connect with what is happening. Moving into the present is like entering your own garden for the first time.

The present moment is always full of treasure. It contains more than you have the capacity to hold. The will of God presents itself at every instant, like an immense ocean. Your heart will receive of the ocean the measure to which it can expand itself, give itself away, be taken over, by trust and compassion.

* *To live the paradox.* Rollo May wrote, 'Every organism has one and only one need in life – to fulfil its own potentialities.' Fear is often necessary for this growth to happen. In fact I think it is true

to say that as long as we keep pushing at the horizons of our limitations, continually trying to explore at the edges of our being, then the emotion of fear is bound to be present. Our passion for the possible will always be accompanied by anxiety. It is so vitally necessary to remember that it is the energy from facing what we dread that pushes us through to the colossal self that we are called to be. Each time we are confronted by some intense fear, we know we have another step to take in our journey to inner freedom. This is the paradox. In the acceptance of our fear lies our freedom. In recognising our brokenness lies our wholeness. Without the pain and loss we would never have to reach down and discover the hitherto unknown depths of rich power and energy within us. The door to our freedom is hidden in the shadow at the end of the cellar of our soul. But our very efforts to catch hold of what we are seeking may prevent us from discovering what is already there. Sheldon Kopp tells this story:

> There is the image of the man who imagines himself to be a prisoner in a cell. He stands at one end of this small, dark, barren room, on his toes, with arms stretched upward, hands grasping for support on to a small, barred window, the room's only apparent source of light. If he holds on tight, straining toward the window, turning his head just so, he can see a bit of bright sunlight barely visible between the uppermost bars. This light is his only hope. He will not risk losing it. And so he continues to strain toward that bit of light, holding tightly to the bars. So committed is his effort not to lose sight of that glimmer of life-giving light, that it never occurs to him to let go and explore the darkness of the rest of the cell. So it is that he never discovers that the door at the other end of the cell is open, that he is free. He has always been free to walk out into the brightness of the day, if only he would let go. (p 143)

* *To be committed* is to be empowered. It is as though the angels of light are waiting until the fundamental option is made before pitching in behind the brave one. To be half-committed is not to be committed at all. Only when the boat is actually pushed out do the winds and the waves move in behind the traveller. There is another face of mystery here. Full commitment enlists the energies of all the positive forces, urging, alluring, drawing and inspiring the questing soul onwards.

What happens then is that the Powerful Spirit takes over. We are no longer relying on our 'white-knuckle will-power'. The Divine Ocean floods our being. The last barrier has been breached. The 'yes' of destiny has been uttered. The 'longest stride of soul' has now been taken. From now on it is so difficult to turn back.

W. H. Murray of the Scottish Himalayan Expedition wrote, 'Until one is committed, there is hesitancy, the chance to draw back ... Concerning all acts of initiative and creativity there is one elementary truth – that the moment one definitely commits oneself, then Providence moves too. All sorts of things occur to help that would never otherwise have happened. A whole stream of events issues from the decision, raising in one's favour all manner of unforeseen incidents and material assistance, which no one could have dreamed would have come his way. Goethe put it this way:

Whatever you can do,
or dream you can, begin it.
Boldness has genius,
power and magic in it.'

* *To be taken over* by the New Life is to live with a transformed vision. You soak yourself in the extravagance of God's delight in you. You feel completely protected, completely safe. 'I am an empty canvas, Lord. You paint the picture.' This is total surrender to the Force of Life. It is complete trust in the mysterious power of God.

Divine activity floods the whole universe. It pervades all creatures and all hearts. It flows over them. Wherever they are, there *it* is. It precedes, follows and accompanies them. We have but to allow ourselves to be carried forward on the crest of the wave.

There is a pulsating energy within us. We must be tuned in at all times to this vibrating divinity. It is even possible to visualise it. It explodes from our centre, bringing a lightness and a lift to all we truly encounter. This is total living. It is living from inside out. The holy shrine of power is within our hearts. Nothing is impossible any more. We *are* all harmony, all beauty, all energy, all compassion. We are already becoming 'copies of the glorious body of God'. And the light and power just flows from us and through us. We are new, we are young and we are shining. All of this we have on the very best of authority: someone who himself was well aware of his light and shadow, his free vision and his 'thorn in the flesh'. It was, of course, St Paul who wrote, 'This Lord is the Spirit. Where the Spirit of the Lord is, there is freedom. And we, with our unveiled faces reflecting like mirrors the brightness of the Lord, all grow brighter and brighter as we are turned into the image that we reflect.'

* *To dance with angels*. St Basil writes: 'The Spirit is like the sun to each person. Through the Spirit hearts are raised, the weak guided, the strong made perfect. Even as bright and shining bodies, once touched by a falling ray of light become even more glorious and themselves cast another light, so too souls that carry the Spirit become spiritual themselves and bless others with new graces. This grace enables them to see the future, to understand mysteries, to grasp hidden things, to have minds filled with beauty and to dance with angels. So is their joy unending, so is their perseverance unfailing, so do they acquire likeness to God, so – most sublime of all – do they themselves become Divine.'

* *To be many*, to be part of, to be networked, to believe in a conspiracy of lovers urgently at work around the world, loving it, saving it, redeeming it, transforming it. The artists, the contemplatives, the poets – all those ordinary mystics whose creative energy and power have come from their acquaintance with pain and emptiness – busily dismantling the establishment sins of our society, revealing the 'culture of death' within the rampant racism, sexism, consumerism and elitism that, like subtle poison, like fool's gold, is eating away at the heart of our mother earth, the beloved child of our Mother God.

To be truly *many* only happens in the context of compassion. Compassion connects. It is at the heart of the 1992 declaration of the Union of Scientists about 'the collision course that human beings and the natural world are on'. It inspires the concern at Rio and Kyoto over the moral implications of environmental destruction through global warming and a long and terrible litany of ecological abuse. It calls for the abandonment of a greedy tradition that sees human beings only as those with rights, because all members of the earth community are sacred and worthy of our best energy. To be *many* leads inevitably and inexorably to celebration. Celebration needs people. Compassion and celebration make a good dancing duet.

* *To be One*, to be absorbed into God, to be no longer separate, to be taken over –this is the final state of being. To be like a speck falling into the well having surrendered all; not to be a dancer before God but to be God's dance, to be danced by God – such images draw us into the deeper spaces of divine intimacy. Nor should we leave these notions for the saints only. We were intrinsically grafted on to God's heart before we were born and we yearn all our lives for the ecstacy of such union once again. In fact all our unitings can be understood in the light of our restless longing for total oneness.

Precious energy is lost each moment in defending, resisting, proving, wanting – all ways of cutting ourselves away from the flow of God, of separating ourselves from the whole, of placing ourselves 'over-against' the sacred energy at the heart of life. Put negatively, we are talking here about the death of the 'ego' – that shadow of pride within us that carries the illusions, the expectations, the conditioning, the attachments – everything that betrays our true nature by leading us astray with alluring promises of false fulfilment.

We have only to sincerely wish for God to be 'all in all' – to stop resisting. Then we will flow in and out of God as the mystics remind us. God became human so that humans could become divine. To be fully alive is to be shining with the radiance of heaven.

My dear people, we are already the children of God
but what we are to be in the future
has not yet been revealed;
all we know is this, that when it is revealed
we shall be like him. (1 Jn 3:2)

Notes

PART ONE

1 Teilhard de Chardin, *Le Milieu Divin* (Collins 1960), p 59
2 Michael Skelley, *The Liturgy of the Word: Karl Rahner's Theology of Worship* (A Pueblo Book: The Liturgical Press 1991), p 100
3 Karl Rahner, *Theological Investigations* vol 5 (Darton, Longman and Todd 1966), p 185
4 Karl Rahner, 'Secular Life and the Sacraments' (*The Tablet* vol 225 no 6822 ,1971), p 237
5 Hermann Hesse, *Siddharta* (Bantam 1974), pp 150-152
6 Karl Rahner, 'Considerations on the Active Role of the Person in the Sacramental Event' in *Theological Investigations* vol 14 (Seabury 1976), pp 166-167
7 James Mackey, 'Grace' (*The Furrow* vol XXIV no 6, 1973), p 341
8 Sean Fagan, 'Sacraments in the Spiritual Life' (*Doctrine and Life* vol 23 no 8, 1973), p 42
9 Skelley, op. cit., p 71
10 ibid. p 80
11 Matthew Fox, *Sheer Joy: Conversations with Thomas Aquinas* (Harper Collins 1992), passim
12 Matthew Fox, *Original Blessing* (Bear and Co 1983), p 119
13 Dermot Lane, *Christ at the Centre* (Veritas 1990), p 136

PART TWO

1 Skelley, op cit., p 128
2 Lane, op.cit., p 66
3 John Macquarrie, *In Search of Deity: An Essay in Dialectic Theism* (SCM Press 1984), p 67
4 Lane, op. cit., p 71
5 ibid., p 76
6 ibid., p 62
7 Gerard Hughes, *Oh God Why?* (Bible Fellowship 1993), pp 138, 149
8 Alan Jones, *Passion for Pilgrimage* (Harper Collins 1995), p 83
9 Gregory Baum, *Man Becoming* (Herder and Herder 1971), p 144
10 ibid., p 156
11 ibid., p 160
12 Skelley, op. cit., p 80
13 Fox, (1983), p 162

PART THREE

1 Vincent Donovan, *The Church in the Midst of Creation* (SCM Press 1989), p 63
2 Thomas Kala, *Meditation on Icons* (St Paul's Press 1993), p 71
3 Lane, op. cit., p 94
4 Timothy Radcliffe, 'Briefing' (Catholic Media Office, Oct 1996)
5 Bishops' Conference of England and Wales, 'The Common Good' (Gabriel Communications, Oct 1996)
6 Lane, op. cit., p 96
7 ibid., p 97
8 ibid., p 97
9 Ronald Rolheiser, *The Catholic Herald* July 1993
10 Harry Williams, *True Resurrection* (Mitchell Beazley 1992), pp 10, 11
11 Karl Rahner, *The Eternal Year* (Burns and Oates 1964), pp 90, 91
12 ibid., p 80
13 ibid., p 94
14 ibid., p 94
15 M. C. Richards, *Centering* (Wesleyan University Press 1964), p 59
16 Ben Okri, *Birds of Heaven* (Phoenix Paperback 1994), pp 9-12

PART FOUR

1 Albert Nolan, *Jesus before Christianity* (Darton, Longman and Todd 1982), pp 124, 125
2 Edward Schillebeeckx, 'Christian Faith and the Future of the World' in *The Church Today*, p 82, quoted in G. Baum, op. cit., p 63
3 Tony Kelly, *An Expanding Theology* (E. J. Dwyer 1993), p 169
4 de Chardin, op. cit., p 123-126
5 Lane, op. cit., pp 144, 145
6 Daniel O'Leary, *Year of the Heart* (Paulist Press 1990), p 30
7 John Haught, *Mystery and Promise: A Theology of Revelation* (Michael Glazier: Liturgical Press 1993), p 158
8 ibid., p 158
9 ibid., p 159
10 ibid., p 161
11 Lane, op. cit., p 155
12 Sally McFague, *Models of God* (SCM Press 1987), p 77
13 Willigis Jager, *Search for the Meaning of Life* (Triumph Books 1995), p 63
14 Matthew Fox, *Meditations with Meister Eckhart* (Bear and Co 1983), p. 14
15 John McQuarrie, *Principles of Christian Theology* (SCM Press, 1966), p. 398
16 Vatican Council II, *The Dogmatic Constitution on the Church*, par. 26.
17 Sean McDonagh, *To Care for the Earth* (Bear and Co 1987), p 171.
18 Thomas Berry, *The Ecological Age*, Whole Earth Papers no 12 (Global Education Associates 1979), p 8

19 ibid., p 5
20 Rubern Alves, *Tomorrow's Child* (Harper and Row 1972), quoted in
    Patricia Mische, 'Toward a Global Spirituality,' Whole Earth Papers
    no. 16, p 11
21 Matthew Fox, *A Spirituality Named Compassion* (Harper and Row
    1979), p 17
22 ibid., p 19
23 Carlos Valles, op.cit., p 94
24 Matthew Fox (1979), p 33
25 ibid., p 89
26 Henri J. M. Nouwen, *Circles of Love* (Darton, Longman and Todd
    1988), p 39
27 Article, 'The Shrinking World' in *Bottom Line Research* vol 10, no 3
    (February 1989)
28 Guy Murchie, *The Seven Mysteries of Life* (Houghton Mifflin Co.
    1987), p 649
29 ibid.
30 T. C. McLuhan, (compiler), *Touch the Earth* (Sphere Books 1973), p 54
31 Marilyn Ferguson, *The Aguarian Conspiracy* (Paladin, Granada
    Publications 1982), p 418
32 Joseph Campbell (with Bill Moyers), *The Power of Myth* (Doubleday
    1988), p 22
33 Dorothee Soelle, *To Work And To Love: A Theology of Creation* (Fortress
    Press 1984), p 137
34 James B. Nelson, *Embodiment: An Approach to Sexuality and Christian
    Theology* (Augsburg Publishing House 1978), p 18
35 Dorothee Soelle, op. cit., p 134
36 Matthew Fox (1988), pp 166-167
37 Daniel O'Leary, *Year of the Heart* (Paulist Press 1989)
38 Jolande Jacobi and R. F. C. Hull, eds., *C. G. Jung: Psychological
    Reflections* (Princeton University Press 1978), p 105